The American Crisis

Books on the Civil War Era

Steven E. Woodworth, Assistant Professor of History,
Texas Christian University
SERIES EDITOR

The Civil War was the crisis of the Republic's first century —the test, in Abraham Lincoln's words, of whether any free government could long endure. It touched with fire the hearts of a generation, and its story has fired the imaginations of every generation since. This series offers to students of the Civil War, either those continuing or those just beginning their exciting journey into the past, concise overviews of important persons, events, and themes in that remarkable period of America's history.

Volumes Published

James L. Abrahamson. *The Men of Secession and Civil War, 1859–1861* (2000). Cloth ISBN 0-8420-2818-8 Paper ISBN 0-8420-2819-6

Robert G. Tanner. *Retreat to Victory? Confederate Strategy Reconsidered* (2001). Cloth ISBN 0-8420-2881-1 Paper ISBN 0-8420-2882-X

Stephen Davis. *Atlanta Will Fall: Sherman, Joe Johnston, and the Yankee Heavy Battalions* (2001). Cloth ISBN 0-8420-2787-4 Paper ISBN 0-8420-2788-2

Paul Ashdown and Edward Caudill. *The Mosby Myth: A Confederate Hero in Life and Legend* (2002). Cloth ISBN 0-8420-2928-1 Paper ISBN 0-8420-2929-X

Spencer C. Tucker. *A Short History of the Civil War at Sea* (2002). Cloth ISBN 0-8420-2867-6 Paper ISBN 0-8420-2868-4

Richard Bruce Winders. *Crisis in the Southwest: The United States, Mexico, and the Struggle over Texas* (2002). Cloth ISBN 0-8420-2800-5 Paper ISBN 0-8420-2801-3

Ethan S. Rafuse. *A Single Grand Victory: The First Campaign and Battle of Manassas* (2002). Cloth ISBN 0-8420-2875-7 Paper ISBN 0-8420-2876-5

The Mosby Myth

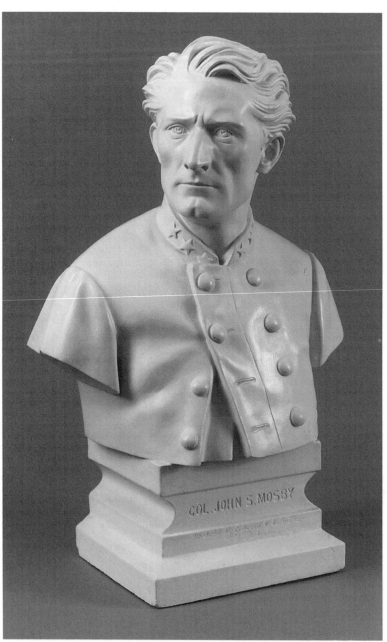

Bust of Col. John Singleton Mosby by E. V. Valentine, 1865. *Courtesy of Valentine Museum, Richmond, Virginia*

The Mosby Myth
A Confederate Hero in Life and Legend

The American Crisis Series
BOOKS ON THE CIVIL WAR ERA
NO. 4

Paul Ashdown
and
Edward Caudill

A Scholarly Resources Inc. Imprin
Wilmington. Delaware

Scholarly Resources Inc.
104 Greenhill Avenue
Wilmington, DE 19805-1897
www.scholarly.com

Library of Congress Cataloging-in-Publication Data

Ashdown, Paul, 1944–
   The Mosby myth : a Confederate hero in life and legend /
Paul Ashdown and Edward Caudill.
      p. cm. — (The American crisis series ; no. 4)
   Includes bibliographical references (p.) and index.
   ISBN 0-8420-2928-1 (alk. paper) — ISBN 0-8420-2929-X
(pbk. : alk. paper)
   1. Mosby, John Singleton, 1833–1916. 2. Guerrillas—Confed-
erate States of America—Biography. 3. Soldiers—Confederate
States of America—Biography. 4. United States—History—Civil
War, 1861–1865—Underground movements. 5. Mosby, John
Singleton, 1833–1916—Influence. 6. Mosby, John Singleton,
1833–1916—Legends. 7. Popular culture—United States—
History—19th century. 8. Popular culture—United States—
History—20th century. I. Caudill, Edward. II. Title. III. Series.

E467.1.M87 A83 2001
973.7'45'092—dc21
[B]   2001020808

∞ The paper used in this publication meets the minimum require-
ments of the American National Standard for permanence of paper for printed library materials, Z39.48, 1984.

For Barbara and Lance

For Daniel and Robert

ACKNOWLEDGMENTS

We are grateful to the School of Journalism and Public Relations and the College of Communications at the University of Tennessee for providing support. We had almost as many helpers with this book as Mosby had Rangers. We owe special gratitude to our editors, Steven Woodworth and Matthew Hershey, and to James Ramage, author of the incomparable *Gray Ghost: The Life of Col. John Singleton Mosby,* who graciously supported our project and offered perceptive editorial suggestions. Here are some of our own Rangers who rode the distance with us:

Barbara Ashdown	Ervin L. Jordan Jr.
Lance Ashdown	Leona Keen
Martin Blum	Diana King
Mary Capouya	Michaela Mauder
Daniel Caudill	Linda Pote Musumeci
Robert Caudill	Chan Patrick
Cordy Cole	Nina Pohlmann
Kathryn Coombs	Teresa Roane
Christopher Craig	Regina Rush
James Crook	David Sachsman
Will Fontanez	Austin Sperry
Sarah Gregory	Dwight Teeter
Ken Haney	Ed Tolson
Tim Hartmann	Patricia Walenista
Terri Hudgins	Dagmar Weiler
Mary Ison	Kathie Wilson

About the Authors

Paul Ashdown (Ph.D., Bowling Green State University) and Edward Caudill (Ph.D., University of North Carolina at Chapel Hill) are professors of journalism at the University of Tennessee, Knoxville. Ashdown is the editor of *James Agee: Selected Journalism* (1985) and has written and lectured extensively about the press, popular culture, and the Civil War. Caudill is the author of *Darwinism in the Press: The Evolution of an Idea* (1989) and *Darwinian Myths: The Legends and Misuses of a Theory* (1997) and the co-author of *The Scopes Trial: A Photographic History* (2000). He is the associate dean for graduate studies, College of Communications.

CONTENTS

FOREWORD

IN 1957, WHEN I WAS thirteen years old, my family moved from Florida to a Chicago suburb. Homesick for the South, I began watching *The Gray Ghost*, a television series about the Confederate partisan ranger John Singleton Mosby. Virginia (actually California) did not look much like Florida, but at least the program was exciting. The Civil War for me then was only a boy's action story, and *The Gray Ghost* was high adventure, without complexity. The television Mosby seemed an unambiguously romantic American hero despite his pale butternut tunic and all those unfurled Rebel battle flags.

At the end of each program a credit line appeared for the author of two books on which the series was said to be based. Many years later I wrote to Virgil Carrington Jones and asked for details about *The Gray Ghost*. He told me how he had come to write his books and to serve as a consultant to the series, and how surprised and disappointed he was when the program was not continued after its first season. While I was working on an article about the series in 1978, Jack DeWitt, its chief writer, called to tell me his version of why the series had been shelved. One reason, he claimed, was that the Civil War was just too controversial in 1957 and 1958 during the school desegregation crisis in Little Rock, Arkansas, and that television was too timid. I finished my article and then forgot about Mosby for almost twenty years while I tended to other projects, including a teaching assignment in Germany. Late one night I went for a long walk along the "castellated Rhine," south of Bonn, which "Drachenfels frowns over like a spectre," in the words of Lord Byron. I could see the outline of the gloomy mountain, where Siegfried slew a dragon, and its ruins rich in Gothic lore across the river and for some reason I started thinking about Mosby, who fought some epic battles against his own dragons, although mostly in distant Virginia. Maybe I remembered Byron's lines from *Don Juan*:

I want a hero: an uncommon want
When every year and month sends forth a new one
Till, after cloying the gazettes with cant,
The age discovers he is not the true one.

Contemplating heroes, myths, and Mosby during this outré midnight amble, I came up with the idea for this book.

Fortunately, I share an office suite at the University of Tennessee with Edward Caudill. Our many common interests in history, the Civil War, popular culture, journalism, literature, language, myths, and metaphors began to converge as we spun some theories about what we called the Mosby Myth during several Canadian fishing trips. His insights gave depth and form to my own desultory musings. Accordingly, we joined forces and set out in cautious pursuit of the elusive Gray Ghost. Find Mosby, we agreed, and we might yet capture some secret dispatches and discover new meanings in American myths that remain with us today.

Two things occurred during the late summer and fall of 2000 to make me realize just how close to us Colonel Mosby's war still is. First, I visited one of Mosby's residences, the Brentmoor House, in Warrenton, Virginia. At the time the house was empty, and its future uncertain, as townspeople debated plans to turn the gloomy old mansion into a museum to stimulate tourism. Not everyone was comfortable with the idea. Mosby had not lived in the house for very long and had left soon after his wife died in one of its upstairs bedrooms. The house seemed truly haunted, not by literal spirits but by the weight of the troubling past, its unresolved questions, the living legacy of the Civil War, and the continuing mystery surrounding the man they called the Gray Ghost who once lived there. I found it difficult to extricate the historical Mosby from a myth that enveloped him like a thick Virginia mountain fog. Perhaps he was entirely myth, a possibility that occurred occasionally to Union soldiers during the Civil War.

Second, I met eighty-five-year-old Brig. Gen. (Ret.) Paul Tibbets one night at a book-signing session in Knoxville, Tennessee. Like me, General Tibbets had spent much of his youth in Miami and had attended the University of Florida. He, himself the subject of a good many myths, was the pilot of the *Enola Gay*, the B-29 that had flown over Hiroshima, Japan, on the morning of August 6, 1945, and dropped the atomic bomb. As I read my signed copy of Tibbets's autobiography, *Return of the Enola Gay*, I was surprised to learn that he knew Gen. George Patton before the war. As a boy, Patton had been befriended by John Mosby. I was two handshakes away from the Gray Ghost. The Civil War was that close.

P.A.

FOREWORD

A FEW SUMMERS AGO I was on a weekend jaunt with my sons, then nine and thirteen, that took us to south central Tennessee. The real purpose had been to go fishing, and fortunately success was not measured by the number of fish boated. At midday we gave up. Leaving the lake area, I noticed signs for the Shiloh Battlefield. There was general agreement that we should "check it out." As we wound our way to the park office, two boys who had had no previous discernible interest in American history, let alone the Civil War, were transformed by landscape, historical possibilities, and their own imaginations into twenty-four-hour aficionados of that great American tragedy. Picking up maps of the battle, Danny set about explaining to me the positions that the troops and cavalry and cannons must have been in, and how even at this moment one could sense ghostly bullets and artillery fusillades flying over our heads. At a shallow pond in the red-clay soil, Robbie noted how the water was still discolored from all the bloodshed. And so it goes for much of America, an inexplicable fascination with the Civil War, perhaps based more on our imaginations and appreciation of tragedy than on reading and study. This is the case for much of American "knowledge" of history—from movies, television shows, pulp fiction, and other culture factories. All of them are great conveyors of drama, although almost always and intentionally short on historical fact.

Those creators of culture too often are given insufficient attention for the ways in which they create and shape figures and events in American history. Historians are justifiably suspicious, for example, of the accuracy of newspaper accounts of battles. Those stories, however, often become the foundation for enduring perceptions about history. The American press is problematic as a primary source for much of our history, but it is critical to our endeavors to trace the contours of culture. It panders to and helps create public prejudices, selectively includes and excludes the facts of national and local life, sometimes whimsically, sometimes with cynical calculation, but always to address an

audience. Col. John S. Mosby seemed to be everywhere and unbeatable. His brilliant and unconventional tactics were exaggerated in the press, and his ability to elude Union troops seemed
uncanny. And so the seeds of a myth were planted in press accounts that reflected the bewilderment and frustration of Northern military leaders, or the fleeting glory and enduring
belligerence of the Confederate States of America.

My interest in Mosby and his myth came in roundabout fashion. My approach to the Civil War and its figures has always been
more as the educated layman, not the scholar or the passionate
reenactor. My previous work has focused largely on a very different issue and group of people—Charles Darwin, the theory of
natural selection, and its reception in the British and American
press and culture. *Darwinian Myths: The Legends and Misuses of a
Theory* (1997) grew out of earlier work on Darwin, evolution, and
the American press, *Darwinism in the Press: The Evolution of an
Idea* (1989). Both works use newspapers and magazines extensively and dwell at length on the misinterpretations and misap-
plications of Darwinism and natural selection.

In the course of writing those volumes, I built substantial files
on what the science-history purist would deem simply as errors
in stories about Darwin or evolution. The purists are right—and
wrong. They forget that it is not the function of the press to con-
vey faithfully the nuances of complex ideas. Perhaps popular
outlets ought to do so, but that is not what happens. Hence, the
historian deals with the reality of a complex institution, one that
brings with it the general values—good and bad—of the culture
in which it resides, an institution able to pick at political scabs
while salving society's abrasions, to chart births and deaths with
actuarial coldness while opining about city zoning with passion
and fervor. It sells information, ideas, and prejudice. Mosby was
"good press," an exciting story, an individual appealing to contrarian and individualist instincts, an entertaining ghost story.
Mosby's myth, like Darwin's theory, took on a life of its own at
some point, a life over which Mosby had little or no control, one
that resided in a culture, not in a house.

Mosby's story improved over time, as historians and audiences dug ever deeper into the details and complexity of war.
The factually suspect news account of Mosby and his Rangers

grew eventually into the Mosby Myth. And Mosby's own contribution to his myth was enhanced by his long life that spanned at least two "eras" in American history. Of particular importance was his living into the twentieth century, at the beginning of modernism, and being able to address that new audience. His longevity meant that his myth was grounded in one era and written for another.

Mosby is not only a window on his times but also on our own. In Mosby, one can see the paradoxes in the conflict that eventually tore the nation apart—loyalty to state or to nation, but not to both. He fought for the South and after the war went to work for the Federal government he had opposed. He personifies that regional pride, grounded primarily in emotion and mythology, which is set against the cold, logical, industrial world that was emerging. And Mosby demonstrates an affinity for that industrial efficiency in his conduct of war, while nurturing an image of reckless, dashing valor.

Paul Ashdown came to me several years ago with an idea for a book about Mosby, a figure admittedly far afield of my previous research but congruent with that research in its focus on myths. I believed that he had a good idea, if it had not already been done. He assured me it had not, at least not in quite the way that he envisioned it. This did not really surprise me because historians and biographers often make little use of the press and other popular media. They have good reasons, including verifiability of facts and the clear prejudices and purposes of sources that may be at odds with the historian's craft. However, for those attracted to the harder-to-define but engaging topic of "culture," such sources are history, even the B-grade movies and hack fiction that critics disdain and audiences love.

True to Paul's perception, Mosby is a wonderful study in the creation and maintenance of myths in our popular culture. The historical Mosby is dragged time and again from history's too somber cellars to be employed in high-drama morality tales and to reaffirm our collective love of the dramatic cliché, whether it be the cowboy, the individualist, the daring soldier, the loyal trooper, the deadly gentleman, or any number of other stock characters constructed from history's raw material.

E.C.

Introduction

NO GALLANTRY OR VILLAINY seems to have been beyond his mythical powers. Although Confederate Col. John Singleton Mosby (1833–1916) was only one of a number of heroes to emerge during the Civil War, he holds a singular place in the American imagination as the fabled Gray Ghost of the Confederacy, a cavalry officer who operated almost with impunity behind Union lines near Washington. "No other figure of the Civil War became during his lifetime such a storybook legend," the literary critic Edmund Wilson wrote. When Mosby died, the *Literary Digest* recalled that during the war people in the North used his name to frighten naughty children and that the masses believed he was "some sinister spirit which brooded over places when things went wrong." Yet Mosby's legacy is a complex, unresolved matter, tenuous, shifting, and always subject to reinterpretation. For some, he remains the irrepressible rebel with a cause, the horseman who emerges from the forests to protect the embattled farmer and his household and bring retribution to the invader. For others, he is a thoroughly repugnant character, little more than a horse thief, train robber, and brigand. English historian Paul Johnson describes Mosby as a myth-figure in the North who was supposed to have "planned all the big railroad robberies, long after the war." Mosby claimed the right to attack railroads as legitimate military targets regardless of the consequences. Defending his torching of a train in 1863, Mosby wrote: "There was nobody but soldiers on this train; but, if there had been women and children, too, it would have been all the same to me. Those who travel on a road running through a military district must accept the risk of the accidents of war. It does not hurt people any more to be killed in a railroad wreck than having their heads knocked off by a cannon shot."[1]

Whether patriot or scoundrel, military mountebank or tactical genius, epic hero or unwelcome ghost of a repressive society best forgotten, he remains what he always was: a fascinating story and a fascinating storyteller who must be approached obliquely, stalked with the same guerrilla tactics that he made famous during the Civil War. Often too much has been made of him, or too little. He is a shadow man, a specter who still haunts the national attic.

FEUDAL LORD?

As the administrative power of the Richmond government receded with the intrusion of the Federal armies into Virginia, Mosby became a kind of military regent within "Mosby's Confederacy," the portions of Loudoun and Fauquier Counties in which he exercised nominal control. Just how much control became the source of yet another myth. It was reported that his men collected taxes, enforced local ordinances, broke up illegal stills, and protected citizens from the depredations of desperados and deserters who tried to take advantage of the absence of civil and military authority. As an attorney, Mosby supposedly served as a one-man judiciary. He was governor, judge, provost marshal, jury, sheriff, prosecutor, and magistrate as well as executioner. He was said to have arrested deserters, runaway slaves, moonshiners, and transients entering the mythical regency without permission. One resident told the *Richmond Examiner* that "old Fauquier was now under the reign of a king, who heard petitions, settled disputes, and by his justice and legal knowledge gained universal approbation, and . . . the country had never during the memory of man been so cheaply and ably governed."[2]

Alexander Hunter, a Confederate soldier, claimed that there "has never been an instance in free America where a man was greater in his realm, for two whole years, than czar or sultan. . . . When the pale, thin, statuesque soldier, wearing a major's star, unclosed his thin lips and gave an order, not even the power of the United States nor that of the Confederate States of America could change it within his kingdom." But this image is perhaps an instance of an old soldier's memory dulled by time and over-stimulated by the demand for war stories.[3]

John Esten Cooke, a captain on Maj. Gen. James Ewell Brown (Jeb) Stuart's staff and one of the South's most distinguished writers, described this region in *Wearing of the Gray*, a volume of somewhat fanciful sketches he published shortly after the war. For Cooke, who overreaches his sources, "Mosby's Confederacy" was similar to the lands along the Scottish border once contested by the Picts and the Anglo-Saxons. "Mosby was king there," he wrote, "and his liegemen lived as jovial lives as did the followers of Robin Hood in Sherwood Forest, in the days of Merry England." It is a good story, but how much of it can be verified? Very little, according to Mosby's biographer, James A. Ramage. Mosby was indeed a protector and defender of an aggrieved people in a ravaged landscape between two warring armies, but Ramage finds no documentation supporting fantastic claims that Mosby was a self-appointed viceroy who exercised broad judicial powers. Ramage thinks it more probable that Mosby was too focused on his military duties to get involved in petty legal affairs. Also, as a careful attorney, Mosby would have been reluctant to become entangled in disputes that could have resulted in postbellum legal complications. At any rate, if Mosby was a king, he was a king whose subjects turned on him after the war and roughly expelled him from his own kingdom.[4]

THE MAKING OF A MYTH

The philosopher and pundit Walter Lippmann once stated that "the distinguishing mark of a myth is that truth and error, fact and fable, report and fantasy, are all on the same plane of credibility." In that sense, Mosby became a myth even during his own lifetime. The Mosby Myth began with Mosby himself. He had cultivated the romantic image of a cavalier, complete with a plumed hat and scarlet cloak. And yet he could say that there was "no man in the Confederate army who had less of the spirit of knight-errantry in him, or took a more practical view of war than I did." His dramatic capture of a sleeping Union general, Edwin H. Stoughton, and other audacious acts attracted widespread attention through the press. He was often wounded and almost captured on several occasions. At times he seemed immortal. Before he was famous he had been captured and exchanged; the Union forces thus missed an opportunity to keep him locked up in a Federal prison for the duration of the war.

After the war, Mosby knew that he had become a myth, but the myth was not always one of his choosing. In his *Reminiscences* he wrote:

> Among the survivors of the Army of the Potomac there are many legends afloat, and religiously believed to be true, of a mysterious person—a sort of Flying Dutchman or Wandering Jew—prowling among their camps in the daytime in the garb of a beggar or with a pilgrim's staff, and leading cavalry raids upon them at night. In popular imagination I have been identified with that mythical character.
>
> I can now very well understand how the legendary heroes of Greece were created.
>
> As for myself, it was for a long time maintained that I was a pure myth, and my personal identity was as stoutly denied as that of Homer or the Devil. All historic doubts about my own existence have, I believe, been settled; but the fables published by the Bohemians [journalists] who followed the army made an impression that still lives in popular recollection.[5]

The Mosby Myth was also taken up by Herman Melville in his epic poem, "The Scout toward Aldie," called by one scholar "a small-scale version of *Moby-Dick*." Perhaps what attracts us to Mosby today is the same elusiveness that was his trademark during the Civil War, as reflected in Melville's poem:

> All spake of him, but few had seen
> Except the maimed ones or the low;
> Yet rumor made him every thing—[6]

Like Mosby himself, the Mosby Myth has been used for "*every thing*." It is, in one of its manifestations, a cultural myth that helps bind communities at various times. The myth is based on, but transcends, the historical Mosby. What primarily distinguishes Mosby from other celebrated figures of the conflict is that he was not a general, admiral, or a political figure, and he operated with a relatively small command. And unlike Confederate generals Stuart or John Hunt Morgan, who equaled or exceeded Mosby in horseback heroics, Mosby survived the war—and not only survived but also lived well into the twentieth century. Union general George Custer fought against Mosby and became an equally mythical figure, yet Custer died in defeat at the Little Big Horn not long after the war. Luck ran out for Custer but not for

Mosby. Perhaps Custer is better remembered only because he lost his last battle.

Mosby's myth, like the man himself, is ephemeral—difficult to put into specific terms, emerging freely from the pages of history books and the popular media for a quick assault on the audience's imagination, only to fade quickly into the forests of American war history. He is both his own myth and an American myth. His individualism and freedom from tradition, especially military tradition, were critical to his success and consonant with the values of the larger American culture. Mosby was a contrarian, a rebel in all respects, not just for a few years in the 1860s but also in his politics, his tactical thinking, even in personal relationships, and so he was of admirable temperament for a nation born in rebellion. He was a man of principle, dedicated to reform and justice, which stood clearly in contradiction to fighting for the preservation of slavery, which he later renounced. He rebelled even against the conduct of the Rebellion, impatient, as Richard Weaver has observed, with the strictures of the Confederate government, which valued proper form over consequence, rules and regulations over pragmatic necessity.[7]

This work will look at Mosby's life as a story largely told by the man himself and as the one constructed for him in newspapers, magazines, novels, and film, the carpenters of a culture's mythology. Mosby's myth traveled the slippery path of cultural values on the firm footing of events. It was conveyed across generations in popular media that are usually given limited attention by historians and biographers. The myth arose because it was useful and malleable, and it endures because it is congruous with national values and mythologies. Mosby was in many respects a microcosm of the larger national mythology, which embraced individualism and rebellion, the conquest of frontiers, whether geographic or political, constantly recommitting itself to idealized notions of democracy, and taking full advantage of practical politics and economics. The legend endures, too, because Mosby is paradoxical and principled, a rebel who ultimately accommodates himself to the larger political system.

Mosby's myth is neither wholly tragic nor triumphant. He lived to fight again and again, but his side lost the war. His personal experiences were often extraordinary, yet hundreds of thousands of men fought courageously and shed their blood. Mosby seemed oddly unconscienced by his cause as he went to work in Republican administrations and even renounced slavery and the postwar habit of many Southerners to look continually backward. His personal sorrows were often made bearable by the residual goodwill many felt toward him. Mosby's myth is perhaps exceptional in that it is compelling to so many generations of Americans in so many places. He is an adventure story, a paradox, a rebel, a reformer.

Michael R. Anderson contends that Mosby's importance as a cultural myth is linked to the decline of the Southern code of honor after the Civil War. That code grew weaker in the wake of increasing secularism and egalitarianism during the Gilded Age, but the myth endured. "The importance of Mosby as a representation of this lost 'honorable' code of living has survived his historical and regional context. Despite efforts by critics to de-mystify Mosby, his legend survives to this day as a prototypical American hero—fiercely independent, innovative in his practice yet stubborn in his ideals."[8]

PARADOX

Because he was a paradox, opinions about Mosby differed sharply. "There was a rich vein of humor running through his nature so close to the surface that it required but little digging to reach it, and no schoolboy ever enjoyed a bit of fun with keener relish than Mosby," wrote James Williamson, a private in Mosby's Rangers. Alexander Hunter saw him differently. "His power over his men was complete, but they did not love him. He had no magnetism; he was as cold as an iceberg, and to shake hands with him was like having the first symptoms of a congestive chill." But Hunter, writing in 1912, also claimed that historians had yet to do justice to Mosby. "He was in warfare what Poe was in literature: absolutely unique; and like Poe his fame will grow." Mosby won the support and admiration of Gen. Robert E. Lee, despite Lee's suspicion of partisan warfare. Both before and after the war, Mosby was a strong Unionist. During the war, Gen. Ulysses S. Grant called him a brigand and once ordered that his men be captured and hung without trial. Grant later befriended Mosby, who had helped get Grant elected president.

Seen by some as an unprincipled political opportunist and a grifter, Mosby became an outcast in the very region he had defended. He continued to pursue causes that became personal crusades, while his large public persona brought attention to his wartime exploits. He served as U.S. consul in Hong Kong and fought corruption in the foreign service. The Department of the Interior sent him to the Great Plains to enforce fencing laws. His insistence on the value of the pistol as a cavalry weapon and his guerrilla tactics during the Civil War contributed to the postwar myth of the Wild West gunfighter. Michael W. Taylor has asserted that a stable-yard shootout in the Shenandoah Valley involving four of Mosby's Rangers and a single Union officer in 1865 "was more than a match for the Wild West's most famous shootout," the 1881 gunfight at the O.K. Corral in Tombstone, Arizona. In the Civil War gun battle, however, two of Mosby's men were killed and two were wounded, their fast draws having failed them during that day's combat. In old age, looking a bit like a long-in-the-tooth sheriff from the pages of a dime novel, Mosby was a familiar figure on the streets of Washington, where he worked, quietly, as a Justice Department attorney.[9]

ULTIMATE REBEL

Mosby enhanced his image by lecturing, publishing articles, and writing letters about his military service. The *New York Herald* praised him as "a writer of peculiar piquancy and power." He held opinions, often inconsistent, about everything and had a talent for lawyerly argument and disputation. Mosby popularized the term "solid South" to describe the ascendancy of Democratic politics in the states of the old Confederacy. In his popular dictionary of slippery political catchwords, *New York Times* columnist William Safire says that, while Mosby did not originate the term, he gave it "political excitement" and boosted the prospects of the Republican Party. According to Safire, the term stuck around for a century. Ever the contrarian, Mosby eventually even rebelled against time itself in his opposition to modernism. He quarreled with Americana indiscriminately, even taking on college football, which he saw as a kind of schoolyard cockfight. "If there be a single vein, however, that surfaces with regularity in the corpus of Mosbiana left us," wrote Kevin H. Siepel, one of his later biographers, "it is that of contrariness—not necessarily a refractoriness for its own sake, but a mind-set that frequently took on that appearance." And yet there was always another reflection in the mirror, a Mosby less a contrarian and more an idealist, a man who always stood for something beyond rebelling against convention. In his own mind, at least, the world was too often rebelling against John Singleton Mosby.[10]

The rapidly changing turn-of-the-century world was a good era for Mosby's myth. It was a time when writing mattered, and Mosby was a good writer. Newspapers were at their zenith in terms of circulation and political power. Circulation soared into the millions for some, and a few notable papers were even given credit—probably too much—for starting the Spanish-American War. Magazines and muckrakers promoted reform, and accomplished it, most notably in the direct election of senators, regulation of oil and rail monopolies, and enactment of pure food and drug laws. The printed word prevailed, and Mosby was as much at home with words as he had been in the woods and fields of Northern Virginia a half-century earlier.

THE MYTH AND THE MILITARY

Mosby's myth also is a testament to his substantial military legacy, both as a tactician and an inspiration to others. Baron Robert von Massow, a Prussian aristocrat who had served briefly with Mosby during the Civil War, became the leader of the Prussian cavalry forces, fought in several wars, and commanded a German army corps on the eve of the First World War. The old general praised Mosby in 1910 as the ideal Confederate commander and perhaps drew on the colonel's methods as he helped shape the modern German army.[11]

When Mosby worked as a railroad lawyer in San Francisco, he befriended a youngster whose family had contributed numerous soldiers to the Confederacy. The boy's name was George S. Patton, later a lieutenant general in the U.S. Army. He, too, became a mythic warrior, renowned for lightning speed, aggressiveness, and tough-guy tactics in the Second World War. According to one of his biographers, Martin Blumenson, Patton had a mystical strain. "Several sets of ghosts haunted Patton throughout his lifetime and exerted a powerful influence on him," he wrote. One was the Gray Ghost himself, and Patton paid close attention when Mosby talked about cavalry raids and the importance of mobility. A creation of postwar combat memoirs, biographies, media coverage, and, especially, the 1970 film *Patton* with George C. Scott, the mythical Patton, ostensibly haunted by the ghosts of his gray-clad Confederate ancestors, offered yet another séance with the Lost Cause as he swept through North Africa and Europe brandishing ivory-handled revolvers, communing with spirits, and battling demons—the real Nazi ones and those he imagined.[12]

In 1899, Winston Churchill wrote *The River War* about his experiences as a young officer in the Sudan. Churchill had survived the Battle of Omdurman in 1898 by following Mosby's advice to fight with a revolver rather than a sword, and he testified in his book to the efficacy of Mosby's cavalry tactics. Churchill advocated arming all British troops with revolvers and doing away with outmoded lances and sabers. Mosby, according to Churchill, was a soldier ahead of his time. Taking note of the then little-known Churchill's support for Mosby's practices in his book, the *Baltimore News* and the *Richmond Dispatch* commented in 1902 that Mosby's "career is full of much that is valuable to the military historian." Just how much is valuable is mere speculation, but in the creation of a myth, possibilities are sometimes more interesting than actual occurrences. Might the history of the twentieth century have been very different if Churchill had ridden into the fray with a sword and not with a Mauser pistol?[13]

The Mosby Myth was invigorated during the Second World War by Virgil Carrington Jones, a Virginia journalist. Writing the preface to his biography *Ranger Mosby* in wartime Washington, DC, eight decades after Mosby had menaced the capital, Jones remarked that the press reported almost daily the amazing activities of commandos in Europe and Asia and that these "feats described were those of Mosby, moved up three-quarters of a century." Mosby's prototypes, he argued, were Robin Hood and

Francis Marion, the Revolutionary War "Swamp Fox." Jones's *Gray Ghosts and Rebel Rangers*, published in 1956, extolled Mosby's tactics as a guerrilla fighter at a time when insurgent and counter-insurgent units were training to fight the Cold War. Mosby has been compared to Lawrence of Arabia and called a precursor of the modern warrior. A Liberty ship, the *John S. Mosby*, saw service during the Second World War. The U.S. Army to this day honors Mosby with a reserve unit, the 310th Theater Army Area Command, based at the J. S. Mosby Reserve Center at Fort Belvoir, Virginia. The unit was deployed in the Balkans in 1996 and 1997.[14]

CATS AND CONSPIRACIES

Mosby continued to appear in literature, popular history, art, film, and television throughout the twentieth century. "He was the stuff of which Hollywood movies are made and indeed might have figured in one since he lived long enough to see *Birth of a Nation*," according to Paul Johnson. He did. *The Old Soldier's Story*, in which Mosby gets the better of General Grant, appeared in 1909. In his midseventies, Mosby put on his faded butternut gray uniform again and appeared as himself in the film *All's Fair in Love and War*, released in 1910. Another Mosby adventure, *The Pride of the South*, appeared in 1913. F. Scott Fitzgerald mentioned Mosby in his celebrated novel *Tender Is the Night*.[15]

Jones's books became the inspiration for a 1957–58 CBS television series, *The Gray Ghost*, which attempted to portray Mosby as a national hero on the eve of the Civil War Centennial. The program's very existence, according to J. Stephen Lang, "says something about Mosby's appeal. How many Civil War officers besides the generals are known today? Very few." *The Gray Ghost*, however, was not continued after CBS encountered opposition from groups that found any program ostensibly glorifying the Confederacy to be offensive. *The Gray Ghost* was the only television series during the Centennial celebration period that attempted to deal with the military aspects of the Civil War in the Eastern Theater based on the campaigns of an actual historical figure. After *The Gray Ghost*, television writers increasingly decontextualized the Civil War and the Lost Cause by moving it to the mythical West, where politically and culturally sensitive issues growing out of sectionalism could be more easily absorbed into the Western genre's narrative of progress and reconciliation.[16]

Mosby resurfaced in the 1960s as the hero of a Walt Disney film, *Mosby's Marauders*, which transformed the Civil War into a boy's adventure yarn. Western novelist Ray Hogan published eight novels featuring Mosby between 1960 and 1966. Saul Bellow made oblique use of Mosby in the title story of his 1968 collection, *Mosby's Memoirs and Other Stories*. The Mosby Myth even made a cameo appearance in a popular children's book, *Mosby, the Kennedy Center Cat*, in 1978. The author, Beppie Noyes, used as the inspiration for her story a renegade cat, nicknamed Mosby, that had taken up residence during the construction of the Kennedy Center in Washington.

Interest in the historical Mosby was revived with biographies and unit histories by Jonathan Daniels, Anne Welsh Guy, Susan Provost Beller, Kevin H. Siepel, Jeffry D. Wert, and James A. Ramage, and two controversial studies by William A. Tidwell: *Come Retribution: The Confederate Secret Service and the Assassination of Lincoln* and *April '65: Confederate Covert Action in the Civil War*. Secretary of War Edwin Stanton claimed, after the Lincoln assassination, that Mosby knew of the plot and was seen in the city with John Wilkes Booth. At the time of Abraham Lincoln's murder, Mosby was actually negotiating with Union Maj. Gen. Winfield Scott Hancock. Although Mosby's possible role in the Lincoln assassination is dubious, sufficient questions are raised to reshape again the Mosby Myth. After all, he had once sent Lincoln a lock of his hair with the jest—at least Lincoln reportedly took it as one—that he would soon come to shear the president. Robert Skimin, in *Gray Victory*, a 1988 novel of alternative history, developed the theme of Mosby as a spymaster by casting him as chief of military intelligence in a Confederate Army that has won the war. Best-selling historical novelist John Jakes suggested that Mosby had knowledge of a plot to murder Lincoln in *On Secret Service*, published in 2000.[17]

WHY MOSBY?

A writer for the *Louisville Courier-Journal* in 1920 could make the outrageous claim that as an elite fighting unit, Mosby's

Rangers "would probably rank with the crack organizations of all time without discounting the three hundred Spartans, Caesar's Tenth Legion, Hannibal's Numidians, the Welsh Knifemen at Poitiers, Custer's Seventh Cavalry or France's *Régiment L'Estranger.*" Even Mosby would probably have winced at such bombast, and he certainly would have howled at being compared to the ill-fated Custer. Keith Poulter, editor of *North & South*, a leading Civil War publication, takes issue with such claims that Mosby ranks among history's greatest chieftains. Placed in historical context, Mosby hardly had the impact of a Mao Tse-tung, the Vietcong, or the Spanish guerrillas in the Peninsular War. Not only did Mosby fail to influence the outcome of the war, but he also made no decisive contribution to a single major battle or, arguably, a single campaign. And, according to Poulter, "Mosby's Confederacy" was a geographic postage stamp in comparison to Kansas and Missouri, where large-scale guerrilla operations raged before and during the war. While acknowledging that if the South could have cloned a hundred Mosbys, it might have won, Poulter argues that we remember Mosby primarily because he was a great publicist who stayed active throughout the war. His raids were never far from major Eastern population centers that supported widely circulated newspapers, and he was always a good newspaper story.[18]

Perhaps Mosby's greatest significance lies in what he did *not* do. He did not carry on a protracted guerrilla war after the surrender of the primary Confederate armies. He saw no future in extending the war but worked to bring about reconciliation. In *Race and Reunion: The Civil War in American Memory* (2001), David W. Blight credits Mosby with dissenting from the prevailing Lost Cause mythology in the postbellum South. "Mosby," he says, "set a high standard for candor." Slavery, Mosby insisted, was the cause of the war, and he refused to wallow in lost causes or tamper with hard truths as he saw them. "If such honesty and spirit of debate had prevailed in Southern confrontations over the Lost Cause, the career of Civil War memory in America might have been different. That it did not and could not tells us much about the tragic interdependence of race and reunion. That the Mildred Rutherfords prevailed in Southern memory over the John Mosbys demonstrates how and why the Lost Cause left such an enduring burden in national memory." Rutherford was the historian general of the United Daughters of the Confederacy from 1911 to 1916 who, according to Blight, sought vindication of the Confederacy "with a political fervor that would rival the ministry of propaganda in any twentieth-century dictatorship." That a distinguished historian would position Mosby in opposition to major currents in Southern mythology illustrates the controversial legacy of the Gray Ghost down to the twenty-first century.[19]

Although his life and exploits have been well documented, the source of the mythical Mosby remains evasive. Mosby worked at shaping his legacy and was cleverly aware of what he was doing. From his days as a student until the end of his life, he understood the value of manipulating others' perceptions. His guerrilla tactics may have been as valuable for the perceived danger they created—and the attendant deployment of Union resources disproportionate to the size of the target (Mosby)—as for the actual losses inflicted in terms of casualties and supplies. He artfully exploited the press to help him create dread and to exaggerate his deeds. This strategy does not deny the reality of his extraordinary military feats, but focuses instead on how a mere colonel—on the losing side, operating in only a few counties, and with a force ranging from a few dozen to no more than a few hundred men—could inspire so much interest in the press and, later, in film, novels, television, and even among scholars. Any myth eventually takes on a life of its own, transcending its origins to suit the purposes of the culture that embraces, enlarges, and sustains it. Mosby's myth was no different.

Tidwell said of Mosby: "He was famous because he was successful, and he was successful because he was smart, lucky, and a good leader." Perhaps there is a tautology to be considered here as well. Mosby was famous because he was successful, but he was also successful because he was famous. The Mosby Myth continues to intrigue us because it represents something grandly irrepressible and yet paradoxical in the American spirit.[20]

Perhaps this is what prompts a St. Louis attorney to host an annual John Singleton Mosby Memorial Celebration to commemorate Mosby's release from jail shortly before Christmas in 1853. Mosby had been convicted of shooting a medical student, which the attorney, with tongue firmly in cheek, one hopes, claims as sufficient reason to hold Mosby, also an attorney, in high regard. "I'm a plaintiff's attorney, so I have my share of run-ins with the medical profession," the St. Louisian said. And perhaps, too, the Mosby Myth is what motivated a forty-nine-year-old sometime Civil War reenactor, Jeff Smith, to don a gray woolen uniform on April 21, 1997, and begin a 180-mile ride on horseback from Wolcott, Connecticut, to Narragansett, Rhode Island. Waving a Confederate battle flag fastened to the six-foot pole that he clutched in a white-gloved hand, he told startled observers that he was Col. John Singleton Mosby. And so he and countless others continue to haunt, and be haunted by, the Gray Ghost. They would do well to recall Stoughton's exchange with Mosby the night he was captured. Mosby woke the sleeping general by slapping him on the buttocks and said: "General, did you ever hear of Mosby?" Stoughton: "Yes, have you caught him?" Mosby: "No, I am Mosby—he has caught you."[21]

NOTES

1. Edmund Wilson, *Patriotic Gore* (New York: Oxford University Press, 1962), 307; *Literary Digest*, July 15, 1916; Paul Johnson, *A History of the American People* (1997; reprint, New York: HarperPerennial, 1999), 478; John S. Mosby, *Mosby's War Reminiscences and Stuart's Cavalry Campaigns* (1887; reprint, New York: Pageant Book Co., 1958), 145.

2. James J. Williamson, *Mosby's Rangers* (New York: Ralph B. Kenyon, 1896), 105; John Scott, *Partisan Life with Col. John S. Mosby* (1867; reprint, Gaithersburg, MD: Butternut Press, 1985), 398; A. Monteiro, *War Reminiscences by the Surgeon of Mosby's Command* (1890; reprint, Gaithersburg, MD: Butternut Press, n.d.), 93–94; Sylvia G. L. Dannett and Rosamond H. Burkhart, *Confederate Surgeon, Aristides Monteiro* (New York: Dodd, Mead & Co., 1969), 187; Civil War list of slave prisoners in Eastern District Military Prison, Richmond, Virginia, 1864, John Singleton Mosby (hereafter cited as JSM) Papers, University of Virginia; Jeffry D. Wert, *Mosby's Rangers* (New York: Simon & Schuster, 1990), 124–25.

3. Alexander Hunter, *The Women of the Debatable Land* (Washington, DC: Corden Publishing Co., 1912), 40–41.

4. John Esten Cooke, *Wearing of the Gray*, ed. Philip van Doren Stern (1867; reprint, Bloomington: Indiana University Press, 1959), 467; James A. Ramage, personal correspondence with the authors, November 16, November 27, 2000.

5. Walter Lippmann, *Public Opinion* (1922; reprint, New York: Free Press, 1965), 80; *Mosby's War Reminiscences*, 23–24, 80, 117.

6. Stanton Garner, *The Civil War World of Herman Melville* (Lawrence: University Press of Kansas, 1993), 319; Wilson, *Patriotic Gore*, 326; Aaron Kramer, *Melville's Poetry: Toward the Enlarged Heart* (Rutherford, NJ: Fairleigh Dickinson University Press, 1972), 64.

7. Richard M. Weaver, *The Southern Essays of Richard M. Weaver*, ed. George M. Curtis III and James J. Thompson Jr. (Indianapolis: Liberty Press, 1987), 165.

8. Michael R. Anderson, "Col. John Mosby and the Southern Code of Honor." On-line American Studies class project, University of Virginia, 1997, http.//xroads.virginia.edu/~class/AM483_97/projects/anderson/literary.html.

9. Williamson, *Mosby's Rangers*, 97; Alexander Hunter, "The Women of Mosby's Confederacy," *Confederate Veteran* 15 (1907): 258; idem, *Women of the Debatable Land*, 39; Virgil Carrington Jones, *Ranger Mosby* (Chapel Hill: University of North Carolina Press, 1944), 306; Joseph G. Rosa, *The Gunfighter: Man or Myth?* (Norman: University of Oklahoma Press, 1969), 37–39; Michael W. Taylor, "In a Small Virginia Stable Yard, a Quick-Shooting Union Lieutenant Bested Five of Mosby's Rangers," *America's Civil War* 13, no. 6 (January 2001): 12.

10. *New York Herald*, August 12, 1876; William Safire, *The New Language of Politics: A Dictionary of Catchwords, Slogans, and Political Usage* (1968; reprint, New York: Collier Books, 1972), 618–19; James A. Ramage, *Gray Ghost: The Life of Col. John Singleton Mosby* (Lexington: University Press of Kentucky, 1999), 391; Kevin H. Siepel, *Rebel: The Life and Times of John Singleton Mosby* (1983; reprint, New York: Da Capo Press, 1997), xviii.

11. Massow to Mosby, May 8, 1910, and undated newspaper clipping, JSM Scrapbooks, University of Virginia.

12. Ladislas Farago, *Patton: Ordeal and Triumph* (New York: Ivan Obolensky, 1963), 50–51; Martin Blumenson, *Patton: The Man behind the Legend, 1885–1945* (New York: Berkeley Books, 1985), 17, 29–31.

13. Winston Spencer Churchill, *The River War, An Historical Account of the Reconquest of the Soudan*, ed. Col. F. Rhodes, 2 vols. (London: Longmans, Green, and Co., 1899), 1:349–50; *Baltimore News*, July 18, 1902; *Richmond Dispatch*, July 27, 1902.

14. Jones, *Ranger Mosby*, viii; Jones, *Gray Ghosts and Rebel Raiders* (1956; reprint, New York: Galahad Books, 1995); Garner, *Civil War World of Herman Melville*, 306.

15. Johnson, *History of the American People*, 477–79; Jack Spears, *The Civil War on the Screen and Other Essays* (South Brunswick, NJ: A. S. Barnes, 1977), 87; F. Scott Fitzgerald, *Tender Is the Night*, ed. Malcolm Cowley (1943; reprint, Harmondsworth, England: Penguin, 1955), 168.

16. J. Stephen Lang and Michael Caplanis, *Drawn to the Civil War* (Winston-Salem, NC: John F. Blair, 1999), 176; Paul Ashdown, "Confederates on Television: The Cavalier Myth and the Death of 'The Gray Ghost,' " *Studies in Popular Culture* 2, no. 1 (Spring 1979): 11–22; Greg Biggs, "The Gray Ghost Story," *Blue & Gray Magazine* (April 1994): 31–33.

17. *The War of the Rebellion: A Compilation of the Official Records of the Union and Confederate Armies*, 70 vols., 4 series (Washington, DC, 1880–1901), Series 1, 46 (3): 838 (hereafter cited as OR); *Mosby's War Reminiscences*, 82.

18. George A. Jones, "A Mosby Partisan Ranger," *Louisville Courier-Journal*, May 16, 1920; Keith Poulter, "A Word in Edgeways," *North & South* 3, no. 1 (November 1999): 18–19.

19. Jay Winik, *April 1865: The Month That Saved America* (New York: HarperCollins, 2001); David W. Blight, *Race and Reunion: The Civil War in American Memory* (Cambridge, MA: Harvard University Press, 2001), 279, 297–99.

20. William A. Tidwell, with James O. Hall and David Winfred Gaddy, *Come Retribution: The Confederate Secret Service and the Assassination of Lincoln* (Jackson: University Press of Mississippi, 1988), 135.

21. Steve Clark, "Lawyer Says Mosby's Finest 'Deed' Was Shooting Med Student," *Richmond News Leader*, October 18, 1990; Claudia Van Nes, "A Confederate Hero in Connecticut," *The Hartford Courant*, May 9, 1997; Jeff Smith's story is told at *http://www.mosbysrangers.com*; John Mosby, "One of My War Adventures," *Belford's Monthly* (n.d. [1891]), quoted in Williamson, *Mosby's Rangers*, 40.

Part One

Satyr's Child

Memory's self is so beguiled
That Mosby seems a satyr's child.
—Herman Melville, "The Scout toward Aldie" (1866)

CHAPTER ONE

PHANTOMS OF THE PAST

I sing of warfare and a man at war.
—Virgil, *The Aeneid* (trans. Robert Fitzgerald, 1983)

Men fight from sentiment. After the fight is over
they invent some fanciful theory on which they
imagine that they fought.
—John S. Mosby, letter to Reuben Page, June 11,
1902, *Letters*

As HE REMEMBERED his early life in old age, Col. John Singleton
Mosby began to write a story. Although he had not finished *The
Memoirs of Colonel John S. Mosby* before his death in 1916, he did
find an ending. "I have given," he wrote, "as faithful an account
as Aeneas did to Dido of events—all of which I saw and part of
which I was." Ever the classicist, Mosby knew the power of myth,
and he knew that classical literature was largely the story of war.
Mosby, like Aeneas, was a warrior who set forth with a band of
doughty followers to found a new nation. And like Aeneas, Mosby
became a literary, mythic creation, but of his own invention. A
life conjured from memory is never the same as a life actually
lived. It is not historical. He had become the Gray Ghost of the
Confederacy, but before the spectral vapors of metaphoric glory
had swirled around him, he had been young Jack Mosby, a child
of Virginia. And, according to Virgil Carrington Jones, who published in 1944 what for many years was the standard biography
of Mosby, "Little that is known of Mosby's life before he reached
manhood sets him apart from other young Virginians who came
up during those turbulent years before the war." As an old man,
Mosby visited the site of what had been the log schoolhouse in
Fry's Woods adjoining his family's farm. The toppled chimney

and scattered rocks "raised up phantoms of the past." He followed a path to find the spring where he had drunk cool water
from a gourd when he was a barefoot schoolboy. "The spring was
still there and the running brook, but all of my schoolmates had
gone," he wrote, with what must have been more than a glimpse
of mortality.[1]

The sentiment is personal, the memories phantasmagoric and
detached from history. The present is defined in terms of what is
absent from it. The past, like the spring, is elemental, mythic, and
eternal. The present, a running brook, a mere filigreed vein of a
deeper tributary, is full of ghosts.

A VIRGINIA BOYHOOD

"I was born December 6, 1833, at the home of my grandfather, James McLaurine, in Powhatan County, Virginia. He was a
son of Robert McLaurine, an Episcopal minister, who came from
Scotland before the Revolution," he began. For Mosby, the story
of his life started, simply and directly, with a time, a place, and a
heritage. Mosby's Scottish heritage came with a family story that
he was descended from Rob Roy MacGregor, so we can be fairly
sure of the reason for his childhood fondness for the novels of Sir
Walter Scott. Later, and with a nod to Robert Burns, he would
call his Rangers his "Tam O'Shanter Rebels." On his father's side,
the family traced its origins to England. The name had originally
been de Moresby, probably of Norman origin. Edward Mosby
emigrated to what was then the Virginia Colony in 1635, more
than a century before Robert McLaurine arrived from Scotland.
Both families had prospered, acquiring moderate-sized farms
worked by slaves in the Piedmont. The families were connected
in ecclesiastical and commercial affairs, and land changed hands
among them.[2]

Mosby's parents were strong influences, especially his mother,
Virginia, who bore eleven children and lived to the age of eighty-
one. Alfred Mosby was almost twenty-four when Jack was born,
and Virginia was eighteen. Jack was their second child. His first
home was in Nelson County near the Blue Ridge Mountains.
When he was seven, the family moved to Albemarle County and
soon settled at Tudor Grove, a house and a farm of some four

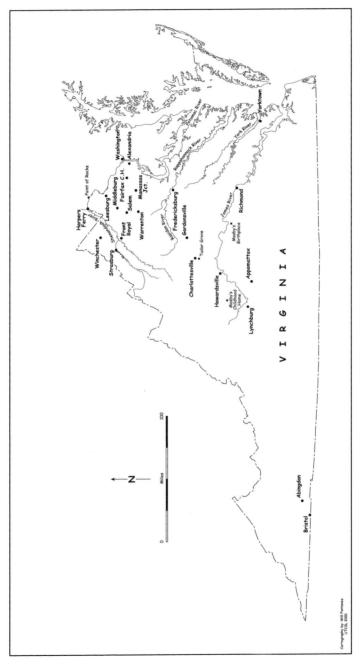

"VIRGINIA IS MY MOTHER." Mosby came to know Virginia well during his lifetime. Born near Richmond and raised within sight of Jefferson's Monticello, he practiced law in Bristol before the war, and lived his final years across the Potomac in Washington. His body was brought back to Warrenton for burial.

hundred acres a few miles south of Charlottesville. What is especially interesting about this farm is its proximity to Monticello,
an icon of American Revolutionary democracy, and what Mosby
eventually thought of that closeness:[3] "I recollect that one day I
went with my father to our peach orchard on a high ridge, and
he pointed out Monticello, the home of Thomas Jefferson, on a
mountain a few miles away, and told me some of the history of
the great man who wrote the Declaration of Independence."[4]

This powerful image of a father and his son gazing at the
American temple of the Enlightenment suggests that Mosby, from
the perspective of old age, saw himself imbued with the symbols
of Jeffersonian democracy, his continuity with the past, and Virginia, his beloved homeland. Jefferson had died in 1826, not long
before Mosby's earliest memory of Monticello, perhaps bringing
to an end the Revolutionary era. Mosby may have admired
Jefferson, but in 1915, when Jefferson's reputation was somewhat
in eclipse and Alexander Hamilton's was in the ascendancy, he
said he had always been a Hamiltonian. There was room enough
in his political philosophy for both. He judged that Alexander
Hamilton "was in ability far above any man this country has produced." Jefferson represents another kind of American story, a
myth of democracy's origins that transcends the gritty truth of
the nation's political beginnings. In grounding his own myth in
this greater and more enduring truth, Mosby slips on the mantle
of American Revolutionary democracy as he would later wrap
himself in the classical truths of antiquity. And the fact that, in
the next several paragraphs, he discusses his early education in a
log schoolhouse suggests both his Jeffersonian respect for education and his backcountry determination in acquiring it, combin-
ing the Sage of Monticello with the Horatio Alger myth that was
popular when he wrote his *Memoirs*. He recalls, for example, that
he and his sisters walked every day "to this rude hut . . . often
through a deep snow, to get the rudiments of an education." He
had briefly attended another country school, where two incidents
occurred that he later considered significant.[5]

The first concerned a black child, presumably one of the family slaves. Virginia Mosby, fearing Jack was too young to be on
his own, had the child accompany her son to and from school.
One day Mosby asked the child to stay with him through the day.

During a recess, older boys hoisted the child onto a block and put him through a mock slave auction. Mosby thought his companion had been sold "and was greatly distressed at losing such a dutiful playmate. We went home together but he never spent another day with me at the schoolhouse." The second event involved the schoolmaster, who became intoxicated one day during his lunch break, passed out along a road, and was carried back to the schoolhouse by the students to finish the lessons. "The school closed soon after; I don't know why," Mosby quipped. An object lesson, perhaps, for he avoided hard liquor throughout his life. Later he developed a fondness for coffee, and during the Civil War he would ride for miles to try to find a freshly brewed cup. He was said to be as excited by coffee, in scarce supply in wartime, as other men were by whiskey.[6]

Mosby's boyhood reading shows a preference for military heroes. He mentions two pictures that left a lasting impression on him. One depicted the British general James Wolfe dying in the arms of a soldier on the Plains of Abraham in Quebec in 1759 during the French and Indian Wars, and the other depicted Maj. Gen. Israel Putnam fleeing British dragoons in 1779. He also recalls reading a biography of Francis Marion by Mason Locke Weems and remembers how he shouted when he "read aloud in the nursery of the way the great partisan hid in the swamp and outwitted the British. I did not then expect that the time would ever come when I would have escapes as narrow as that of Putnam and take part in adventures that have been compared with Marion's." Parson Weems also wrote infamously unreliable biographies of Washington and other American heroes, books full of bloated parables and moralistic blather. Mosby's early exposure to American history, therefore, tilted heavily toward the mythic.[7]

His education was furthered by a young woman his father had employed as a governess for Mosby's sisters. She was an outspoken abolitionist from Massachusetts. His brother-in-law, Charles W. Russell, added this note in the *Memoirs* to clarify Mosby's views: "Colonel Mosby never had a word to say favorable to slavery—a fact which may be attributed to the influence of Miss Abby Southwick. . . . All the Mosby family were, and remained, devoted to Miss Southwick. She and young Mosby had

numerous talks on the subject of slavery and other political topics. At the close of the war she immediately sent money and supplies to the family and told them how anxiously she had read the
papers, fearing to find news that he had been killed.[8]

Mosby said he still cherished "a strong affection for the slaves
who nursed me and played with me in my childhood. That was
the prevailing sentiment in the South—not one peculiar to myself—but one prevailing in all the South toward an institution
which we now thank Abraham Lincoln for abolishing." From the
perspective of the twenty-first century, a reader cannot help but
speculate on the meaning of these words, which seem to say that
even though slavery was wrong, it was not really so bad for the
slaves. Later in life, Mosby had no use for slavery, saw it as the
direct cause of the war, and saw emancipation as liberating more
whites than blacks because it overthrew an oligarchy of
slaveholders. "In retrospect," he wrote in 1902, "slavery seems
such a monstrous thing that some are . . . trying to prove that
slavery was not the cause of the war. Then what was the cause?"
But his own personal experiences of slavery seem retrospectively
sentimental, and one wonders what form the discussions with
Miss Southwick actually took in the Mosby household. His story
about seeing his black companion being bartered on the stump
seems more amusing to him than repugnant.[9]

At about the age of ten, Mosby began attending a school in
Charlottesville. Although he was often an indifferent student, he
had a talent for Latin and Greek, could recite Tacitus and
Thucydides, and claimed he was a walking dictionary of the classics. "I was born a Greek," he said. Perhaps, like Achilles, Mosby
believed he was destined to die young and gloriously. But, unlike Achilles, he was to live to a ripe old age. He also enjoyed
literature, especially the works of Washington Irving. By the age
of sixteen, he was sufficiently prepared to begin studies at the
University of Virginia. He says little more in the *Memoirs* about
his early life, but he does leave his future biographers some important clues. He had a passion for hunting and arose early on
Saturday mornings so he could spend as much time as possible
shooting game in the fields and woods. He found any form of
athletics distasteful and claimed never to have seen a ball game.
He also recalls, with what sounds like considerable resentment,

that he was "very delicate and often heard that I would never live to be a grown man. But the prophets were wrong, for I have outlived nearly all the contemporaries of my youth." The family doctor feared Mosby was vulnerable to consumption because he was frail and could not gain weight. Virginia Mosby claimed that her son, at the age of nineteen, was "of a very weak delicate constitution" and had been "delicate from his birth."[10]

His delicacy, however, did not preclude physical combat. He mentions that he once was whipped by a teacher for fighting at the log schoolhouse. He was vulnerable to bullying, and this gave Mosby's biographers an important key to his personality. By fighting back against bullying, Mosby developed his early aggressiveness and propensity to violence. James Ramage concludes that Mosby developed a "bipolar personality," revered and pampered at home but tormented and belittled at school. Winning or losing fights mattered less than showing his courage and his unwillingness to be abused. Mosby once said he had lost every fight except one, which came to a premature end when someone separated the antagonists before Mosby could claim a victory. He came to regard others with suspicion and hostility. His strength and self-confidence came from his determination to be a formidable adversary. When war came, Mosby was emotionally ready to do battle. "I was glad to see that the little men were a match for the big men through being armed," he wrote in 1911. Virgil Carrington Jones provides a colorful, if somewhat ludicrous, analogy: "He was a battler by instinct, and he graduated from fist to firearms with the same easy evolution that the Southland swung from a haven of mint juleps and honey to a battlefield of rotting bodies."[11]

By the time Mosby entered the University of Virginia in 1850, he had developed into a capable scholar with a capacity for mayhem. In *Patriotic Gore*, his classic study of the motives, myth, and literature of the Civil War, Edmund Wilson expresses a great deal of interest in Mosby. He writes that the "ideal of education that Jefferson had hoped to encourage in founding the University of Virginia was sometimes to realize itself in unpredictable ways through temperaments quite alien to Jefferson's. Edgar Allan Poe had been such a case, and Mosby was another." Jefferson believed young men at his university should not be excessively restricted by academic rules, and the students tried hard to oblige. Gambling, fighting, horse racing, drinking, bell ringing, and firing off pistols were all too common, and some townspeople thought the students were completely out of control.[12]

Mosby continued to excel in Latin, Greek, literature, and history. He was usually quiet and introspective. But outside the classroom he, too, acquired a reputation as a "graceless scamp" and a troublemaker. He was a great horseman who took on all comers in a race and rode his horse through Charlottesville at a speed considerably faster than the laws permitted. On April Fools' Day he broke a gunstock over the head of a constable he thought was being unnecessarily rough with a fellow student he had apprehended during some hijinks. This action led to an indictment for assault and a fine. These shenanigans, however, only foreshadowed the notorious incident that led to Mosby's imprisonment and early rustication from the university.[13]

JAILHOUSE LAWYER

The trouble began innocently enough, and, in Wilson's condescending view, it was "a typically absurd Southern quarrel." Mosby and a medical student, George Turpin, both wanted the same violinists to perform on the same evening. Mosby had invited them to play at a party at Tudor Grove. Word later reached him that Turpin had made remarks to which Mosby took exception. Mosby wrote a letter to Turpin, who responded by threatening to beat him. The problem from Mosby's point of view was that Turpin was a dangerous character who had slashed one man with a knife and beaten another senseless with a rock. Turpin was larger and stronger than Mosby and might well have killed him in a fight. So Mosby took precautions, borrowing a small pepperbox pistol. The inevitable confrontation occurred at Mosby's boardinghouse. Several witnesses later claimed Turpin rushed at Mosby, who drew his pistol and shot Turpin in the neck. A doctor was summoned and removed the bullet. Turpin survived but Mosby was later arrested at Tudor Grove and jailed. Turpin claimed Mosby shot before he moved toward him. Mosby was indicted on charges of malicious and unlawful shooting. Conviction on the first count could have put him in the penitentiary for a decade.[14]

The trial concluded about two months after the shooting. Mosby was convicted of the lesser charge of unlawful shooting, a misdemeanor, and sentenced to a one-year term to be served in the county jail. Mosby's prospects at this point in his life seemed grim. Aristides Monteiro, a classmate who would later serve as a surgeon in Mosby's Rangers, said of him: "Of all my University friends and acquaintances this youthful prisoner would have been the last one I would have selected with the least expectation that the world would ever hear from him again." Ironically, however, the jail term worked to Mosby's advantage. William J. Robertson, the Commonwealth's attorney who had prosecuted him, one day saw him in his cell reading a book. "What are you reading?" Robertson asked. "Milton's 'Paradise Lost' and I hope soon to enjoy 'Paradise Regained,' " Mosby replied. Robertson suggested that Mosby should do some writing, but Mosby said that he had decided to study law: "The law has made a good deal out of me. I am now going to make something out of the law." Siepel suggests that Mosby's sudden interest in the law may have been a response to "the power of words. He'd been locked up, after all, by words, not by pistols or swords." But the young classicist and literary scholar already knew their power. And when words proved insufficient, he had learned the power of a pistol. A complementary explanation is that Mosby was learning how to make the most out of any situation presented to him, a pragmatic tendency that came to fruition during the war. If the law was going to lock him up, he would use the time to unlock the mysteries of the law.[15]

Mosby's objective was more than just researching the statutes to look for loopholes that might exonerate him. Robertson gave Mosby access to his law library, and he began preparing to pass the bar exam and take up the practice of law after his release. Meanwhile, nine jurors signed a petition requesting a pardon for Mosby, and his attorneys and his father obtained almost three hundred signatures on a separate petition for a pardon. Several physicians offered the opinion that Mosby was too frail to serve out a jail term. His parents made repeated appeals to the governor, who eventually pardoned Mosby two days before

Christmas in 1853. According to Russell, "Mosby's conviction affected him greatly, and he did not include an account of it in his story because—or at least it would seem probable—he feared that the conclusion would be drawn that he was more like the picture painted by the enemy during the war, instead of the kindly man he really was."[16]

But he felt no remorse. In 1911, Mosby wrote that he had "never done anything that I so cordially approve as shooting Turpin." He claimed that soon after the shooting, Turpin went to Alabama where someone poisoned him. Whatever the lingering consequences of the ordeal, Mosby passed the bar exam after studying for many months in Robertson's law office. One of the examining judges, ironically, was Richard H. Field, who had presided over the trial that had resulted in Mosby's conviction. Later, during the Civil War, Mosby and Field enjoyed a laugh together when the judge told him, "I always believed you did exactly right in shooting that fellow," and Mosby replied, "Why in the devil, then, didn't you tell the jury so?" He bore Field and Robertson no animus, a pattern of behavior he followed throughout his life when he felt an adversary had treated him fairly. Toward those who had treated him unfairly, he carried a grudge to the grave.[17]

BORDERLANDS

Mosby opened his first law office in the little village of Howardsville in Albemarle County in 1855 and practiced there until November 1858, with few clients. In June 1856, however, he met the young woman who was to become his wife. Pauline Clarke was nineteen years old and the daughter of a prominent attorney and former congressman from Kentucky who had been the Democratic Party's candidate for governor. They were married by a Roman Catholic priest in Nashville, Tennessee, on December 30, 1856. One of the guests, by some accounts, was Tennessee's U.S. senator, Andrew Johnson, the future president. The couple's first daughter, May Virginia, was born March 10, 1858; their first son, Beverly, was born October 1, 1860. Mosby never became a Roman Catholic, but he had no objection to his children being taught in Catholic schools or to Pauline's devotional life. He wore throughout the war a small cross she had given him.[18]

Mosby looked for a better place to build his law practice. He had considered Memphis, but settled on Bristol, which straddled the Virginia-Tennessee border. He had planned to practice law in Bristol as early as 1855. In the fall of 1856, Bristol had become an important rail terminus linking the Virginia & Tennessee Railroad with the East Tennessee & Virginia, both parts of a rudimentary trunk line that would extend rail transportation from Richmond to New Orleans by the time of the Civil War.[19]

Passengers changed trains in Bristol merely by walking across Main Street, which was the state border. Mosby's law office on the Virginia side was close to the train station, and he would have had a keen awareness of the railroad's importance to the city. Mosby had come of age with the railroads in the Virginia of his day, and the nascent railroad industry would figure prominently in his future in unexpected ways. By the time of the Civil War, railroads were seen as a symbol of unity as the young nation expanded, and there was much talk in Bristol of progress and opportunity as the trains clattered into town. Mosby took advantage of the dual court systems and practiced in both Washington County, Virginia, and Sullivan County, Tennessee. The railroad stimulated commerce, and commerce stimulated litigation. The city suited Mosby, who would find border regions and sectional disputes congenial throughout his life. He was a man who appreciated subtleties and ambiguities, and there was a strange dualism in his nature. Borders were places of conflict, and Mosby throve on conflict.[20]

STORM CLOUDS

Whatever tranquillity Mosby found in Bristol was short lived, as local affairs were engulfed in the gathering sectional crisis. At first the talk was merely the political bluster of a national election year. Mosby recalled that the summer of 1860 brought "omens of war at this time, but nobody realized the impending danger." During a summer court appearance in Abingdon, Virginia, a friend persuaded Mosby to join the Washington Mounted Rifles, a militia unit soon to come under the command of Capt. William E. "Grumble" Jones.[21]

Mosby wanted no part of secession and voted in favor of Stephen A. Douglas, the Northern Democratic candidate. His was one of only 56 votes cast for Douglas in Washington County. John Breckinridge, the Southern Democrat, led the field with 1,178 votes, followed by John Bell, on the Unionist ticket, with 916 votes. In Mosby's view, William L. Yancey, the firebrand Alabama secessionist, was most responsible for splitting the Democratic Party, which gave Lincoln the presidency and severed the Union. When Mosby had approached Yancey during the campaign to ask him to debate Tim Rives, a noted orator who supported Douglas, he was rebuffed. "I shall never forget the arrogance and contempt with which he treated me," Mosby wrote years later. How he arrived at his political views is a matter of some conjecture. J. Austin Sperry, editor of the *Bristol News* and the *Knoxville Register*, recalled that Mosby had initially been reticent: "So guarded had been his political utterances that but few of the villagers knew with which of the parties to class him, when he suddenly bloomed out as an elector on the Douglas ticket. This seemed to fix his status as a Union Democrat. I say seemed, for I am now inclined to think his politics was like his subsequent fighting—independent and irregular."[22]

Mosby continued to oppose secession as Deep South states began to follow South Carolina out of the Union. In mid-January he happened to meet Sperry in the street. Mosby said he had concluded from the editorial in the day's paper that Sperry was "a secessionist *per se.*" Sperry replied that Mosby had drawn the wrong conclusion and that he was a secessionist "by the logic of events." Mosby then said he was glad to hear it, because he would enjoy "hanging a disunionist *per se.* Do you know what secession means? It means bloody war, followed by feuds between the border States, which a century may not see the end of." Sperry asked which side Mosby would take in the event of war. "I shall fight for the Union, Sir—for the Union, of course, and you?" Sperry said if he met Mosby in battle, he would run him through with a bayonet. "Very well," Mosby replied. "We'll meet at Philippi," quoting from Shakespeare's *Julius Caesar.* (Philippi was the

Macedonian city where Brutus and Cassius were defeated by Antony and Octavian in 42 B.C.)[23]

Mosby was attending court in Abingdon on April 15 when news came that Lincoln had called for 75,000 volunteers to put down the rebellion. He recalled that "in the delirium of the hour, we all forgot our Union principles in our sympathy with the pro-slavery cause, and rushed to the field of Mars." Two days later the Virginia convention, which had been debating the issue for months, passed an ordinance of secession. "Nobody cared whether it was a constitutional right they were exercising or an act of revolution. At such times reason is silent and passion prevails," Mosby wrote. Shortly thereafter he walked into Sperry's office wearing the militia uniform he had been issued by Captain Jones. "Why, Mosby," Sperry said. "This isn't Philippi, nor is that a Federal uniform." Said Mosby: "No more of that. When I talked that way, Virginia had not passed the ordinance of secession. She is out of the Union now. Virginia is my mother, God bless her. I can't fight against my mother, can I?" Or, as he put it later in his *Memoirs*, "Virginia went out of the Union by force of arms, and I went with her." He elaborated in his *Reminiscences* that "it is a mistake to suppose that the Virginia people went to war in obedience to any decree of their State, commanding them to go. On the contrary, the people were in a state of armed revolution before the State had acted in its corporate capacity. I went along with the flood just like everybody else."[24]

BARRISTER IN BUTTERNUT

Mosby remembered his first days as a soldier as a quixotic prelude to an epic drama that ended in tragedy. Before he could join his company at its barracks and campground in Abingdon, he first had to settle his legal and personal affairs. Jones gave him permission to remain in Bristol for a time. He still had a court appearance in Blountville, Tennessee, to take care of, and he wanted to collect some fees from his clients before he marched off to defend Virginia from the Yankee hordes. He complained half a century later that many of these clients still owed him money. After he said goodbye to his wife and children, he told one of his former Rangers years later during a visit to Bristol that he had already fought his hardest battle.[25]

He learned several things shortly after he returned to Abingdon. Lonely and hating camp life, he committed a minor disciplinary infraction and was briefly under arrest. As the company's "frailest and most delicate man," he already had a reputation as a slouchy rider and an indifferent soldier. He asked Jones for a transfer to an infantry unit, but before anything could be done the unit was ordered to Richmond. The unit he had wanted to join was composed of many Bristol men, and it eventually was commanded by Stonewall Jackson. He said later that, if his transfer had been approved, he likely would have remained a private throughout the war. Even more likely, he would have been killed.[26]

Mosby also learned that if he was ever to become a soldier, his best chance was to learn all he could from Jones, a tough professional from Washington County. He was crude, profane, cranky, hot tempered, a strict disciplinarian, and, in Mosby's eyes, an imposing officer. He looked after his men and had them well prepared for battle. "Jones was always very kind to me," Mosby recalled. He and Jones would often converse at the end of the day in Jones's tent, the difference in their rank apparently of no great matter. Jones patiently answered Mosby's questions about cavalry tactics and military strategy. Mosby later wrote, "To the lessons of duty and obedience he taught me I acknowledge that I am largely indebted for whatever success I may afterwards have had as a commander." If Robertson had made Mosby a lawyer, "Grumble" Jones was about to set him on the path to becoming the Gray Ghost.[27]

"THE FIELD OF MARS"

They left Abingdon on May 30, 1861, more than a hundred riders strong, slogging toward Richmond in a spring rain, their new cavalry sabers jangling at their sides, and the cheering crowds waving them on to glory. "Our march to the army was an ovation," Mosby recalled. "Nobody dreamed of the possibility of our failure and the last scene of the great drama at Appomattox." By the time the column reached Wytheville several days later, news of a skirmish at Fairfax had been reported by the newspapers. "We were greatly excited by the news of the affair. Our people had been reading about war and descriptions of battles by historians and poets, from the days of Homer down, and were filled with enthusiasm for military glory. They had no experience in the hardships of military service and knew nothing, had no conception, of the suffering it brings." In Richmond, Jones managed to equip some of his troopers, including Mosby, with the already-scarce Sharp's breech-loading carbines.[28]

The morning after his arrival, and almost three weeks after leaving Abingdon, Mosby posted a letter to his mother. Despite sleeping on the ground most nights, "I never before had such luxurious sleeping. I had no sign of a cold, although it rained a good deal of the time. I fattened every day." He was beginning to thrive on military life. It seems unlikely such a sickly young man could have turned himself into a redoubtable soldier in such a short time, and his insistence on reassuring his worrying mother that he was surviving the rigors of what had been up to that point little more than a camping trip points to another possible explanation. Mosby's former health problems might well have been psychosomatic. Told repeatedly that he was frail and delicate and overprotected by his family, he had thought of himself as physically unimposing. Now that he was in the cavalry where his size was an advantage, and where he was surrounded by hardy characters such as Jones, he almost immediately began to feel better. His mood lightened and he became more vigorous. This becomes increasingly evident in the first letters he wrote Pauline: "My health is as good as it can be"; "I live very well & enjoy perfect health"; "my health is better than it ever was in my life"; "I am living first rate now."[29]

Soon after he arrived in Richmond, Mosby ran into Tim Rives, the orator who had campaigned with him for Douglas. Rives offered to introduce Mosby to Gov. John Letcher and to recommend him for a military commission. But Mosby declined. He said he did not have enough training to be an officer, and, in any case, if he had to remain a private to serve under Jones, then he would remain a private. Captain Jones soon took his command to Ashland and provided the training Mosby was looking for. Jones not only could teach him the craft of soldiering, but he could also explain the axioms of warfare. If Mosby could master Greek and Latin, he could also learn the conjugations of combat from a professional soldier he respected. While he was at Ashland, Mosby was joined by one of his family's slaves, Aaron Burton, who stayed with him throughout the war. Mosby's mother had received Burton as a present from her father. In an interview he gave at the age of eighty-six when he was living in Brooklyn. Burton was generous in his recollection of Mosby. "I raised Colonel Mosby," he said. "I loved him and was with him in all his battles. When the war was over Colonel John told me that I was free and could go and do as I pleased. . . . He is a good man, and was a great fighter." Mosby helped him find work after the war, and occasionally sent him money. Burton may well have had great affection for Mosby. If, on the other hand, he did not, he would have been unlikely to express it in print while Mosby was sending him money. What is significant is that Burton's comments as reported in the press sustain Mosby's own stance toward slavery. After the war, he never denied that slavery was wrong or that it was the root cause of the war, but at the same time it was important to his myth that at least he be regarded as a generous master.[30]

GRAPESHOT AND GLORY

In July the company left camp for the Shenandoah Valley to join Jeb Stuart's First Virginia Cavalry regiment, which was providing a screen for Gen. Joseph E. Johnston's troops around Winchester. At Bunker Hill, on July 9, Mosby saw Stuart for the first time and was greatly impressed. Like Jones, Stuart was a professional, but, unlike Jones, he had panache. "His personal appearance bore the stamp of his military character, the fire, the dash, the energy and physical endurance that seemed able to defy all natural laws," Mosby wrote. In Stuart, he found a "heaven-born" knight who seemed to have emerged from the pages of Elizabethan romance. Although they were about the same age, Mosby thought at first that "the distance between us was so great that I never expected to rise to even an acquaintance with him." It was not just Stuart's chivalric presence that appealed to Mosby—there was plenty of that in the Confederate army's officer corps. He

came to see Stuart as a practical man who "possessed the qualities of a great leader of cavalry. He never had an equal in such
service. He discarded the old maxims and soon discovered that
in the conditions of modern war the chief functions of cavalry
are to learn the designs and to watch and report the movements
of the enemy." Writing this after the war, Mosby might well have
been describing his vision of himself.[31]

Two days later Jones led a scouting party near Martinsburg
and came upon some Union foragers. Mosby was in a squad that
captured two men who had fled into the woods. After securing
the prisoners, the squad unsuccessfully tried to provoke a fight
with Union pickets. A week later the First Virginia began moving
toward the Manassas battlefield, bivouacking on July 20 near
Ball's Ford after a sixty-mile forced march in the rain. Mosby was
one of six men issued Colt pistols by Jones, who told them they
would be assigned to the most dangerous missions. That night,
Mosby and his friend Fount Beattie lay on blankets under a
canopy of pine trees and heard their first picket firing with fore-
boding. Maybe, they considered, this would be their last night
beneath the stars.[32]

In the morning the six were sent into the woods near Bull
Run to reconnoiter before the company crossed the stream. Finding no Union forces to impede the crossing, Mosby was given the
first position in the first column of four riders as the company
rode into action. "Nothing afterwards occurred in my military
career that gives me more satisfaction to remember," he recalled.
Stuart divided his command, and Mosby's unit was never fully
engaged in the main action. Taking up a position in support of a
battery on Henry House Hill, where Jackson earned the appella-
tion "Stonewall," they were exposed for several hours to a hail of
grapeshot and exploding shells as they maneuvered to prevent
the battery from being flanked. At the end of the day, Mosby's
unit swept through its own infantry and pursued the routed
bluecoats until dark in what he called "the most memorable panic
in history." They returned with whatever spoils and provisions
they could carry.

The next day, Mosby crossed the battlefield with a message
to Stuart. He wrote Pauline a grisly description of the harrowing

scene: "In confused heaps were lying men and horses, adversaries and friends. But to hear the groans of the wounded and to see their ghastly wounds was more heart-rending than to look on the dead whose sufferings were over."[33]

Moving to Fairfax Court House on July 23, Mosby was amazed by country that "looked very much like Egypt after a flood of the Nile—it was strewn with the debris of [Brig. Gen. Irvin] McDowell's army." Mosby had survived his first battle—and the South's first great victory. His letters reveal that he was excited by combat, confident of further success, and supplying himself well with Yankee plunder. He concluded his letter of July 24 to Pauline: "We are now marching on to bombard Washington City." He expected the war to be over by the end of the year. And yet, after the war, in a lengthy analysis of the battle, he argued that the Confederate cause was lost at Bull Run because its advantage had not been exploited. He reasoned, as a cavalryman, that if the available cavalry units, including Stuart's, had been ordered across the Potomac at Seneca, they could have moved toward Baltimore, cut communications and isolated Washington, and possibly ended the war.

He had a hyperbolically high opinion of Southern cavalry, comparing the Confederate horsemen to ancient Persians, Cossacks, and "the Parthian horsemen who drove to despair the legions of Crassus and Antony." He overlooked the fact that Stuart's command was already exhausted by the time it reached the battlefield and that some cavalry units had been engaged in a sharp and bloody action. Even in a supporting role, he had ridden his "horse nearly to death on the battlefield," and that was before the pursuit of the retreating troops and the recovery of discarded booty. The South had lost some 2,000 soldiers in the fight, units were disorganized, and there were serious transportation and logistical problems in the wake of the battle. And yet Jackson reportedly claimed he could have taken Washington with 10,000 men. Whatever wisdom was possible in hindsight, it is clear that opportunities were lost, and that, by the end of the fighting at Manassas, Mosby was already beginning to think he knew more than many of the generals and politicians who were directing the war.[34]

"I COULD NOT BUT FEEL SOME REGRETS"

With both armies salving their wounds after Manassas, the next few months were comparatively quiet. This gave Mosby more time to study how to be a soldier and to learn the contours of the Northern Virginia countryside near Washington. He was not familiar with this part of the state, so his scouting and picket duties would prove valuable later. He spent most of his time on duty as a vedette along the Potomac River. One rainy August night near Falls Church, Mosby and two more vedettes were surprised by the sound of cavalry coming from the Union lines. He fired in the direction of the approaching horsemen and then scuttled back toward his own company. In the confusion, his horse tripped over a cow lying in the road, hurling Mosby to the ground and then rolling over on him. Knocked unconscious, he was taken to Falls Church by his companions who assumed he was dying.

When he awoke the next day, he was "bruised from head to foot, and felt like every bone in my body had been broken." He was sent to a hospital. The riders whom Mosby had heard in the night were Confederate cavalrymen who had failed to tell the patrols the route they would take on returning to their own lines. Mosby recovered and made light of the accident, but he had had his first of many close calls. Others, and perhaps Mosby himself, began to think he was immortal. As he recovered from his injuries, however, the somber reality of the political aspects of the war must have been heavy on his mind. Ascending to the top of Munson's Hill when he returned to picket duty in mid-September, he could see the Capitol a half-dozen miles away across the dark artery of the Potomac and the U.S. flag flying over the fortifications of the besieged city. "I thought of the last time I had seen it," he wrote Pauline, "for you were there with me, and I could not but feel some regrets that it was no longer the Capitol of my Country, but that of a foreign hostile foe."[35]

Those regrets, however, did not prevent Mosby from taking a sometimes perverse delight in shooting his enemies. His letters betray a cool indifference to firing at pickets, which was clearly a violation of international, Federal, and Confederate law, although one apparently ignored by both sides. He wrote that he was more eager to shoot enemy soldiers than he ever was to fire on squirrels. He seemed unmoved at finding a love letter in the pocket of a Brooklyn soldier he had shot through the head during a raid, and instead he described the overall engagement as "the most dashing feat of the war."[36]

SCOUTING FOR STUART

Mosby's fortunes began to change one morning in February 1862, when Stuart, by then a general, asked for a member of his command to accompany two young women who lived at Fairfax Court House to a position of safety farther within Confederate lines. Mosby was selected because he knew the father of one of the women. He took them by carriage to Centreville in a snowstorm and reported back to Stuart, who invited him to spend the night at his headquarters rather than walk back to his unit late at night in the snow. General Johnston and Maj. Gen. Gustavus Woodson Smith were also there, and Mosby was asked to join them at meals. At first reluctant to enter into the conversation, Mosby gradually became more comfortable with the setting and bantered with Johnston before riding back to camp. Here, again, we see Mosby adjusting and adapting to a new situation.

When he got back to camp, Jones appointed him a first lieutenant and adjutant of the First Virginia Cavalry. He wrote Pauline that the appointment was "a good stepping stone for future promotions and it is no small credit to me to be promoted from the ranks over the heads of those under whom I started." He was already becoming conscious of his status in the army and his ability to enhance his reputation. Mosby said that why Stuart made him his guest that night remained a mystery, but he always marked that occasion as the beginning of his great friendship with the general, which began to flower after his appointment as adjutant. And, more important, he was about to become Stuart's favorite scout. What forged the peculiar bond between them, at least in Mosby's eyes? Stuart had learned quickly that he could trust Mosby, who could be daring and resourceful. But perhaps, too, Stuart was charmed by Mosby's table talk, his wit and erudition. Mosby, in his own way, possessed a sometimes appealing sort of cunning. The two soldiers, forever yoked in Confederate mythology, may well have enjoyed each other's bonhomie, but at a deeper level each found the other useful.[37]

Mosby's first assignment involved scouting Maj. Gen. George McClellan's diversionary maneuvers west of the Potomac around Warrenton Junction. With a small squad, Mosby was able to get behind the Union forces facing Stuart and Johnston. His scouting reports supported other intelligence Stuart was gathering, all pointing to the conclusion that the bulk of McClellan's army was heading for the Peninsula, a district in southeast Virginia between the York and James Rivers. Stuart commended Mosby in official dispatches. In Mosby's mind, at least, this exploit was of huge import, and in his *Reminiscences* he lamented that he had "not been so fortunate as to have a poet to do for me on this occasion what Longfellow did for the midnight ride of Paul Revere." Mosby was eager to establish his reputation in the pantheon of American heroes. After all, Revere, too, was a rebel. Mosby's stock, however, was rising fast in 1862, at least with Stuart and Jones, but then another event soon cost him his commission. The Confederate Congress had passed legislation requiring the election of officers below the rank of general, and Lt. Col. Fitzhugh Lee was elected to replace Jones as colonel of the First Virginia, then stationed near Yorktown. Mosby immediately resigned as adjutant, knowing that he was no favorite of Fitz Lee, who disapproved of him and had recently threatened to have him arrested if he ever again called a bugle a horn. He made much of this petty incident after the war, writing with characteristic grandiosity: "I lost my first commission on the spot where Cornwallis lost his sword." He added that if he had been retained as adjutant, he likely would never have became the Gray Ghost. Stuart, who may have been chagrined by Mosby's sudden demotion, and still appreciative of his talents, assigned him to his personal staff as a scout. "In this way I began my career as a partisan, which now, when I recall it through the mist of years, seems as unreal as the lives of the Paladins."[38]

He soon had the chance to justify Stuart's confidence. On the morning of June 9, 1862, Stuart summoned Mosby to breakfast and outlined the situation on the Peninsula as he saw it. Johnston had been wounded at the bloody but inconclusive Seven Pines battle, which had at least served the purpose of checking

McClellan's advance on Richmond, and had been replaced by Gen. Robert E. Lee. Lee fortified the Confederate lines so a small force could keep McClellan's army at bay while he hammered McClellan's right flank north of the Chickahominy River. His plan was to bring Jackson's army from the Shenandoah Valley to strike at the enemy's rear. But first he had to probe McClellan's right flank to see how he was protecting his supply lines. Stuart asked Mosby to take a few men and find out if McClellan was fortifying his positions on the Totopotomoy Creek, which flows into the Pamunkey River, the anchor of his right wing. Mosby discovered a gap in McClellan's line guarded only by "a mere shroud of cavalry pickets." He returned to Stuart, who was relaxing beneath the boughs of a tree, and sprawled on the grass to explain what he had found.

"A CARNIVAL OF FUN"

Who deserves credit for what happened next is a matter of conjecture. Mosby claimed he had given Stuart the idea to exploit the gap in the lines. Stuart asked Mosby to write a report, which Stuart conveyed to General Lee along with a proposal that he ride completely around McClellan. Lee studied the report and sent Stuart off to find the gap and make what he could of it. In his *Reminiscences*, Mosby, at work at building his own legend, disputes the later claim of Maj. Heros Von Borcke, the Prussian soldier of fortune on Stuart's staff, that he and Stuart had already learned of the gap in McClellan's lines from a spy they had contacted during a behind-the-lines ride on the night of June 8. Mosby proclaimed Von Borcke a Baron Munchausen and dismissed his story as fiction. Ramage concludes, however, that Mosby "did not suggest the idea of the raid, but [that] his scouting provided a fresh, reliable intelligence foundation." *Baron Munchausen's Narratives of His Marvelous Travels and Campaigns in Russia* was first published in London in 1785. It purports to be an account of the adventures of a mendacious Hanoverian nobleman. By calling Von Borcke a Baron Munchausen, Mosby is depicting the Prussian soldier as a liar—but an amusing one. He thought much more highly of his own Prussian baron, Robert von Massow.[39]

Early on the morning of June 12, Stuart left Richmond with 1,200 troopers on what was to become his celebrated three-day, 100-mile circuit of McClellan's entire army. Feinting toward the Shenandoah Valley, they bivouacked that night near Hanover Court House, and when Stuart sent him out with an advance scouting party the next morning, Mosby "saw that my idea of a raid on McClellan's lines was about to be realized." Just outside the village, the squad ran into a Union cavalry force that scattered before it could be engaged. Near Linney's Corner, Mosby charged with the Ninth Virginia into the ranks of the Fifth U.S. Cavalry and engaged in brief saber and hand-to-hand fighting that drove the Federals back. Stuart, now fully committed to the encircling maneuver, sent Mosby and two scouts ahead of his main body.

Using the element of surprise to its fullest effect, Mosby took prisoners, destroyed or captured supply wagons, cut telegraph lines, and found two supply schooners being unloaded on the Pamunkey River. Stuart had them burned. Riding alone near Tunstall Station, Mosby surprised a squadron of the Eleventh Pennsylvania Cavalry. Knowing Stuart's advance guard was not far behind, and that his horse was too exhausted to outrun the Pennsylvanians if they decided to pursue, he simply drew his saber and waved it in the air, as if he were leading a sizable force. The bluff worked, and the troopers retreated as soon as they heard the Confederate horsemen approaching. The raiders pressed forward, attacking a train, looting supply depots, and burning wagons through the night until "the heavens were lurid with the light reflected from the burning trains, and our track was as brilliant as the tail of a comet." It had all seemed absurdly easy, and years later Mosby would write that the "summer night was a carnival of fun I can never forget. Nobody thought of danger or of sleep, when champagne bottles were bursting, and Rhine wine was flowing in copious streams. All had perfect confidence in their leader. In the riot among the sutlers' stores 'grim-visaged war had smoothed his wrinkled front,' and Mars resigned his sceptre to the jolly god."[40]

He returned to Richmond a hero. Lee praised him in his congratulatory orders. Stuart lauded him in his report and recommended him for promotion. The *Richmond Dispatch* called him "the gallant Lieutenant," even though he was still a private. The *Abingdon Virginian* boasted that Mosby, the local lawyer, "is evidently of the same stuff that [Col. John Hunt] Morgan and [Col. Turner] Ashby and such men are made of." Mosby told Pauline the raid was "the grandest scout of the war. I not only helped to execute it, but was the first one who conceived and demonstrated that it was practicable. . . . I never enjoyed myself so much in my life."[41]

A PARTISAN IN WAITING

Mosby took no part in the Seven Days battles that followed, and while he rested from his adventures, he gave some thought to what he wanted to do next. On June 20, 1862, Stuart had written Secretary of War George Randolph, requesting that Mosby be given the captaincy of a company of sharpshooters in his brigade, but nothing had come of it. Mosby, in any case, had bigger plans. McClellan's Peninsula Campaign was a failure, but a new threat was developing in the Northern Virginia counties where Maj. Gen. John Pope was putting together a new Union army from units scattered in front of Washington. The bombastic Pope proposed to move south while living off the land and giving little attention to what was behind him. Moreover, he promised to quell rebellious Virginians by imposing harsh treatment on civilians. As Mosby saw it, Pope "had opened a promising field for partisan warfare and had invited, or rather dared, anybody to take advantage of it." Accordingly, he approached Stuart with a scheme. He wanted a dozen men "to make the harvest for the laborers were few, and do for Pope what he would not do for himself, take care of his rear and communications for him." (The Biblical allusion is to Matthew 9:37–38: "Then saith he unto his disciples, The harvest truly is plenteous, but the laborers are few; Pray ye therefore the Lord of the harvest, that he will send forth labourers into his harvest.") Mosby argued that his plan could succeed for several reasons. He knew the territory because he had served there during the first year of the war. Pope would have little choice but to detail his cavalry to protect his communication lines if they were being harassed by Mosby's band. And that would peel off troops from Pope and constrict his movements as he tried to forage through the countryside. More important, Mosby would spread confusion and panic behind the lines. Pope's plans would have to change, and his offensive strength would be reduced. Pope had raised the stakes through his threats to lay waste to the countryside. Maybe it was time to give him his own bitter medicine.[42]

Just what happened next and why is something of a mystery. Stuart turned Mosby down, which puzzled and angered him. Years later the incident still rankled, and Mosby wrote that he had had "to beg for the privilege of striking the enemy at a vulnerable point. If the detail had been given me, I would have started directly to cross the Rapidan to flank Pope, and my partisan war would have begun then." Mosby's biographers have come to different conclusions as to why Stuart hesitated. James Ramage suggests Stuart may have thought the plan had little chance for success. Mosby, after all, was not proposing a raid but a sustained operation in enemy territory. Virgil Carrington Jones and Kevin Siepel seem to conclude that Stuart basically had favored the plan. Stuart did tell Mosby he would write Stonewall Jackson a letter recommending him as a scout, but not, according to Ramage, specifically endorsing the partisan scheme. Stuart's reason was that he was reorganizing his cavalry and had no men he could give Mosby, but that Jackson might be able to detach some cavalry or infantry for the endeavor. Other explanations are also possible. Stuart may have thought that by sending Mosby to Jackson he might yet get him back if Jackson opposed the plan. Or he may not have wanted to upset Fitz Lee, his chief subordinate, who despised Mosby and had no use for irregular tactics. Perhaps Stuart even thought Mosby was becoming a little too full of himself. He knew what Mosby could do as a scout, but that plan at that time may have sounded preposterous.[43]

And what of Mosby's motivation? Ramage suggests that he had been excited earlier by the Partisan Ranger Act passed by the Confederate Congress on April 21, 1862. The act authorized the chartering of partisan bands that could operate behind enemy lines while remaining part of the regular army. The partisan rangers would receive the same pay as regular troops but they would also be permitted to sell their plunder and keep the profits. An additional incentive for Mosby to participate would have been his freedom from regular army routine. He had gotten a taste of the partisan life on his raid with Stuart, and Ramage argues that, although Mosby himself was not greedy, he saw what an incentive plunder could be to hungry soldiers and how "avarice could be harnessed as a means to success." Moreover, he had relished the shock tactics that had stunned and terrified the sutlers and the disorganized cavalrymen he had attacked during the raid.[44]

Jones notes that Southern newspapers were enthusiastically behind the Partisan Ranger Act. Mosby, he imagines, "saw rich stores waiting to be snatched, wagon trains burning in the moonlight, prisoners captured by bold action. To him came a conviction stronger than that of Robin Hood, more daring than that of Marion." He speculates that Mosby "dreamed of himself at the head of a separate command, an energetic following, one that would serve at his bid, would dash into daring feats without waiting for deliberative council of superior officers." Here, perhaps, is where history and romance begin to ride off in different directions. Whatever Mosby's reasons and whatever Stuart's concerns, Mosby took the general's offer of a letter to Jackson and called it "the best I could get." But was service under Jackson really the weaker option? Jackson himself was coming to the conclusion that the only way to defeat Union forces was by organizing small bands of hard-fighting, highly mobile troops to launch counterinvasions into the North. He had told a cavalry officer that this kind of warfare "best suits the temper of our people and the dash and daring of the Southern soldier, and I would right now seize the golden moment to show the North what they may expect." Mosby, it would seem, might well have been given a warm reception by the aggressive general.[45]

BACK TO PRISON

Jackson by this time had begun operations around Gordonsville at the junction of the Orange & Alexandria and Virginia Central Railroads to check Pope. Mosby and a courier left Stuart on July 19 and rode off for Gordonsville by way of the Beaver Dam Station on the Virginia Central. After spending the night with a farmer, he had just sent the courier on to Jackson's headquarters at dawn with his horse and settled down outside the depot to wait for a train that was expected within the hour, when a New York cavalry regiment arrived and took him prisoner. In his haversack was a copy of Napoleon's *Maxims of War*— a gift from Stuart to Jackson—and Stuart's letter of introduction. One of the cavalrymen wrote an account of the incident that appeared later in a regimental history: "During an affray we captured a young Confederate, who gave his name as Captain John S. Mosby. By his sprightly appearance and conversation he attracted considerable attention. He is slight but well formed; has a keen blue eye and a blond complexion, and displays no small amount of Southern bravado in his dress and manners. His gray plush hat is surmounted by a waving plume, which he tosses, as he speaks, in real Prussian style."[46]

If this is true, it may have been colored by a later perception of Mosby, who possibly anticipated the rank he would probably have received if his plan to reach Jackson had succeeded. Stuart had already nominated him for a captaincy, which Mosby may have regarded as still pending, and Stuart had called him a captain without commission in his report on the circuitous ride. Or Mosby may have tried to bluff his captors into thinking he was an officer in order to gain better treatment. This deception would have been unnecessary, because the contents of Stuart's letter made Mosby's importance clear. He told his captors at least one other lie, that the train would be guarded, and they did not wait to test him. But he wrote Pauline he had been treated courteously by the officers, one of whom even offered to loan him money. The hat and the plume were part of the costume of Stuart's cavalrymen, who perhaps had been influenced by Von Borcke.[47]

In any event, Mosby was taken to Washington to await his exchange and spent the next ten days in the Old Capitol Prison. Mosby, of course, is not the only subsequently famous man to have been locked up and then released by those he would later torment. Before the end of the war, nevertheless, it must have been especially galling for Union leaders to realize they had once had the scourge of the Capital behind bars and then let him go. This time Mosby read Napoleon's *Maxims* in jail instead of Blackstone's *Commentaries*, claiming that he "rather enjoyed my visit to Washington" because, in addition to catching up on his reading, he continued to do a little scouting.

A MEETING WITH LEE

Mosby boarded a steamer for the journey down the Chesapeake Bay to Hampton Roads. While the vessel lay at anchor for four days before turning up the James River, he saw troop transports and found out they carried soldiers from Maj. Gen. Ambrose Burnside's corps, which had been based in North Carolina. He reasoned that if they were going to reinforce Pope at Aquia Creek, ten miles from Fredericksburg on the main line of the Richmond, Fredericksburg & Potomac Railroad, it probably meant McClellan was withdrawing from the Peninsula. But if they were reinforcing McClellan, that meant Pope might be vulnerable, and McClellan might again try to batter down Richmond's back door. He persuaded the captain of the steamer, a Southern sympathizer from Baltimore, to find out what was happening on shore. The transports were going up the Potomac, and when Mosby saw them passing into the bay by Fort Monroe, he knew the Peninsula Campaign was over—and the next move would be Pope's. Later that morning, on going up the James, he told one of the Confederate exchange commissioners he had vital news for Lee, and he was quickly processed and sent on his way.

He started the dozen-mile walk to Lee's headquarters near Richmond under a broiling August sun but collapsed from exhaustion before he could get there. A cavalryman found him sprawled by the side of the road and got him a horse to ride the rest of the way. When Mosby met General Lee at headquarters, he was as overwhelmed as he had been when he first saw Stuart, remarking that "he was alone and poring over some maps on the table, and no doubt planning a new campaign. Although his manner was gentle and kind, I felt for him an awe and veneration which I have never felt for any other man. He was then the foremost man in all the world, and I almost imagined that I saw one of the Homeric heroes before me."[48]

Lee was impressed with Mosby's information and sent a message to Jackson that night. Jackson, seeing his opportunity, struck at Pope at Cedar Mountain on August 9 before Burnside's reinforcements could arrive, and just four days after Mosby's meeting with Lee. Mosby boasted that his information had brought on the battle, and he could, perhaps, claim some role in setting in motion the campaign that concluded with the Confederate victory at Second Manassas. The Comte de Paris's *History of the Civil War in America* implied that Mosby's information was decisive. The Comte exaggerated Mosby's importance at the time by saying that, when he left the steamer and struck out for Richmond, his "face was well known to every Virginian, and his name to all his companions in arms; it was the celebrated partisan, Colonel John Mosby." This, obviously, is a description given well after the fact. But Ramage notes that Mosby's claim "failed to take into account the synthesis of intelligence from several sources," although his predictions proved correct and his value as a scout was further enhanced. Again, the mythmaking apparatus initiated by Mosby himself had placed him at the center of extraordinary events and given him a decisive role.[49]

Mosby had yet to report to Jackson and was on his way to do so on August 17, 1862, when he met Stuart, who was returning from Richmond to meet Fitzhugh Lee and his cavalry before launching a raid behind Pope's army. But Fitz Lee was not where he was supposed to be, and Stuart, Mosby, and some others spent the night at a house in a deserted village. Just before sunrise, Mosby and another soldier heard the sound of cavalry and went to investigate. They were soon being pursued by a small Union force, and Mosby and Stuart narrowly escaped. After the war, Mosby again poked fun at Von Borcke, who, he claimed, had given himself a heroic role in the day's action, but the Prussian's horse "ran faster than ours and that was the only distinction he won." Mosby fought with Stuart during the ensuing Second Battle of Manassas, a Confederate victory, but still in Mosby's view a "comedy of errors," in which "Lee never again had such an opportunity to destroy an army." During the battle, Mosby was grazed in the head by a bullet. With another soldier, he captured a fine Yankee horse, two saddles, a couple of pistols, two infantrymen, and seven cavalrymen. Nevertheless, he was upstaged by the irrepressible Von Borcke, who, as usual, related "prodigies he performed that were never surpassed by Amadis of Gaul" (the "perfect knight" of sixteenth-century Spanish legend). Competing myths were continually being created and amended, and Mosby was quick to debunk men such as Von Borcke who, he believed, were building reputations on fantasy rather than actual accomplishments. Egregious embellishers such as Von Borcke made easy targets, however, and by correcting such claims, Mosby was implicitly arguing for the veracity of his own accounts in more controversial matters.[50]

THE INVADER

With Lee now poised to launch his first invasion of the North, Mosby rode in the advance guard of the 40,000-man Confederate army that surged across the Potomac on September 4 in a campaign that would lead, almost two weeks later, to a clash with McClellan's army at Antietam Creek, the war's bloodiest one-day battle. Passing through Frederick, Maryland, with the band playing "Maryland, My Maryland," Mosby proudly rode just behind Jackson. During the battle on September 17, Mosby and Stuart rode by Jackson's batteries near the Dunkard Church and the West Wood. As Jackson directed his fire into the flank of the last attacking column after the bloody repulse of Maj. Gen. John Sedgwick's division, Mosby paused "to look at the great soldier who was then transfigured with the joy of battle." Mosby rode on and caught up with Stuart. He took care not to ride over the wounded strewn across the field. "Whole ranks seemed to have been struck down by a volley."

He saw a wounded Federal officer, Col. Isaac J. Wistar, who appeared to be in agony from a wound in his shoulder, and stopped to place a rolled-up blanket under his head. He took a canteen of water from the body of a dead soldier lying nearby and offered the water to another wounded soldier, who told him, "No, take it to my Colonel, he is the best man in the world." This, Mosby wrote, was a speech worthy of Sir Philip Sidney, the English soldier-poet and model of chivalry. He learned after the war that the soldier had died that night. As Mosby turned to leave Wistar after giving him the water, he heard the sudden threshing of Jackson's batteries. "Whose guns are those?" Wistar asked. "I don't know," Mosby replied, not wishing to burden the colonel

with the possibility that his men were being shredded in the ab-
attoir of Antietam. Wistar recovered from his wound, was promoted to the rank of brigadier general, and later became president
of the Pennsylvania Canal Company. Mosby met him after the
war, and Wistar was astounded to learn that it was the famous
partisan who had paused to give him a drink. This incident, and
others like it, shows another side of Mosby as a mythic warrior.
He could be the Good Samaritan and the chivalrous knight who
shows compassion for his enemies and respects courage and sacrifice. Both this aspect of Mosby's nature and the darker, more
ruthless side would be addressed in the literary and cultural
Mosby Myth that arose after the war.[51]

With both armies battered and bloodied in the carnage at
Antietam, the autumn became a time for maneuvering, reorgani-
zation, and recovery that ended with the mauling of the Federal
army at Fredericksburg on December 13. Scouting alone or with
Stuart, Mosby was active during the interval and provided valuable information about the placement of Union forces in Northern Virginia, earning a personal letter of thanks from Lee. During
one scouting mission forty miles behind the Yankee lines, Mosby
happened to be standing near Catlett's Station by the Orange &
Alexandria Railroad and saw General McClellan in a railroad car
on his way to Washington. Investigating further, he learned that
McClellan had been replaced by Burnside, who was moving the
army from Warrenton to the Rappahannock, across the river from
Fredericksburg. Scouting near Manassas, Mosby and a squad of
nine men surprised a like number of cavalry pickets. Mosby ordered his men to dismount and charge while he did a reprise of
the bluff he had managed during Stuart's ride around McClellan
on the Peninsula. Seeing Mosby galloping about and shouting
orders to phantom troopers, the pickets supposed they were about
to be engulfed by a brigade of Stuart's cavalry and fled. Their
flight caused a panic in their own regiment, which hastened from
the area. Mosby boasted to Pauline that he had "stampeded two
or three thousand Yankees," and complained that the Richmond
newspapers had given the well-connected Col. Thomas Rosser
of the Fifth Virginia Cavalry the credit he and his men actually
deserved. Mosby claimed Rosser was twenty-five miles away

from the action. Mosby was becoming increasingly attentive to the way the press covered his exploits and resented its inaccuracies. But he learned later that inaccurate press reports could work to his advantage.[52]

CROSSING THE RIVER

Mosby and Stuart's cavalry had no major role in the Battle of Fredericksburg and soon began foraging while the armies went into winter camp. Weary of inactivity, Stuart launched a Christmas raid with 1,800 troopers to disrupt Burnside's communications with Washington. Leaving Dumfries, Stuart ordered Mosby and his friend Fount Beattie to ride on ahead through a dense forest where there was a danger of ambush:

> Beattie and I went forward at a gallop, until we met a large body of cavalry. As no support was in sight, several officers made a dash at us, and at the same time opened such a fire as to show that peace on earth and good will to men, which the angels and morning stars had sung on that day over 1800 years ago, was no part of their creed. The very fact that we did not run away ought to have warned them that somebody was behind us. When the whole body had got within a short distance of us, Stuart, who had heard the firing, came thundering up with the 1st Virginia cavalry. All the fun was over with the Pennsylvanians then. There was no more merry Christmas for them.[53]

When he returned, Stuart let Mosby stay behind with a squad to attack Union outposts along the Alexandria, Loudoun & Hampshire Railroad. During the next few days he captured twenty cavalrymen, their horses, and weapons. Impressed with Mosby's success, Stuart let him cross the Rappahannock at Fox's Mill with a band of fifteen men on January 24, 1863, to operate in the area around Middleburg just within the protection of the Bull Run Mountains and some twenty miles west of the defensive cavalry screen that encircled Washington. "It looked as though I was leading a forlorn hope, but I was never discouraged. In general my purpose was to threaten and harass the enemy on the border and in this way compel him to withdraw troops from his front to guard the Potomac and Washington," he wrote. A few days later Mosby and his band assembled near Aldie to launch their first raid.[54]

NOTES

1. His brother-in-law, Charles W. Russell, edited Mosby's manuscript, supplementing it with letters, notes, comments, and quotations from newspaper articles; Jones, *Ranger Mosby*, 18; John S. Mosby, *The Memoirs of Colonel John S. Mosby* (1917; reprint, *Mosby's Memoirs* [Nashville: J. S. Sanders, 1995]), 3–4 (hereafter cited as *Mosby's Memoirs*).

2. *Mosby's Memoirs*, 1; Ramage, *Gray Ghost*, 11–17; Jones, *Ranger Mosby*, 15; James H. Mosby, *Our Noble Heritage: The Mosby Family History* (Evansville, 1957), quoted by Ramage, *Gray Ghost*, 13; Siepel, *Rebel*, 20–21.

3. Jones, *Ranger Mosby*, 29.

4. *Mosby's Memoirs*, 1–2.

5. Ibid., 3; JSM to Spottswood Mosby, December 23, 1915, *The Letters of John S. Mosby*, 2d ed., ed. Adele H. Mitchell (n.p., Stuart-Mosby Historical Society, 1986), 239 (hereafter cited as *Letters*); Bernard Mayo, *Myths and Men* (Athens: University of Georgia Press, 1959), 58–60.

6. *Mosby's Memoirs*, 3.

7. Ibid., 4.

8. Ibid., 5–6; Jeffry D. Wert, *Mosby's Rangers* (New York: Simon & Schuster, 1990), 78.

9. Mosby to Reuben Page, a lawyer and judge who served with Mosby in the Washington Mounted Rifles (hereafter cited as JSM to RP), June 11, 1902, *Letters*, 111–14; Mosby to Samuel Chapman, September 30, 1909, JSM Papers, Duke University.

10. *Mosby's Memoirs*, 6; Jones, *Ranger Mosby*, 20; Ramage, *Gray Ghost*, 19; *Mosby's Memoirs*, 5–6; Virginia Mosby to Virginia governor Joseph Johnson, n.d., Joseph Johnson Papers, Mosby Pardon File, Archives Research Services, Library of Virginia.

11. *Mosby's Memoirs*, 7; Ramage, *Gray Ghost*, 18–19; JSM to William Sam Burley, January 18, 1911, Box 2, Burley Family Papers, University of Virginia, quoted by Siepel, *Rebel*, 23; Jones, *Ranger Mosby*, 18.

12. Wilson, *Patriotic Gore*, 308; Jonathan Daniels, *Mosby, Gray Ghost of the Confederacy* (Philadelphia: J. B. Lippincott Co., 1959).

13. Ramage, *Gray Ghost*, 19–20; Commonplace Book of Robert G. Kern, March 30, 1853, 3070-a, University of Virginia; Siepel, *Rebel*, 22–24; Dannett and Burkart, *Confederate Surgeon*, 52–53.

14. Wilson, *Patriotic Gore*, 308; Jones, *Ranger Mosby*, 21–22; Ramage, *Gray Ghost*, 21–23; *Mosby's Memoirs*, 6–8.

15. Monteiro, *War Reminiscences*, 12; Siepel, *Rebel*, 29.

16. *Mosby's Memoirs*, 9; "Petitions concerning the Pardon of John S. Mosby in 1853," ed. William M. E. Rachal, *Papers of the Albemarle County Historical Society* (Charlottesville, VA) 9 (1948–49): 13–41.

17. Mosby to Louise Cocke, January 16, 1911, JSM Papers, University of Virginia; Ramage, *Gray Ghost*, 22–28; Jones, *Ranger Mosby*, 23–26, 28; W. Sam Burnley, a typed essay, Burnley Family Papers, University of Virginia Library, JSM Scrapbook, University of Virginia.

18. Virgil C. Jones, "Ranger Mosby in Albemarle," *Papers of the Albemarle County Historical Society* (Charlottesville, VA) 5 (June 1945): 43; Jones, *Ranger Mosby*, 28, 312; Ramage, *Gray Ghost*, 29. Both John and Pauline Mosby later mentioned that Johnson had attended, but Ramage was unable to verify that he was actually there (*Gray Ghost*, 356); JSM to PM, June 30, 1861, *Letters*, 5; JSM to PM, November 3, 1861, JSM Papers, University of Virginia; Siepel, *Rebel*, 291.

19. Siepel, *Rebel*, 293; Jones, *Ranger Mosby*, 27; Bell Irvin Wiley and Hurst D. Milhollen, *Embattled Confederates* (New York: Harper & Row, 1964), 128.

20. Ramage, *Gray Ghost*, 30; James A. Ward, *Railroads and the Character of America, 1820–1887* (Knoxville: University of Tennessee Press, 1986), 30. See also V. N. Phillips, *Bristol, Tennessee/Virginia: A History, 1852–1900* (Johnson City, TN: Overmountain Press, 1992).

21. *Mosby's Memoirs*, 11–12.

22. State of Virginia, Election Records, 1860, Washington County, Library of Virginia; *Mosby's Memoirs*, 14–15, 17; JSM to RP, June 11, 1902, *Letters*, 112.

23. *Mosby's Memoirs*, 17–18; Jones, *Ranger Mosby*, 32–33, 312; Paul W. Brindle, *Ancestry of William Sperry Bunk* (n.p.: privately printed, 1974), 132–35.

24. *Mosby's Memoirs*, 17–20; *Mosby's War Reminiscences*, 6.

25. *Mosby's Memoirs*, 22–27; *Bristol Herald Courier*, June 29, 1958. Quoted by Ramage, *Gray Ghost*, 33.

26. *Mosby's Memoirs*, 22–27; William Willis Blackford, *War Years with Jeb Stuart* (New York: Charles Scribner's Sons, 1945), 14; Jones, *Ranger Mosby*, 38; *Mosby's War Reminiscences*, 8.

27. Jones, *Ranger Mosby*, 33–37; Ramage, *Gray Ghost*, 33–34; " 'Grumble' Jones: A Personality Profile," *Civil War Times Illustrated* (June 1968): 35–36; *Mosby's Memoirs*, 22–23; *Mosby's War Reminiscences*, 206.

28. *Mosby's Memoirs*, 22–30.

29. Jones, *Ranger Mosby*, 41–42; Siepel, *Rebel*, 41.

30. Jones, *Ranger Mosby*, 43; Ramage, *Gray Ghost*, 38–39; unidentified newspaper clipping, n.d., JSM Scrapbooks, University of Virginia.

31. *Mosby's Memoirs*, 31; *Mosby's War Reminiscences*, 206, 218.

32. Ramage, *Gray Ghost*, 37; *Mosby's Memoirs*, 47–48.

33. Siepel, *Rebel*, 38; *Mosby's War Reminiscences*, 212.

34. Jones, *Ranger Mosby*, 49; *Mosby's Memoirs*, 47–85, 89; Ramage, *Gray Ghost*, 37–38; Siepel, *Rebel*, 34–35; JSM to PM, July 28, 1861, *Letters*, 9; James I. Robertson Jr., *Stonewall Jackson: The Man, the Soldier, the Legend* (New York: Macmillan, 1997), 269; *Mosby's Memoirs*, 81–82; *Mosby's War Reminiscences*, 213–14.

35. *Mosby's Memoirs*, 88–90; Ramage, *Gray Ghost*, 39.

36. Ramage, *Gray Ghost*, 39–40; Jones, *Ranger Mosby*, 54; Richard Shelly Hartigan, *Lieber's Code and the Law of War* (Chicago: Precedent, 1983), 58; OR, Series 1, 4 (3), 509–10, 608; Harold Holzer and Mark E. Neely Jr., *Mine Eyes Have Seen the Glory: The Civil War in Art* (New York: Orion, 1993), 59–63; JSM to PM, September 2, 14, November 21, 1861,

JSM Papers, Virginia Historical Society; *Mosby's Memoirs*, 91; *Mosby's War Reminiscences*, 17; JSM to PM, September 14, 1861, *Letters*, 13–14.

37. *Mosby's War Reminiscences*, 19–22; *Mosby's Memoirs*, 100–101, 106; JSM to PM, February 14, 1862, *Letters*, 3–4. The date on this correspondence in *Letters* is February 14, 1861, but the letter was actually written a year later.

38. *Mosby's Memoirs*, 99–109; *Mosby's War Reminiscences*, 22, 215, 218; Ramage, *Gray Ghost*, 42–45.

39. Bruce Catton, *Terrible Swift Sword* (Garden City, NY: Doubleday, 1963), 314–17; *Mosby's War Reminiscences*, 218–22; Ramage, *Gray Ghost*, 46–47, n. 359.

40. *Mosby's War Reminiscences*, 222–32; Ramage, *Gray Ghost*, 47–48.

41. *Richmond Dispatch*, June 17, 1862; *Abingdon Virginian*, June 27, 1862, JSM Scrapbooks, University of Virginia; *Mosby's Memoirs*, 119–20.

42. *Mosby's Memoirs*, 121–26.

43. Ibid., 125–26; Ramage, *Gray Ghost*, 50; Jones, *Ranger Mosby*, 62; Siepel, *Rebel*, 58.

44. Ramage, *Gray Ghost*, 46, 49.

45. Jones, *Ranger Mosby*, 61–62; Mary Anna Jackson, *Life and Letters of General Thomas J. Jackson* (New York: Harper & Bros., 1892), 307–21, quoted by Robertson, *Life and Letters of General Thomas J. Jackson*, 514–15, n. 882.

46. *Mosby's Memoirs*, 127–29.

47. *Mosby's War Reminiscences*, 241–42.

48. *Mosby's Memoirs*, 128–33; *Mosby's War Reminiscences*, 242–45.

49. *Mosby's Memoirs*, 133–35; Siepel, *Rebel*, 61; Ramage, *Gray Ghost*, 54; Louis-Philippe-Albert d'Orleans, Comte de Paris, *History of the Civil War in America*, vol. 2 (Philadelphia: J. H. Coates, 1876), 255.

50. *Mosby's Memoirs*, 135–43; *Mosby's War Reminiscences*, 245–50; JSM to PM, September 5, 1862, *Letters*, 26.

51. *Mosby's Memoirs*, 144–45; Robertson, *Stonewall Jackson*, 616; Isaac J. Wistar, *Autobiography of Isaac Jones Wistar, 1827–1905* (New York: Wistar Institute of Anatomy and Biology, 1937), 407–9, 475–76; Ramage, *Gray Ghost*, 55; Siepel, *Rebel*, 63–64.

52. JSM to PM, November 15, 1862, December 9, 1862, *Letters*, 27–28; Ramage, *Gray Ghost*, 56–57.

53. *Mosby's War Reminiscences*, 27–28.

54. *Mosby's Memoirs*, 149–50; Jones, *Ranger Mosby*, 69–71; Ramage, *Gray Ghost*, 58–59.

CHAPTER TWO

THE NAME ON THE WALL

Strategy is only another name for deception.
—John S. Mosby, *Mosby's Memoirs* (1917)

THE VIRGINIA COUNTIES in which Mosby intended to operate compose a region of sublime beauty. In 1863 about forty-three thousand people were living on small farms and in rustic villages scattered across the rolling countryside. The variegated terrain of Fauquier and Loudoun Counties was as conducive to myth-making and romance as it was to partisan combat. Rarely has war been fought in a more congenial setting, and across a water-color landscape with more euphonious names: Raven Rocks, Aldie, Silcott Springs, Ashby's Gap, Sugarland Run, Bluemont, Orlean, Catoctin, Rappahannock. From the high tors, knolls, wooded crests, and spurs of the Blue Ridge Mountains a horse-man could survey a broad expanse of rich, pastoral territory seamed with stone walls, runneled with deep river gorges, creeks, and valleys, and dappled with apple and peach orchards, vine-yards, cornfields, cantilevered barns, and rolling pastures.

Stately eighteenth-century brick and pale stone seigneurial mansions with gabled roofs, columns, porticoes, and trellised gardens spangled with flowers served as the residences of many of the state's oldest families. Oak Hill, once the three-story country home of former president James Monroe, with imposing Doric columns, stood in a grove of oaks, yellow locusts, and poplars near Aldie. Stands of walnut, pine, sycamore, and chestnut trees formed natural boundaries between fields full of prancing thoroughbreds. Goose Creek, to which the Indians had given a name meaning the river of swans, followed a fifty-mile northeasterly course across both counties from its source in Fauquier to the

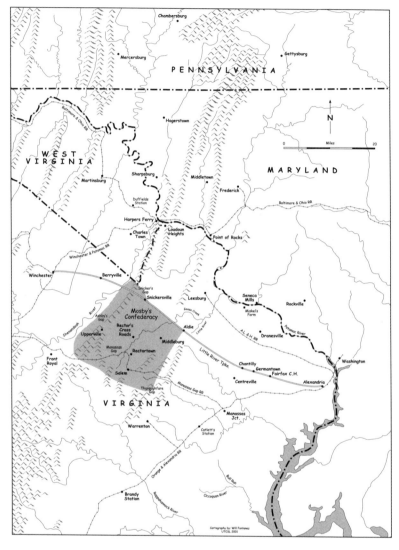

"MOSBY'S CONFEDERACY," the shaded area on the map, became a kind of mythical regency during the war where Mosby was said to have presided like Robin Hood in Sherwood Forest. But the area remained contested terrain throughout the conflict and Mosby's band ranged well beyond its confines. By attacking communications and supply lines near Washington, Mosby was able both to frustrate Union military and political leaders and to create dramatic news stories for journalists who often had little to report between major engagements.

Potomac. The Alexandria, Loudoun & Hampshire and the Manassas Gap railroads meandered westward across the countryside.

Plumes of mist rose from mountain ramparts bisected by a series of strategic gaps and sheltering swales through which a gray rider could pass by night to the fords and bridges of the Shenandoah River. A broad valley spread southward from the Potomac between the Blue Ridge and the Bull Run mountains. In the larger towns, compact brick and stone structures on well-kept streets served as shops, residences, offices, churches, and public buildings. During the winter months, a white shroud would be drawn across a land scented with wood smoke from a thousand fieldstone chimneys.

This was an ethereal tableau where a handful of horsemen could seem ghostly legions to cold, frightened men in blue from Vermont, Pennsylvania, and New York huddled around melancholy campfires in an alien land. But, oddly enough, initially the land was alien to Mosby as well. After the war, Mosby said, "It is generally supposed that I resided there before the war; the fact is that I never was in that section of Virginia until I went there as a soldier. The Union soldiers knew just as much about the country as I did." As Mosby put it later, the two counties were "the Flanders of the war," without natural defenses and open to the whim of the invader. Nor could he enjoy "such shelter there as Marion had in the swamps of the Pedee [Pee Dee]," but what it did have was "a highly refined and cultivated population, who were thoroughly devoted to the Southern cause," and Mosby resolved to protect them without making his presence the source of their destruction. Nevertheless, as Jeffry Wert points out, "In the end, the presence of the Rangers in the region was a double-edged sword."[1]

RASCAL RANGERS

On January 28 the Rangers met shortly before dawn at Mount Zion Church, a mile and a half from the village of Aldie, and on a path through the frozen woods rode Mosby, his horse cantering through the fresh snow beneath a sky becoming the color of tarnished pewter. Not then, but soon after, a story was abroad that his horse left no tracks. The Rangers rode a dozen miles east down the Little River Turnpike toward Chantilly Church, capturing eleven vedettes. Another Federal lookout tried to escape across the pallid fields, and Mosby put two bullets in him. The band returned through Aldie to Middleburg farther west on the turnpike. The incursion was like removing pawns from a chessboard, and Mosby sent the captured men back to their camp with signed paroles and a taunting message for their colonel, Sir Percy Wyndham. Mosby's men had kept the horses and confiscated the weapons, and Wyndham had called Mosby a horse thief. "I did not deny it," he wrote, "but retorted that all the horses I had stolen had riders, and that the riders had sabres, carbines, and pistols." The weapons, Mosby complained, were obsolete, and he requested that next time Wyndham provide his men with Colt revolvers.

Wyndham was an English soldier of fortune who fought by what Mosby considered outdated rules of war. He had resolved to annoy Wyndham as much as possible. The next morning at daybreak, Wyndham retaliated by striking at Middleburg, Mosby's first base of operations. Mosby narrowly escaped capture and rounded up a dozen men to attack Wyndham's rearguard. Mosby again escaped during the skirmish that followed and dared Wyndham to shoot him as he sat on a fast horse at the end of a lane. This angered Wyndham even more, and he charged that Mosby was not fighting fairly. Mosby tried to justify his actions:

> The complaints against us did not recognize the fact that there are two parties of equal rights in a war. The error men make is in judging conduct in war by the standards of peace. I confess my theory of war was severely practical—one not acquired by reading the Waverley novels—but we observed the ethics of the code of war. Strategy is only another name for deception and can be practised by any commander. The enemy complained that we did not fight fair; the same complaint was made by the Austrians against Napoleon.[2]

Wyndham's next move was to set up an ambush for Mosby by placing thirteen pickets around a roaring campfire near an abandoned railroad depot in Fairfax County. If the raiders attacked the camp, a camouflaged cavalry squadron was supposed to pick them off. But Mosby approached stealthily and captured eleven men and killed one before the trap was sprung. The next ploy was to place a half-dozen sharpshooters in some wagons. When the train approached Middleburg, Mosby's troopers stampeded the cavalry screen, and as the Federal riders came within range of the wagons, the startled marksmen, assuming they were Confederates, cut them to pieces with Spencer repeating rifles. In any event, the ruse could not have stopped Mosby, who was off making a raid near Dranesville.

Next up was Maj. Joseph Gilmer, who swooped down on Middleburg on the night of March 1 with two hundred mostly drunken cavalrymen of the Eighteenth Pennsylvania to avenge Mosby's attacks on cavalry outposts. He rousted old men from their beds and carried them off along with some black women and children. Looking "more like a procession of Canterbury Pilgrims than cavalry," according to Mosby, Gilmer's column headed to Aldie, with Mosby and seventeen partisans in pursuit. The next morning, Gilmer abandoned his charges and fled when he saw fifty troopers of the First Vermont Cavalry sent from Dranesville to sweep the countryside of guerrillas. He assumed they were Mosby's men and took off in the direction of Centreville. Gilmer was court-martialed, found guilty of drunkenness on duty, and cashiered from the army. Mosby mentions in his *Memoirs* that Gilmer encountered the First Vermont at the point where the Braddock Road crossed the Little River Turnpike and notes that a young George Washington had marched along the Braddock Road during the French and Indian Wars. By including such details, Mosby is reminding his readers of his connection with grand historical themes and of his continuity with the earlier Virginia Revolutionaries enshrined in the national consciousness.

The First Vermont then rode toward Aldie. Mosby and his Rangers approached Aldie from the west, rode through the little village, and suddenly came upon some dismounted troopers of the First Vermont feeding their horses at a brick gristmill. Mosby's bay was startled and galloped on at full speed, out of control. Seeing another body of cavalry ahead, Mosby jumped from his horse to avoid capture. But, again, the Union cavalry panicked when it saw the plumed rider and his horse coming wildly toward them. The bizarre encounter resulted in the capture of nineteen

Union men, including two captains, and twenty-three horses. According to Mosby, his horse chased the Union cavalry twenty-five miles to their camp, where it presumably was captured. "I have said that in this affair I got the reputation of a hero; really I never claimed it, but gave my horse all the credit for the stampede." To Mosby, war was "not always grim-visaged, and incidents occur which provoke laughter in the midst of danger." Mosby had the literary skills to make the most of these Falstaffian moments, which may not have seemed so humorous to the victims. He was, he wrote Pauline, having "a gay time with the Yankees." If Robin Hood had his Merry Men, Mosby was creating a whooping band of Rascal Rangers.[3]

The Aldie Mill, where Mosby and his men surprised troopers of the First Vermont Cavalry on March 2, 1863. They were, he later wrote, "as much shocked as if we had dropped from the sky." Photograph by Paul Ashdown.

"I SHALL MOUNT THE STARS"

By early March, Mosby was on the verge of celebrity. A month earlier he had been praised by Stuart, who had wished him "increasing success in the glorious career on which you have entered," and Lee had noted the "evidence of merit of Captain

Mosby" as he forwarded reports to Richmond. The Middleburg and Aldie skirmishes had caused a local sensation. Mosby was a hero in Middleburg for rescuing the civilians and assisting the Yankees in making fools of themselves. Now he was ready for "a more daring enterprise than any I had attempted." The motivation for the plan was rooted in Mosby's growing hostility toward Wyndham, in whom, declares Wert, Mosby "had found a personal antagonist, a foe who had impugned his honor. The Virginian internalized the conflict and made it his own—'Mosby's War.' Sir Percy Wyndham was George Turpin [his University of Virginia nemesis] clad in Union blue."[4]

What little we know of Turpin suggests that he was the classic bully, and Mosby had despised him for that. Ramage and other Mosby biographers often have insisted that the "bully theory" was a key to understanding Mosby's complex personality. If Mosby did see the ghost of George Turpin in the Union officer, it was clearly time to settle the score.[5]

His opportunity arrived in the presence of a Yankee deserter from the Fifth New York Cavalry, Sgt. James F. Ames. He confirmed what Mosby suspected—there was a gap in the screen protecting Washington in Fairfax County between the Little River Turnpike and the Warrenton Pike. More important, Ames had come from Germantown, only a mile from the town of Fairfax Court House, and five miles within the lines, where Wyndham and Brig. Gen. Edwin H. Stoughton, the twenty-four-year-old commander of an infantry brigade, had set up their headquarters in the comfort of private residences. Their units were elsewhere, leaving them protected only by their personal staffs and a handful of guards. Stoughton and his men knew of the gap in his lines, but no action was taken to close it. Mosby's primary target was Wyndham, but if he could take out the young general also, so much the better.

On the afternoon of March 8, Mosby took Sunday dinner with a friend, Col. Lorman Chancellor. As he mounted his horse to leave, he told Chancellor, "I shall mount the stars tonight or sink lower than plummet ever sounded." Such sangfroid on the eve of adventure was typical of the ever-literary Mosby, but he was disingenuous in his *Memoirs* in adding that he had "no reputation to lose, even if I failed." He did have a reputation to lose, and greater fame to gain, and he was willing to take the risk. It was not an unreasonable risk, however, as Mosby made clear in an article in *Belford's Monthly* published in 1892. "To a man uninitiated into the mysteries of war our situation, environed on all sides by hostile troops, would have appeared desperate," he wrote. "To me it did not seem at all so, as my experience enabled me to measure the danger."

And so with twenty-nine men, who believed they were merely on their way to attack a picket post, Mosby left Dover, two miles west of Aldie, late in the afternoon and headed southeast through melting snow on the Little River Turnpike. At nightfall a light rain began to fall and a mist rose from the woods as they passed unnoticed through the picket lines between Chantilly and Centreville, and rode into the streets of Fairfax Court House at 2 A.M. on the morning of March 9 after cutting the telegraph wires. The dark concealed their gray uniforms from the few sentries who might have raised an alarm if they had thought they were Confederate troops. When hailed, they identified themselves as belonging to the Fifth New York Cavalry, and if a sentinel was too inquisitive, he immediately became a prisoner. In the courthouse square, Mosby detailed the men into squads, some to capture horses, some to find the wanted officers. But Wyndham had left for Washington the previous evening by rail, so attention turned quickly to the alternative prize. Mosby and five or six raiders dismounted in front of a two-story brick house on the edge of the village and knocked on the door. From an open window, someone asked what was wanted, and Mosby replied that he was with the Fifth New York and had a dispatch for the general. The door opened, and Mosby grabbed Lt. Samuel Prentiss by the shirt collar and demanded to be taken to Stoughton. Mosby and three men followed Prentiss up a flight of stairs and entered the sleeping Stoughton's room. Uncorked champagne bottles were scattered about. Mosby gave an account of what happened next:

> As the general was not awakened by the noise we made in entering the room, I walked up to his bed and pulled off the covering. But even this did not arouse him. He was turned over on his side snoring like one of the seven sleepers. With such environments I could not afford to await his convenience or to stand on ceremony. So I just pulled up his shirt and gave him a spank.

Its effect was electric. The brigadier rose from his pillow and in an authoritative tone inquired the meaning of this rude intrusion. He had not realized that we were not some of his staff. I leaned over and said to him: "General, did you ever hear of Mosby?" "Yes," he quickly answered, "have you caught him?" "No," I said, "I am Mosby—he has caught you."[6]

While Stoughton dressed, Mosby took what was probably a piece of charred wood from the fireplace and wrote his name on the wall. He wanted to leave no doubt as to who was responsible for removing the besotted general from his lair.

At 3:30 A.M., Mosby rode out of Fairfax Court House with Stoughton, two captains, thirty other prisoners, and fifty-eight horses, and by morning, after a series of narrow escapes, he and his entourage had arrived in Warrenton, where he was greeted with an ovation. He had pulled off one of the great raids of the Civil War without a single casualty, and the effect was as electric as the whack he had given the general. Mosby knew he had "drawn a prize in the lottery of life."[7]

"YOUR PRAISE IS ON EVERY LIP"

When Lincoln heard the news, he said something to the effect that he could easily make another brigadier general but that good horses were expensive. It was a fine way to make light of this blow to Union morale, and the fear and uncertainty it caused within the army units stationed in Virginia. Northern newspapers generally focused on the weaknesses of the Union command structure and the embarrassment to Stoughton, but Mosby's name was getting into print, and he made the most of his growing fame. Mosby found that his exploits were gaining him a reputation in the Northern press and that he was becoming as well known as several higher-ranking Confederate officers. There are different versions of what Lincoln said, but in all of them he is dismissive of the loss of Stoughton. The general was imprisoned, exchanged in May, and soon left the army. He never recovered from the embarrassment of his capture. He died on Christmas Day in 1868. Mosby apparently corresponded with Stoughton after the war, and Stoughton's brother wrote a letter supporting Mosby's nomination for a consulship.[8]

General Stuart read an announcement of the raid to each cavalry regiment in the Army of Northern Virginia, calling it "unparalleled in the war." General Lee said Mosby "has covered himself with honors." On another occasion the usually diffident Lee proclaimed, "Hurrah for Mosby! I wish I had a hundred like him!" The *Richmond Dispatch* ran a front-page story about the raid, and the *Richmond Enquirer* praised Mosby for his brilliance and gallantry. Most of this bombast was simply Confederate propaganda. A lot was being made out of the capture of a twenty-four-year-old general. Nevertheless, Mosby sent two newspapers containing stories of the raid to Pauline and asked her to pass them on to Stuart in case he had not seen them. He also asked her to buy copies of the Richmond newspapers reporting the raid or Stuart's encomium. Little more than a week after the Stoughton incident, Mosby and forty men surprised a picket post of the First Vermont Cavalry near the Potomac at Ball's Mill. He ordered a rare saber charge during the engagement, which resulted in the capture of four officers, twenty-one enlisted men, and twenty-six horses, all without the loss of a single man of his own force. Lee praised Mosby in a note to Jefferson Davis, who was beginning to hear a good deal about Stuart's paladin.[9]

But what Mosby really wanted was an official commission, and he was deeply offended when Stuart offered him a captaincy in the Virginia state forces. Stuart told him he believed that the War Department would recognize the commission, but Mosby viewed the rank as a kind of honorary title because he knew there were no Virginia state troops. "I want no recognition," he snapped at Stuart. In his *Memoirs* he admitted he meant only official recognition. "I did not affect to be indifferent to public praise," he wrote. "Such a man is either too good or too bad to live in this world." He really did want official recognition, however, and it finally came on March 19, when Lee notified him of his appointment as captain of the Partisan Rangers and then promoted him to major on March 26. The official appointment from Davis technically was only temporary, until Mosby could recruit a Ranger company and get it mustered into the army as a regular cavalry unit. Lee's motivation was to protect Mosby from the bad reputation attached to partisan commands. Davis, Lee, and Johnston viewed partisans as detrimental to regular army discipline and a potential menace to civilians. Moreover, partisan raids would set in motion a chain of reprisals that could turn the war into an unmitigated bloodbath that could not be contained or arrested by professional soldiers. Undoubtedly, too, there was the natural careerist's suspicion of amateurs meddling in affairs they could not properly understand, not to mention the suspicion that partisan warfare was profoundly ungentlemanly.[10]

Eventually, however, the government yielded to growing pressure, supported by many newspapers, to dispense with formalities and legislate the partisans into existence. By September 1862, partisan units were operating under the Partisan Ranger Act in eight states. Within a few months the War Department was flooded with complaints about the depredations of the partisans. The eventual solution was to try to keep the partisans within regular army commands, to refrain from creating new units, and to disband those that could not be controlled. Accordingly, Stuart wrote Mosby and told him to

> by all means ignore the term "Partizan Ranger." It is in bad repute. Call your command "Mosby's Regulars," and it will give it a tone of meaning and solid worth which all the world will soon recognize, and you will inscribe that name of a fearless band of heroes on the pages of our country's history and enshrine it in the hearts of a grateful people. . . . Your praise is on every lip, and the compliment the President has paid you is [as] marked as it is deserved.[11]

But Mosby rejected Stuart's advice and ignored the flattery, complaining that he had recruited his partisans within the provisions of the Partisan Ranger Act, under which they were entitled to share in the spoils of war. Mosby and Stuart were looking at the situation in quite different ways. As a professional soldier, Stuart had every reason to distrust the term "Partizan Ranger," with its suggestion of irregular activity outside the normal boundaries of army discipline. It was a question of order versus disorder, of professionals versus amateurs. The very name "Mosby's Regulars" was too bureaucratic. From Mosby's point of view, everything hinged on the name of his command. He and Stuart were essentially addressing two different audiences. Stuart was worried about what his superiors, solid West Point military men, would think. Mosby was thinking of how he was going to recruit "a fearless band of heroes," a hot-blooded bunch of boys with romantic ideas of chivalric soldiering and a pragmatic eye on the spoils of war. It was the difference between Sir Walter Scott's novels and *Hardee's Tactics*, the standard drill manual. If he was going to go down in history as the Gray Ghost and not the Old Gray Goose, he needed a unit with panache.

After the war, Mosby took pains to explain that he had always had Lee's sanction in his capacity as commander of the Army of Northern Virginia, of which Mosby's battalion was a part. His independence, he argued, was due to the great discretionary authority that Lee and Stuart gave him, so that it was never necessary to constrict him with orders. He argued that the Partisan Ranger Act was an extension of a martial tradition that had permitted the division of maritime prizes. He and his men, accordingly, were like land-based privateers. There was nothing novel in applying the principle to land forces, he claimed, citing the Duke of Wellington's division of spoils after the Battle of Waterloo as one of several precedents. Such principles had been further established during the American Revolution as well. The Partisan Ranger Act went even further, however, by authorizing specific government payment for captured resources.[12]

Mosby knew greed was a powerful inducement for the men under his command and that the "peculiar privileges given to my men served to whet their zeal. I have often heard them disputing over the division of the horses before they were captured, and it was no uncommon thing for a man to remind me just as he was about going into a fight that he did not get a horse from the last one." Mosby himself chose not to share in the plunder but set up a disciplined system that permitted those who had distinguished themselves in a particular operation to have the first claim on the spoils. The spoils system, John Scott explained, was the "cohesive force in the Ranger service." Ranger James Williamson claimed the system did not make the men wealthy because they had to pay their own expenses. Yet a raider could pocket the equivalent of a private's pay for a year simply by capturing one cavalryman and selling his horse and equipment. So the soldier's chances of profiting from military service were far greater in a partisan command than in a regular unit. Accordingly, Mosby could be selective in choosing the men he wanted for his battalion.[13]

Mosby realized the importance of the Partisan Ranger Act for protecting his reputation after the war. Like a good attorney for the defense, he marshaled his evidence. His independence was necessary because he was often far removed from the Confederate lines. The division of spoils was a practical response to the increasingly desperate situation faced by the Confederacy and its chronic shortage of resources. The act enabled him to recruit and motivate tough fighters who might otherwise have been lost to the Confederacy. Without the Act, his would have been an ordinary cavalry unit. Without the act, he would have had little defense against charges that he was a highwayman, a common horse thief, and a train robber, and his men little different from the unaffiliated border ruffians who took advantage of the civil

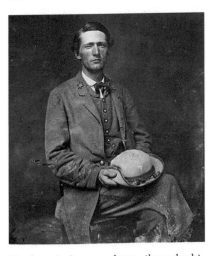

disorder to loot and pillage for personal gain. Even with the Partisan Ranger act, the Mosby Myth was a delicate, highly nuanced narrative that needed constant cultivation, and it was fortunate for Mosby that he, and many of his most credible supporters, lived long enough to make his case convincingly. A lesser commander might have lost control not only of his command but also of his place in the annals of war.

His fame in its ascendancy, the redoubtable Major Mosby gained the authority to raise his doughty band of Rangers. He scraped together a tough, efficient partisan unit and fought politically to gain legitimacy for his command. *Library of Congress*

Mosby took advantage of the fame he had gained in capturing Stoughton to build his fighting force. But first he had to clear up the matter of the nature of his commission.

He wrote Stuart to say that he could not accept his appointment without the authority to enlist his men under the terms of the Partisan Ranger Act. Stuart sent Mosby's letter to Lee, who replied that Mosby had not been given authority to raise partisan troops. His commission was limited to himself alone and did not automatically sanction the men under his command. Mosby appealed to Secretary of War James Seddon, who, impressed with what Mosby had accomplished, saw the advantage of having him empowered under the Partisan Ranger Act. By June 10, Mosby had the formal authority he requested, and Stuart and Lee put up no more resistance. Mosby, evidently, was able to trade on his reputation to circumvent his senior commanders—and that without antagonizing them. As a soldier, at least, he was showing considerable political skill.[14]

"CHILDREN OF THE MIST"

The men Mosby recruited to make up his Ranger battalion were a diverse lot. They included convalescents who could still ride and fight despite a variety of injuries. Some had served in the Black Horse Cavalry, a unit made up mostly of men from Fauquier County. One man in ten had some previous Confederate military service. Some were farmers, some men too young, or too old, for regular service. Others had just drifted away from other army units, although Mosby had been admonished by Stuart not to enroll deserters. A few were men Mosby had transferred from other units. He recruited soldiers of fortune from Canada, England, Scotland, Ireland, Germany, and other countries. Some, like Mosby, were lawyers; some, like Mosby's friend Dr. Monteiro, were physicians. Mosby's adjutant, Samuel Chapman, was a Baptist minister, and clergymen were well represented at battalion reunions after the war. Some Rangers had been cadets at the Virginia Military Institute. James Heiskell was the grandson of President James Monroe. Whenever they could safely affect the accouterments of military foppery, they adorned themselves in garish cloaks, gold braid, and raffish plumes. They boarded comfortably in family homes or roughed it in graveyards, huts, hay ricks, forests, fields, barns, and caves until summoned for action. "My men had no camps," wrote Mosby. "If they had gone into camp, they would have all been captured. They would scatter for safety, and gather at my call, like the Children of the Mist."

The Federal army adopted the wrong strategy to combat Mosby's Rangers, because they were not bandits and highwaymen but partisan soldiers. As the Rangers became better trained and organized, they adopted tactics that would have been well beyond mere bushwhackers and cutthroats. By underestimating their strength and demeaning their abilities, the Federals were slow to develop countermeasures against them. The army could not fight ghosts and "mist," but it could learn to fight a battalion of skilled partisans with a very corporeal commander. Wert estimated that between 80 and 90 percent of the partisans were Virginians, with the largest concentration coming from Fauquier, Loudoun, Fairfax, and Prince William Counties. The largest number of non-Virginians came from Maryland, and a few men from New York, New Jersey, and Pennsylvania also joined the command. Their average age was about twenty-three, three years younger than the average age of the soldiers in the regular army.

Rangers found the pistol a more effective weapon than the saber in close engagements. Sketch by James E. Taylor; Williamson, *Mosby's Rangers*, frontispiece.

At the end of the war, Mosby had seventeen boys under sixteen in his command, including one youngster who had enlisted at the age of fourteen. Mosby said the younger Rangers were his most daring fighters.[15]

The exact number who served under Mosby during the war cannot be accurately determined, but Wert claims that at least 1,900 men served between January 1863 and the end of the war. Some Rangers did fight for plunder, but many were simply caught up in what they saw as the romance of war. "The true secret was that it was a fascinating life, and its attractions far more than counterbalanced its hardships and dangers," according to Mosby. But he added that patriotism, as well as love of adventure, also impelled them. "If they got rewards in the shape of horses and arms, these were devoted, like their lives, to the cause in which they were fighting. They were made no richer by what they got, except in the ability to serve their country." Monteiro said that during his three years of military service, he had never witnessed "more true courage and chivalry, or a higher sense of honor blended with less vice, selfishness and meanness than I found during my official intercourse with the Partisan Battalion."[16]

GUNFIGHT AT MISKEL'S FARM

Those who served with Mosby would need all the true courage they could muster to avoid destruction during his next major escapade, which might have spelled the complete destruction of his inchoate command. Returning empty-handed from what was to have been a raid against Federal outposts at Dranesville on March 31, 1863, Mosby and about seventy Confederates pulled together from different units stopped about two hours before midnight to spend the cold night at Miskel's Farm in Loudoun County, some two miles off the Leesburg & Alexandria Turnpike and one-half mile from the Potomac River near its junction with Broad Run. They had found no opportunities for a productive engagement at Dranesville, because Federal units had pulled back closer to Alexandria. But the Yankees had been tipped off as to Mosby's movements, and at midnight five companies of the First Vermont Cavalry under the command of Capt. Henry Flint began moving westward on the turnpike from Difficult Run to trap Mosby at Miskel's Farm. But Dick Moran, one of Mosby's men who had been visiting a friend on a farm road near the turnpike, had seen the 150 Vermonters. At sunrise he had just arrived at Miskel's Farm to raise the alarm when the column thundered up the fenced lane leading to the two-story clapboard farmhouse and its hay barn.

A high plank fence surrounded the snow-covered barnyard with a gate to the lane leading to the turnpike. Flint had divided his column, placing Capt. George Bean in command of a fifty-man reserve unit. He ordered Bean to close and barricade the gate behind Flint's lead squadron and circle around behind the barn. Flint then deployed his men in a semicircle and ordered a saber charge. Mosby, meanwhile, saw Flint coming through the gate, buckled on his sidearms and ordered his men to bridle their horses. He found protective cover behind a fence while his confused soldiers scrambled down from haylofts and raced to their tethered animals, drew two .44 caliber Colt pistols, and with several other men opened fire as the troopers came within range. "As Capt. Flint dashed forward at the head of his squadron, their sabres flashing in the rays of the morning sun, I felt like my final hour had come," Mosby admitted.

But his time had not yet come. Six bullets cut Flint from his saddle, and he fell bleeding into the snow. At least a dozen more soldiers tumbled from their mounts. Rallying twenty of his men who had managed to mount their horses, Mosby charged into the faltering ranks of the Vermonters with both guns blazing. Offered a horse by one of his men, he mounted and led the counterattack into the collapsing right flank of the ill-fated squadron. His men "responded with one of those demoniac yells which those who once heard never forgot, and dashed forward to the conflict 'as reapers descend to the harvest of death,' " he recalled. Mosby, evidently, was in full voice as well, as John Munson, one of his Rangers, recalled, noting that "the Mosby yell—to which no person has yet been able to do full justice—rose on the wings." Munson's mythmaking is in full voice here as well, as the famous Rebel Yell is now identified with Mosby. The Union horsemen then panicked and stampeded toward the locked gate, bunching up until it collapsed. Bean had had enough of Mosby and was one of the first through the gate. Trapped in the narrow space between the fences, the Yankees were shot and clubbed by the enraged Confederates, who "like so many furies were riding and shooting among their scattered ranks."[17]

Samuel Chapman, the preacher Mosby described as "a sort of military Calvin," was in the vanguard of the assault, shooting two Federals and hacking his way through the ranks with a saber after he had emptied his two pistols. Chapman's fury amused Mosby, who wrote that, even at "that supreme moment in my life, when I had just stood on the brink of ruin and had barely escaped, I could not restrain the propensity to laugh." The pursuit of the fleeing Federals continued for several miles down the pike all the way to Dranesville, where two sutlers' stores were appropriated. Three out of four Union soldiers who had fought in the skirmish were casualties, eighty-two of them as captives.

One of Mosby's men was dead and three were wounded. Bean was later discharged by the army for cowardice.[18]

The fight showed Mosby's inexperience as a commander. He conceded as much in his report to Stuart, in which he admitted that he had "not taken sufficient precautions to guard against surprise." He added, as mitigating factors, the fact that he had ridden upwards of forty miles in snow and mud on the previous day and that his men and horses were exhausted. "The entire affair was a mistake on Mosby's part," said John Divine, a Leesburg, Virginia, historian who commented on the skirmish during a *Civil War Journal* cable television broadcast in the mid-1990s. "He had ridden into a trap. . . . Mosby too learned a lesson: never camp in a place with only one entrance." He had failed to place a sufficient screen to protect his command, and, as he later admitted, "We were in the angle of two impassable streams and surrounded by at least four times our number, with more than half of my men unprepared for a fight." He exaggerated the ratio, but he knew that he had had a close call and was also aware that he seemed to be continually blessed with good luck. This gave him additional confidence. Had Moran not reached Mosby in time, and had the Vermonters dismounted and not divided their column before attacking, Mosby's unit might have been slaughtered or forced to surrender. That events turned in their favor further established the Mosby Myth.[19]

REBEL IMMORTAL

Within a single month, and not yet thirty years old, Mosby had become immortal. Wert claimed that from the moment Mosby had awakened Stoughton, he was "one of the most famous soldiers in America." The Fairfax raid became the signature incident in the Mosby Myth. It has been cited prominently in virtually every Mosby memoir and biography. Cooke includes the story in *Wearing of the Gray*. It was the subject of Ray Hogan's novel *Night Raider*, the subject of the first episode of *The Gray Ghost* television series in 1957, the centerpiece of the Walt Disney 1967 film *Mosby's Marauders*, and the subject of a chapter, "A Gray Ghost Captures a General," in a 1998 volume, *Daring Raiders*, by David Phillips. Both the Fairfax raid and the Miskel's Farm skirmish were given ample attention in the *Civil War Journal* episode on Mosby. The Stoughton raid and the accompanying vignette about Mosby appears in the best-selling companion to the Ken Burns *Civil War* documentaries.[20]

The Miskel's Farm skirmish had been one of the most dramatic small-unit actions of the entire war. In 1895 the Civil War artist James E. Taylor (1839–1901), who had made eyewitness drawings of some of Mosby's raids for *Frank Leslie's Illustrated Newspaper*, produced a dramatic sketch of the Miskel's Farm encounter. In the foreground, Chapman, rising in his stirrups, holds his saber aloft and is about to strike a hatless Federal trooper. Beneath him several wounded men and horses lie contorted on the ground. The wounded men appear bewildered and in agony. Behind Chapman and near the center of the sketch, on a rearing white horse, is Mosby, who has just fired his revolver into the head of a dismounted officer, presumably Captain Flint. Mosby is fully dressed and wearing his plumed hat. At the extreme right, a determined Union soldier appears to be fleeing on horseback with a Confederate soldier in pursuit. The flag of the First Vermont, the barn, and the farmhouse are all clearly visible. Like Mosby, all the Confederate soldiers are in uniform and all have

The engagement at Miskel's Farm was one of the most dramatic small-unit engagements of the war. This fanciful sketch of the skirmish shows Mosby, pistol in hand, near the center of the action. Sketch by James E. Taylor; Williamson, *Mosby's Rangers*, 53.

their distinctive plumes. Taylor's sketch mythologizes the conflict to reveal the heroism of the Confederates. A more accurate
rendition would have depicted the Confederates as they more
likely were—hatless, half-dressed, many probably still in long
underwear. Nothing in the sketch indicates that the Confederates were surprised by the attack or that they had launched an
improvisational countercharge.[21]

SHADBAKES AND SABERS

In the early spring of 1863 the Civil War was reaching its crucial phase. As the snows melted and the warming sun shone crim-
son and gold in the hills of Northern Virginia, Lee had his cavalry
feelers out below the Rapidan River, probing for Maj. Gen.
Joseph Hooker's advancing Federals in the expanse of dense,
second-growth timber known as the Wilderness. Stuart detailed
Mosby to skirt the flanks of the massive Union army, watch for
moving divisions, and, if possible, capture a train supplying
Hooker's cavalry. Mosby was detained by Union cavalry on a
sweep from Fairfax Court House, and before he could move again,
scouts had located Hooker at a clearing in the dense forest called
Chancellorsville.[22]

Mosby could hear the guns of the Chancellorsville battle as
he led some one hundred men on a raid with the intention of
striking Hooker's supply line at the Orange & Alexandria Railroad junction near Warrenton. On the bright, warm morning of
May 3, he was distracted from his main mission when he saw an
opportunity to surprise several hundred First West Virginia cavalrymen who were relaxing in an open field, and enjoying the
sounds of the distant fight as if it were a fireworks display. It
looked like another easy victory as the Confederates bore down
on the unsuspecting West Virginians. But the cavalrymen re-
grouped and made a stand in several nearby buildings. Mosby's
men were able to drive most of them out, but one hundred or so
regathered in a large frame structure and kept firing. Mosby
reached a window and emptied two Colt revolvers into the
crowded lower room. Then Chapman and three men burst
through a door, and the Union soldiers on the first level surren-

dered, but those in the upper rooms resisted. Mosby dragged some bales of hay into the lower rooms and set the building on fire. The Union soldiers staggered outside as the building filled with smoke. While Mosby's men gathered prisoners and spoils and chased horses, a large Fifth New York Cavalry squadron supplemented by units of the First Vermont Cavalry appeared and routed the Confederates, who, this time, fled rather than fought. Mosby himself was nearly captured.

"I committed a great error in allowing myself to be diverted by their presence from the purpose of my expedition," Mosby said. He should, he saw in retrospect, have marched around the cavalrymen and struck a blow at Hooker's supply wagons concentrated at his rear on the Rappahannock. He imagined the demoralizing effect that the sight of the blazing supply wagons might have had on Hooker's already hammered forces. By the time he was able to reorganize his command to make another attempt on Hooker's supplies, Hooker had moved his forces out of the Wilderness. Mosby tried to explain this defeat in his *Reminiscences*. He pointed out that his force was a mere "aggregation of men casually gathered," and not a unified group of carefully selected partisans under his command. They had fought bravely, but as individuals. They had begun as raiders, and they had finished as a mob. He admitted his error in ordering the charge and engaging a force larger than his own. But he amplified what he might have accomplished. Had he actually been able to get behind Hooker's army and wipe out his supply trains, the Confederate victory at Chancellorsville would have been a worse defeat for the Union army. While admitting a major error in a minor skirmish, he was suggesting he could have played a crucial role in a major battle, and thus magnified his own importance.[23]

Emboldened by their success at Warrenton, and determined to redeem the army's defeat at Chancellorsville, the Union cavalry increased the pressure on Mosby, whom they were coming to despise. He was being called a highway robber, a marauder, a bushwhacker, a guerrilla, and a terrorist. Traps were set for Mosby, with mixed results. Throughout May the Rebels paid a stiff price for their raids. Several dozen of Mosby's men were captured, wounded, or killed, but he continued his attacks on the Orange

& Alexander Railroad, burning its bridges and blocking the tracks. On May 27, Stuart gave Mosby a twelve-pound bronze mountain howitzer, and Mosby assigned Chapman to train a crew in the use of the cumbersome weapon. On May 30, with fewer than fifty men, he attacked a train near Greenwich, but again had to fight the First Vermont, the Fifth New York, and the Seventh Michigan. In trying to protect the cannon, Mosby's men lost some of their mobility and their nerve. "Some of the men who had joined me, thinking that they were going on a picnic, had already left to fry their shad and eat the confectioneries they had got on the train. . . . Realizing the desperate straits we were in, I wished I was somewhere else," he wrote. In the ensuing fight, Mosby was slashed on the shoulder with a saber and bore the scar for the remainder of his life. His pursuers captured the cannon. The raid had been a qualified success, and he did manage to tie down thousands of Union troops to look for him and to protect the railroads, but the cost to Mosby was high. His disorganized irregular command again was partially to blame.

On the night of June 8, Mosby was staying with his wife and children at a three-story brick house some five miles north of Salem. About midnight a detachment of the First New York Cavalry surrounded the house and searched it. Mosby apparently climbed out the bedroom window and hid in the branches of a tree until the cavalry detachment had left. Turning the tables on Mosby, they took his sorrel mare, which they renamed "Lady Mosby." By June 10, Mosby had recovered from his saber wound, and he finally organized his men into a company of the Forty-third Partisan Ranger Battalion at Rector's Cross Roads on Ashby's Gap Turnpike in Fauquier County. He now had greater authority over his command and was ready to step up his attacks. The next day he struck a Sixth Michigan Cavalry camp at Seneca Creek on the Potomac in Maryland about twenty miles from Washington. Stuart then recommended him for promotion to lieutenant colonel. Mosby returned to Middleburg with his prisoners and looked for Stuart. Early on the morning of June 17, he found him and learned what he had only suspected: Lee's army was on the move into Pennsylvania. The fateful rendezvous with the Union army would come at Gettysburg.[24]

ENIGMA AT GETTYSBURG

Stuart's role in the defeat of the Army of Northern Virginia at Gettysburg has been one of the most widely debated topics of the Civil War. The great cavalry general's tardy arrival on the battlefield, Lee's alleged rebuke of his favorite ("General Stuart, where have you been?"), and Stuart's subsequent defeat in a cavalry engagement on the third day of fighting are all well-known pieces of a historical puzzle. Emory Thomas concludes that Stuart's "protracted raid during the Gettysburg campaign deprived Lee of his 'eyes and ears' and contributed to the Confederate defeat." But the controversy, as Thomas explains, "is only important to the extent that Stuart's actions did or did not affect the outcome of the Battle of Gettysburg." His "best answer to the riddle of Stuart's aberrant performance in the Gettysburg Campaign is the simplest. He was long-term tired before the campaign even began. Stuart then became exhausted to the point of dysfunction as his exertions and stress only increased during the long march toward battle." Stuart had his apologists, and none of them was more fervent than Mosby, who, as Thomas puts it, "was rabid in his defense of his former commander." Mosby devoted much of his postwar career to Stuart's cause.[25]

Mosby and about thirty of his men left Stuart at Middleburg on the afternoon of June 17 and rode toward Aldie, intending to make another raid on Seneca as a diversion while Lee's army moved through the Shenandoah Valley. From a vantage point in the Catoctin Mountains, they saw clouds of dust rising on every road below, indicating that Hooker's army was marching from Fredericksburg toward the Potomac, and thus blocking Mosby's path to Seneca. Looking for an opportunity to disrupt communications and track Hooker's movements, the Rangers kept themselves concealed "like Robin Hood and his merry men, in the green wood until night," and then moved within Maj. Gen. George Meade's lines along the Little River Turnpike. There Mosby captured two staff officers and found documents explaining Hooker's instructions to his cavalry commanders, which indicated that Lee's movements in the valley were still a mystery to the Union general. These documents he sent to Stuart and Lee, who used the information to plan further dispositions of the cavalry screen protecting the Army of Northern Virginia. Mosby continued scouting, and on June 22 was ambushed by Meade's infantry. Three of his men were wounded, but Mosby, who "was not ten steps from the infantry when they fired the volley," escaped and was soon attacking Meade's wagons. In his report, Meade wrote that "the prettiest chance in the world to dispose of Mr. Mosby was lost." Nevertheless, word must have got around that Mosby had been killed. When he rode alone into Fairfax some days later, his acquaintances there "thought when they first saw me that it was my ghost." By then, the Union soldiers were already calling Mosby the Gray Ghost, so perhaps they were not thinking of a metaphor.[26]

Finding Stuart at Rector's Cross Roads, Mosby suggested that Stuart could pass easily through the scattered units of Hooker's army with three cavalry brigades and cross the Potomac at Seneca Ford. On June 24, after again passing through the Union lines with prisoners for Stuart, Mosby reported that the route to the Potomac remained open if Stuart wanted to sweep around Hooker to create a further diversion. From Mosby's point of view, Stuart's plan depended on the position of the two armies remaining roughly constant until he could get through Hooker's army to the river. Mosby expected to link up with Stuart in Loudoun County and take command of his advance guard. But Stuart had to make a wider circuit around Hooker's army when his intended route was blocked by units of Hancock's corps. When Mosby could not find Stuart on the Little River Pike, he turned back and later rode to Pennsylvania through the Shenandoah Valley, assuming Stuart had gone that way, when he found his route to Seneca blocked. Instead, Stuart and his weary riders found their way to Gettysburg two days later than they anticipated. Mosby passed through Hagerstown, Maryland, and looked for Lee's army in Mercersburg, Pennsylvania, but by then it had concentrated at Gettysburg. So Mosby rustled 218 head of cattle and 15 horses and returned to Virginia. He also gathered a dozen blacks and, according to Williamson, brought them along, too.[27] Why he took them, and what he did with them, is unknown, but Confederate troops did capture blacks in Pennsylvania.

GUERRILLA HISTORY

Given the outcome of the battle, and the postwar legend that has it the turning point in the war, it was inevitable that scapegoats for the Southern defeat had to be found. Viewing his own actions as central to Stuart's, Mosby considered himself responsible for Stuart's raid. "Later," according to Ramage, "when Stuart was blamed for contributing to Lee's Gettysburg defeat by being away, Mosby felt that the critics were attacking him as well." Mosby was not responsible for Stuart's decisions. Stuart never suggested that he was, and, in any event, the matter of the cavalryman's route had already been broached before Mosby confirmed that gaps existed in the Union lines. Stuart had Lee's approval, but, as Mosby biographer Jonathan Daniels put it, Lee's order "contained a lot of 'ifs' about what Stuart could do."

After the war, Mosby was convinced he had exonerated himself and Stuart of any blame for the failure at Gettysburg and had shifted the blame to others, including those he thought were covering up the errors of senior commanders. He was not so sure about the judgment of history. "That the inventions of the staff officers have been accepted by historians as true is the most remarkable thing in literary history since the Chatterton forgeries," he wrote, adding that "the history of the world is a record of judgments reversed." (The English poet Thomas Chatterton [1752–1770] wrote a series of poems that he attributed to a fifteenth-century monk, an invention. When the poems were rejected as forgeries, Chatterton took poison and died at the age of seventeen. He later became a literary hero to the Romantics.) Perhaps Mosby was suggesting the staff officers would have been well advised to follow Chatterton's example. In evaluating Mosby's 1908 book *Stuart's Cavalry in the Gettysburg Campaign*, Ramage does not so much take issue with Mosby's general thesis as with his technique of "guerrilla history," an overly tendentious, highly selective interpretation of documents and events as well as an intemperate attack on his critics. James Robertson considers Mosby's book "hysterical in places." Robert Skimin's engaging alternative history novel, *Gray Victory*, places Mosby's defense of Stuart in a courtroom after the war. The real Mosby would have enjoyed this conjunction of loosely reconstructed historical events with the imponderables of speculative fiction, because it further enlarges the Mosby Myth by placing him at the heart of the great battle of the war.[28]

WAGON RAIDS

After Gettysburg, Meade moved into Virginia east of the Blue Ridge Mountains and concentrated his forces near Warrenton, while the Confederates dug in across the muddy Rappahannock. Mosby set up a camp in the mountains some fifteen miles north of Warrenton and swooped down to raid the unprotected sutlers' wagons supplying Meade's army. But Lee was not pleased with the wagon raids as he wanted Mosby to strike at Meade's communications, drive in his outposts, and cut his rail connections. He told Stuart he had heard reports that Mosby's men had auctioned supplies taken from the wagons and that some of the men were deserters who should be returned to their army units. Mosby was trying to keep his men occupied, and the best way to do that was to give them incentives. He was not auctioning plunder and believed he was hindering Meade by attacking his wagons. With only thirty men in his command at the time, and no artillery, he could hardly do much damage to railroads unless Lee expected miracles. Nor were the raids doing much for his reputation in the North. A fanciful sketch depicting the aftermath of one such raid appeared on the front page of *Harper's Weekly.* Mosby's men are shown reveling in the joys of the "jolly god," straddling looted barrels, rifling boxes, and swilling liquor. One simian figure appears to be balancing a book in his left hand, as if mocking reason itself.

Still, to keep Lee happy, he had to modify his tactics. On August 24 he attempted to burn some railroad bridges near Fairfax Court House but ran into detachments of the Second Massachusetts Cavalry and the Thirteenth New York Cavalry. These units were under the command of Col. Charles Russell Lowell, who had been trying to stop Mosby's raids on the wagons. Lowell was greatly frustrated by Mosby and called him "an old rat [who] has a great many holes." During a sharp engagement in which the Confederates drove away the slightly larger Union force and captured a dozen prisoners and eighty-five horses, Mosby was shot in the thigh and groin. A surgeon was able to treat the wound before Mosby bled to death. He was taken to his parents' home near Lynchburg to recover. On August 31 an obituary appeared in the *New York Herald*. He was reported to have been "shot twice in the bowels and breast" and taken, mortally wounded, to Richmond.[29]

GHOST STORY

Like a mythical hero in an ancient epic, Mosby would return to life, thus multiplying not only the frustrations of his more calculating opponents but also their irrational fears. Mosby's bards have given close attention to the psychological effect of his frequent resurrections. In his *Gray Ghosts and Rebel Raiders*, Virgil Carrington Jones writes: "But somehow, in the days following, stories of Mosby's death failed to rest peacefully. . . . Like the ghost of the unrestful dead, they continued to haunt, to be disturbed by denials and counterdenials. The more this tale was repeated, the more it seemed to be substantiated." And so we see the story of the Gray Ghost becoming a ghost story, and it is easy to understand why. The Mosby Myth served the purposes of a credulous, sentimental age as well as a contemporary, scientific era that welcomes a reminder that things sometimes do go bump in the night. Shortly after the war a poet wrote:

> Old tales still tell some miracle
> Of saints in holy writing—
> But who shall say why hundreds fled
> Before the few that Mosby led,
> Unless the noblest of our dead
> Charged with us then when fighting?[30]

Here the myth extends not only to Mosby but to his merry men as well, anticipating the famous story of the Angels of Mons during the First World War in which British soldiers, reeling from German attacks in Belgium, were spelled by the ghosts of English bowmen slain at Agincourt. Certainly hard-nosed commanders such as Sheridan and Grant did not believe that Mosby's Rangers were spooks any more than British Gen. Douglas Haig and King George V thought they could defeat the German army by invoking spirits, but frightened young soldiers facing the possibility of extinction on a foreign field were another matter. Even Lincoln, according to the testimony of many who knew and wrote about him, trembled at the supernatural and is the putative source of more hauntings than any figure in American history. It never really mattered whether Mosby and his spectral band actually galloped through the Virginia night within sight of the lights of Washington, or even whether Mosby prowled with a cloven hoof. Yet today, when the wind rattles the windowpanes, something within us is never quite sure he is not still out there, along with the Headless Horseman and all the other myths and legends of American history.[31]

"A SAD AND SULLEN SILENCE"

After meeting with Lee and Seddon to discuss further operations, Mosby returned to his command on September 21. During his meeting with Seddon in Richmond, Mosby was promised some largely experimental percussion torpedoes that he could use to try to blow up a train on the Orange & Alexandria Railroad. This seems to be what Lee wanted him to do, although there is no evidence that Mosby was ever able to detonate any of the weapons. Lee also suggested that Mosby should try to capture prominent Federal officials if the opportunity presented itself. He soon tried to burn a railroad bridge near Alexandria, scouted enemy positions, acquired horses, mules, wagons, weapons, and prisoners, and narrowly missed capturing the Federally appointed governor of Virginia, Francis H. Pierpont.[32]

During the autumn of 1863, the size of Mosby's band slowly increased, and he divided it into several companies. The raids continued through the Indian Summer days and began to intensify as the weather turned colder and snow fell on the armies huddled against the chilling winds that swept across the Rappahannock and the Rapidan. In January, temperatures fell below freezing and then settled below zero as snow turned to ice. Men pulled blankets tighter around their tunics and thought more of firelogs than fighting; and if they had no shoes or blankets, they moved a little closer to the warmth. But Mosby knew that the weather could also work to his advantage. Now came Capt. Benjamin Franklin Stringfellow, a scout from Stuart's command. Frank Stringfellow had been with Mosby on the Seneca raid and had a reputation for bravery and tall tales. He had a bold plan, and Mosby was interested.

A woodcut depicts the drama and the misinformation that surrounded the emerging legend. As in this illustration, Union cavalry did sometimes recapture wagon trains Mosby had taken. But Mosby and his men rarely used sabers and bullwhips, let alone muskets with unwieldy fixed bayonets, opting more frequently for revolvers, which were easier to use on horseback and offered more firepower than the single-shot musket. However, it was an era of transition—one in which modern weaponry had not yet displaced the mythic accouterments of the heroic cavalryman, especially the image of a mounted man with saber in hand. The pragmatic Mosby quickly saw the uselessness of the blade, but the artists of the era continued to embrace it as an icon of daring and gallantry. *Frank Leslie's Illustrated Newspaper*

The First Maryland Cavalry, an independent command led by Maj. Henry A. Cole, had been making frequent incursions into Mosby's small protectorate and then had settled into a base camp on Loudoun Heights overlooking the junction of the Potomac and the Shenandoah Rivers across from heavily garrisoned Harpers Ferry. In December, Cole had been ordered to occupy the heights across from Harpers Ferry to guard a bridge across the Shenandoah. Stringfellow told Mosby he had found a way to attack Cole's camp from the rear by moving west along the Potomac from the direction of the Short Hills, traversing a dense thicket and then climbing an icy escarpment to reach the eastern point of the snow-covered heights.[33]

On January 9, Mosby led 106 men on a frigid twenty-two-mile ride from Upperville, connecting with Stringfellow and his 10 men in a narrow valley beyond Hillsborough. After the two commanders scouted the camp for a couple of hours, the Rangers led their horses up the snowy mountain, arriving on the crest shortly after 4 A.M. on January 10. Across the broad and dark rivers, the campfires of the Union troops in the Maryland mountains above Harpers Ferry flickered in the cold winter night. James Williamson recalled how the landscape was "clothed in the white robes of winter, and it seemed almost a sacrilege against the beauty and holy stillness of the scene to stain those pure garments with the life blood of man, be he friend or foe." A train whistle screeched, and many of the frostbitten Rangers, thinking Mosby had found the camp too heavily fortified, believed they would be attacking the Baltimore & Ohio Railroad. Cole had as many as 200 men in the camp, so it was imperative that Stringfellow and Mosby use the element of surprise. The plan called for Stringfellow and his 10 men first to capture Cole in the two-story house he was using for a headquarters, while Mosby and his Rangers took care of the men sleeping in tents.

But the raid turned sour very quickly. A sentinel fired on Stringfellow's men, alerting Cole, who began rousing his troops. "All my plans were on the eve of consummation," wrote Mosby, "when suddenly the party sent with Stringfellow came dashing over the hill toward the camp, yelling and shooting. They had made no attempt to secure Cole. Mistaking them for the enemy, I ordered my men to charge." In the confusion, Stringfellow's squad and Mosby's men, all mounted and believing the other to be the vanguard of a countercharge, fired into each other's ranks. This gave Cole's troopers time to grab their pistols and carbines and open up on the Confederates. Some climbed to higher positions and poured a heavy fire onto the scattering intruders. A captain who had rushed to the aid of a fallen Ranger lay dead in the snow. A lieutenant, one of Mosby's original band, was mortally wounded. A former British army captain fell from his horse, bleeding from a bullet wound, and died for the Confederacy. The fight was brutal, with weapons discharged at close range. Hearing a signal gun fired from Harpers Ferry, Mosby ordered a retreat to the valley, and managed to bring out six prisoners and some sixty mounts, but his price for the raid had been a dozen casualties. "The march homeward was indeed a gloomy one," Williamson recalled. "A sad and sullen silence pervaded our ranks and found expression in every countenance. All that we could have gained would not compensate for the loss we sustained."

The *New York Herald*, the *Baltimore American*, and the *Washington Evening Star* reported the repulse of the attack, puffing the size of Mosby's force to four hundred men, and dramatizing the doomed ascent of the raiders to a camp about to be "baptized in blood." Cole was promoted to colonel and proclaimed a hero, and Mosby was promoted to lieutenant colonel just eleven days later, although the raid had been a fiasco. In some ways this raid reprised the Miskel's Farm skirmish, but this time it was the Union that had gained the advantage. John Munson later wrote that the Rangers regarded the raid as "our Waterloo, for the men lost seemed to us worth more than all Cole's Battalion." Bold action carried high risks, but the Loudoun Heights raid was audacious even for Mosby. He had learned thereby that combined commands, night raids, and brutal weather might be too much even for his intrepid Rangers, although he thought he could have overrun Cole's camp if Stringfellow had carried out his part of the mission.[34]

RISKS AND REWARDS

Mosby still had the confidence of Lee, Seddon, and Stuart, and his was one of only two partisan units permitted to continue in service after the Confederate Congress repealed the Partisan Ranger Act on February 14. Lee continued to try to bring Mosby's battalion into regular service but Mosby resisted. "Stuart and Lee failed to appreciate the essence, the cement of Mosby's operation," according to Ramage. "They agreed that Mosby was great, and they both recommended his promotion and continuance where he was. They regarded it as a compliment and favor to make him regular, but he feared being returned to regular duty as much as his men." Mosby's greatest protection, then, was to continue to achieve dramatic results by taking risks. Without continual activity, he would lose the control of his men that was also necessary to keep the good opinion of his superiors. He could not afford to let them fall into brigandage through boredom, nor could he justify his continuing existence as a partisan without multiplying the effectiveness of his command. Mosby knew he had to keep building his reputation, not so much for personal aggrandizement as for the very survival of his mode of warfare. He was in a situation rather like that of the president of a modern corporation who must do whatever it takes to justify market expectations by continuing to pump up the price of the stock with short-term publicity. The Mosby Myth was his martial capital; if he cashed in the myth, he effectively bankrupted the company.[35]

BARON VON MASSOW

On February 22, two days after winning a sharp skirmish with Cole's cavalry, Mosby led 160 men to the vicinity of Dranesville and divided them to ambush a force of about equal size from the Second Massachusetts Cavalry under Capt. James Sewell Reed. Serving with Mosby during the raid was Baron Robert von Massow, a Prussian army lieutenant from an aristocratic family with a pedigree dating back to 1259. He was the son of the chamberlain to the King of Prussia. Massow, who was born in 1839, had served in the Prussian forces for seven years without seeing much action, and, like other soldiers of fortune, he came to Virginia to see what war was really like. He secured a letter of introduction to Mosby from Stuart. He previously had fought in an attack on a wagon train at Bealton Station, which he proclaimed more enjoyable than an English fox hunt, and a raid on a stable near Vienna, which had led him to remark: "Ah, this is not fighting; it's horse stealing." During the Dranesville skirmish, Massow was attired in a cape lined in scarlet over a gray uniform with green trim, and he had two large ostrich plumes extending from his slouch hat. Before the fight, Second Lt. William B. Palmer told him: "Baron, unless you are ready to die this morning, use your pistols and put back that sabre." But the baron demurred, saying, "Palmer, a soldier should always be ready to die." Waving his sword, the baron rode toward Reed, who made a gesture the Prussian took to be a sign of surrender. But as Massow rode by, Reed, still armed, and possibly thinking he was Mosby, shot him in the back. Capt. William Chapman then shot Reed, who died quickly. Massow survived the wound and returned to Prussia. (He later became the chief cavalry officer in the Imperial German Army, commander of the Ninth Army Corps, presiding officer of the German Military Court, and chief of the general staff of the First Army Corps during the First World War. He attained the rank of lieutenant general and died in 1927, sixty-three years after he had fought with Mosby.)

During the First World War, Mosby read a letter to the *London Times* regarding the treatment of Belgian civilians who were shooting German soldiers. The letter suggested that Virginia farmers who served with Mosby had sniped at Federal soldiers. Mosby was indignant and replied, "If you were to ask Massow if he ever was a sniper in the Shenandoah Valley, he would answer you from the mouth of a Krupp gun." Mosby, however, did not seem to object to the term "bushwhacker." In his *Memoirs* he said: "We were called bushwhackers, as a term of reproach, simply because our attacks were generally surprises, and we had to make up by celerity for lack of numbers. Now I never resented the epithet of 'bushwhacker'—although there was no soldier to whom it applied less—because bushwhacking is a legitimate form of war, and it is just as fair and equally heroic to fire at an enemy from behind a bush as a brestwork [*sic*] or from the casemate of a fort." When Mosby learned in 1901 that Massow planned to leave a fortune to the survivors of Mosby's command, he said he had no doubt "there will be at least 100,000 applicants and that it will be shown that I had a greater army than Grant." Whatever Massow learned from Mosby may have had some application in the German army, even if was only the limited usefulness of the saber in combat.[36]

THE BARD AND THE BALLAD

The Mosby Myth sometimes grew in unexpected ways. During the winter of 1864 a twenty-four-year-old Union soldier from San Francisco, William Ormsby, had become smitten with a Virginia woman; he deserted from the Second Massachusetts Cavalry and joined Mosby. He was captured February 5 during a raid, tried, and executed the next day. Ormsby had made a brief speech expressing his loyalty, and Herman Melville used the incident in his famous novella *Billy Budd*.

With the arrival of spring, Mosby spread his men out across Northern Virginia from the Shenandoah Valley to Fairfax County, and from the Potomac south to Warrenton. He continued attacking wagon trains, seizing horses and livestock, scouting Union infantry positions, and fending off attacks from Lowell's cavalry brigade. On April 18, Lowell led some three hundred troopers from Vienna to Leesburg and Aldie in pursuit of Mosby. Accompanying Lowell on the three-day raid was Herman Melville, who knew Lowell and was a cousin of one of his regimental officers. Although Melville had published *Moby-Dick* in 1851, he was not then the literary figure he would become in the twentieth and twenty-first centuries, but only a struggling poet. By the time Lowell returned to Vienna on April 20, he had lost one man and had three others wounded, and he had mortally wounded one of Mosby's men and taken eleven prisoners.[37]

Every mythic American hero usually finds his great bard. Francis Marion had his William Cullen Bryant, Paul Revere his Henry Wadsworth Longfellow, and Lincoln his Walt Whitman. Mosby was immortalized by Melville, the great American epic poet of cosmic angst, who included "The Scout toward Aldie," an 800-line ballad, in his *Battle-Pieces and Aspects of the War*, published on August 17, 1866. Like Longfellow's "Paul Revere's Ride," "The Scout toward Aldie" is a poet's quest for a place in the American national story. Inspired by Lowell's raid and by events Melville may have witnessed, the poem is heavily laden with symbol and metaphor, and the Mosby of Virginia becomes wholly transformed. In a curious footnote, Melville actually praises Mosby for his compassion and detaches him from the

Mosby of the poem, who is satanic, an infernal spirit who lures men to their own destruction.

Critic Stanton Garner has called the poem "a small-scale version of Moby-Dick," and Edmund Wilson contended that, read correctly, the poem "involves a glorification of Mosby. We are made to feel that the colonel has a kind of fatal rendezvous with the sinister ranger, that he is drawn to his opponent by a kind of spell." This, he suggests, offers valuable insight into the war, into the "mutual fascination of each of the two camps with the other, the intimate essence of a conflict which, though fratricidal, was also incestuous." The whole war, then, becomes strangely Melvillean, giving rise "to a formula of romantic fiction which continued to be popular for decades and which produced all those novels and plays in which two lovers, one Northern, one Southern, though destined for one another, are divided by their loyalties to their different flags."[38]

MOSBY AND GRANT

During the final year of the war, Grant took command of the Union armies, plunged a pitchfork into Virginia soil, and gave Mosby all the fight he could handle. The middle prong of Grant's pitchfork, under Meade, was aimed at Lee. The left prong, under Maj. Gen. Benjamin F. Butler, was to strike a key railroad intersection at Petersburg, while Maj. Gen. Franz Sigel was to cut off the Shenandoah Valley in the west. Grant thought he could crush the Confederacy before the end of 1864. On April 15, Mosby had been pursuing cavalry at Warrenton Junction and had left just moments before Grant arrived on an unguarded Orange & Alexandria train from Washington, where he had conferred with Lincoln. When Grant told Mosby the story after the war, Mosby remarked, "Well, if I had got hold of that particular train, maybe I'd be President now and General Grant would be calling on me."[39]

After the war, Mosby maintained that his command had saved Richmond for another six months. He had so annoyed Grant that, on at least one occasion, the general threatened to hang the partisan and his men if he could catch them. But when Grant died in 1885, Mosby said he had lost his best friend. Grant's *Personal*

Memoirs, published in 1886, contained a generous assessment of Mosby: "There were probably but few men in the South who could have commanded successfully a separate detachment in the rear of an opposing army, and so near the border of hostilities, as long as he did without losing his entire command."[40]

But, in 1864, depriving Mosby of that command was one of Grant's objectives. On May 8, dividing his forces, Mosby hit Meade's supply lines by burning Orange & Alexandria Railroad bridges and attacking a wagon train near Belle Plain, while two companies attacked Sigel's wagons in the Shenandoah Valley. On May 11, Maj. Gen. Philip Sheridan, Grant's new cavalry chief, got around Lee's left flank with 12,000 horsemen, raced toward Richmond, and clashed with Jeb Stuart's troopers at Yellow Tavern. Stuart was mortally wounded and died the next day in Richmond. Shortly after the war, Mosby visited Stuart's grave at Hollywood Cemetery in Richmond. He plucked a flower from the ground, placed it on the grave, and wept. Mosby would mourn Stuart for the rest of his life.[41]

NOTES

1. James W. Head, *History of Loudoun County, Virginia* (n.p.: Park View Press, 1908); *Mosby's War Reminiscences*, 39–41; Jones, *Ranger Mosby*, 72–73; Wert, *Mosby's Rangers*, 34–39, 126.

2. Walter S. Newall, *A Memoir* (Philadelphia, 1864), 131; *Mosby's Memoirs*, 151–62.

3. *Mosby's Memoirs*, 152, 156; Jones, *Ranger Mosby*, 73–87; Ramage, *Gray Ghost*, 60–63; Scott, *Partisan Life*, 30–32; Wert, *Mosby's Rangers*, 44–45.

4. OR, Series 1, 25 (1): 5–6; Stuart to Mosby, February 8, 1863, JSM Papers, Library of Congress, quoted by Wert, *Mosby's Rangers*, 42; *Mosby's War Reminiscences*, 26; *Mosby's Memoirs*, 168; Wert, *Mosby's Rangers*, 45.

5. On the "bully theory," see, for example, Ramage, *Gray Ghost*, 18–19, 49.

6. Mosby, "One of My War Adventures," published in *Belford's Monthly* (1892?), and quoted in Williamson, *Mosby's Rangers*, 34–46.

7. Newspaper clipping, JSM Scrapbooks, University of Virginia, quoted by Ramage, *Gray Ghost*, 69; Mosby in Williamson, *Mosby's Rangers*, 44; *Mosby's Memoirs*, 175, 181.

8. *Washington Star*, March 9, 14, 1863; *Baltimore American*, March 13, 17, 1863; *New York Times*, March 11, 12, 1863, quoted by Ramage, *Gray Ghost*, 71; Ramage, *Gray Ghost*, 70–75; David L. Phillips, *Daring Raiders* (New York: Friedman/Fairfax, 1998), 50–61.

9. Stuart, General Orders No. 7, and Lee to Stuart, March 12, 1863, OR, Series 1, 25 (2): 856; Stuart to Mosby, March 27, 1863, *Mosby's War Reminiscences*, 69–72, 92; *Richmond Dispatch*, March 12–13, 1863, quoted by Ramage, *Gray Ghost*, 73; JSM to PM, March 16, 1863, *Letters*, 30–31; Wert, *Mosby's Rangers*, 68–84; Carl E. Grant, "Partisan Warfare, Model 1861–1865," *Military Review* (November 1958): 42–49.

10. *Mosby's Memoirs*, 183, 192; Ramage, *Gray Ghost*, 73.

11. Stuart to Mosby, March 25, 1863, *Letters*, 31, 250; OR, Series 1, 25 (1): 65–66.

12. Ramage, *Gray Ghost*, 73, 106.

13. *Mosby's War Reminiscences*, 81, 86; A. E. Richards, "Mosby's Partizan Rangers," in *Famous Adventures and Prison Escapes of the Civil War*, ed. G. W. Cable et al. (1885; reprint, London: T. Fisher Unwin, 1894); Scott, *Partisan Life*, 324; Williamson, *Mosby's Rangers*, 23.

14. Scott, *Partisan Life*, 75.

15. *Mosby's War Reminiscences*, 44–45, 98; Jones, *Ranger Mosby*, 104–5; Ramage, *Gray Ghost*, 96–97; Wert, *Mosby's Rangers*, 68–84, 328; John W. Munson, *Reminiscences of a Mosby Guerrilla* (1904; reprint, Washington, DC: Zenger, 1983); John H. Alexander, *Mosby's Men* (New York: Neale Publishing Co., 1907), 24; Jones, *Ranger Mosby*, 311.

16. *Mosby's War Reminiscences*, 101; Williamson, *Mosby's Rangers*, 24; Wert, *Mosby's Rangers*, 74.

17. Munson, quoted in *Civil War Journal: The Leaders*, ed. William C. Davis, Brian C. Pohanka, and Don Troiani (Nashville: Rutledge Hill, 1997), 402.

18. Wert, *Mosby's Rangers*, 51–54; *Mosby's War Reminiscences*, 101–12; Ramage, *Gray Ghost*, 77–82; George H. Bean, Compiled Military Service Record, Records of the Adjutant General's Office, RG 94, National Archives, Washington, DC, cited by Ramage, *Gray Ghost*, 82.

19. Mosby to Stuart, *Mosby's War Reminiscences*, 96, 105; Davis, Pohanka, and Troiani, *Civil War Journal*, 402.

20. Wert, quoted in Davis, Pohanka, and Troiani, *Civil War Journal*, 401; Geoffrey C. Ward, with Ric Burns and Ken Burns, *The Civil War: An Illustrated History* (New York: Alfred A. Knopf, 1990), 245.

21. James E. Taylor, *With Sheridan Up the Shenandoah Valley in 1864: Leaves from a Special Artist's Sketchbook and Diary*, ed. George F. Skoch, Martin F. Graham, and Dennis E. Frye (Dayton, OH: Morningside House, 1989); Holzer and Neely Jr., *Mine Eyes Have Seen the Glory*, 146.

22. Ramage, *Gray Ghost*, 83.

23. *Mosby's War Reminiscences*, 130–36; Wert, *Mosby's Rangers*, 58–59; Ramage, *Gray Ghost*, 88.

24. Jones, *Ranger Mosby*, 10; Williamson, *Mosby's Rangers*, 440; Jonathan Daniels, *John Singleton Mosby, Gray Ghost of the Confederacy* (Philadelphia: J. B. Lippincott Co., 1959), 7; *Mosby's War Reminiscences*, 154–62.

25. Emory Thomas, "Jeb Stuart," *Encyclopedia of Southern Culture*, ed. Charles Reagan Wilson and William Ferris (Chapel Hill: University of North Carolina Press, 1989), 703; Emory Thomas, "Eggs, Aldie, Shepherdstown and J. E. B. Stuart," in *The Gettysburg Nobody Knows*, ed. Gabor S. Boritt (New York: Oxford University Press, 1997), 101–21.

26. *Mosby's War Reminiscences*, 171–77; Williamson, *Mosby's Rangers*, 77; Daniels, *Mosby*, 85.

27. Williamson, *Mosby's Rangers*, 79–80; Ramage, *Gray Ghost*, 90–95; *Mosby's War Reminiscences*, 178–79; John S. Mosby, "Personal Recollections of General J. E. B. Stuart," *Munsey's Magazine* (April 1913): 40; J. Matthew Gallman, with Susan Baher, "Gettysburg's Gettysburg: What the Battle Did to the Borough," *The Gettysburg Nobody Knows*, 161.

28. John S. Mosby, *Stuart's Cavalry in the Gettysburg Campaign* (New York: Moffat, Yard and Co., 1908); Ramage, *Gray Ghost*, 94–95, 313–14; ; Daniels, *Mosby*, 87; *Mosby's Memoirs*, 252; James I. Robertson Jr., *General A. P. Hill: The Story of a Confederate Warrior* (New York: Random House, 1987), 214; Robert Skimin, *Gray Victory* (New York: St. Martin's Press, 1988).

29. Wert, *Mosby's Rangers*, 91–93; Ramage, *Gray Ghost*, 112–13; Edward W. Emerson, *Life and Letters of Charles Russell Lowell* (Reprint; Port Washington, NY: Kennikat Press, 1971), 35, 294–96, quoted by Wert, *Mosby's Rangers*, 95; *Harper's Weekly*, September 5, 1863; *Mosby's Memoirs*, 260–61; *New York Herald*, August 31, 1863.

30. Virgil Carrington Jones, *Gray Ghost and Rebel Raiders* (1956; reprint, New York: Promontory Books, 1995), 195; see, for example, Christopher K. Coleman, *Ghosts and Haunts of the Civil War: Authentic Accounts of the Strange and Unexplained* (Nashville: Rutledge Hill Press, 1999); Madison Cawein, "Mosby at Hamilton," quoted in Williamson, *Mosby's Rangers*, 445.

31. Paul Fussell, *The Great War and Modern Memory* (New York: Oxford University Press, 1975), 115–16; Merrill D. Peterson, *Lincoln in American Memory* (New York: Oxford University Press, 1994), 228.

32. JSM to PM, October 1, 1863, *Letters*, 33–34; Wert, *Mosby's Rangers*, 97–98; Ramage, *Gray Ghost*, 115.

33. Ramage, *Gray Ghost*, 120–26; *New York Herald*, January 21, 1864; *Baltimore American*, January 13 and 21, 1864; *Washington Evening Star*, January 11, 1864; Hugh C. Keen and Horace Mewborn, *43rd Battalion Virginia Cavalry: Mosby's Command* (Lynchburg, VA: H. E. Howard, 1993), 101–3.

34. Ramage, *Gray Ghost*, 127–29; *New York Herald*, January 21, 1864; *Baltimore American*, January 13, 21, 1864; *Washington Star*, January 11, 1864; Munson, *Reminiscences*, 241–42; Williamson, *Mosby's Rangers*, 126, 129.

35. Ramage, *Gray Ghost*, 136–37.

36. *Mosby's Memoirs*, 270; Wert, *Mosby's Rangers*, 146–48; Ramage, *Gray Ghost*, 139; Jones, *Ranger Mosby*, 175–76, 307; *Washington Star*, April 19, 1955; *Meyers Konversationslexikon*, 6. Auflage, Band 13 (Leipzig, 1906); Mosby, *Memoirs*, 285; undated newspaper clipping, JSM Scrapbooks, University of Virginia, circa 1901.

37. Garner, *Civil War World*, 307–8.

38. Wilson, *Patriotic Gore*, 324–26; Herman Melville, *Battle-Pieces and Aspects of the War* (New York: Harper and Bros., 1866).

39. Siepel, *Rebel*, 161.

40. OR, Series 1, 43 (1): 811; Ulysses S. Grant, *Personal Memoirs of U. S. Grant* (New York: Charles L. Webster & Co., 1886), 142; Siepel, *Rebel*, 244.

41. Mosby, "Personal Recollections of General J. E. B. Stuart," 40–41.

CHAPTER THREE

SMOKE AND SHADOWS

So in his tale before the attentive crowd
Aeneas' single voice recalled the fates
Decreed by heaven, and his wanderings.
He fell silent at last and made an end.
—Virgil, *The Aeneid* (trans. Robert Fitzgerald, 1983)

There was no Southern soldier as badly hated at the close
of the war as I was. I think if Northern people got reconciled to
me they would to most Southern men.
—John S. Mosby, *Letters* (1904)

IT WAS ONE YEAR after the fatal third-day charge at Gettysburg, and once again Confederate troops were sweeping through the lower Shenandoah Valley. Lt. Gen. Jubal Early's Second Corps, including the remnants of Jackson's old division, had defeated Maj. Gen. David Hunter's army at Lynchburg and then headed north to Maryland, crossing the Potomac on July 5, 1864. Mosby had been active since Stuart's death, fighting Hunter in the Valley after the Union general replaced Sigel, foraging, tangling with the Sixteenth New York Cavalry, and destroying a railroad depot. Mosby learned of Early's movements on July 2 and took 250 men to break communications between Washington and Harpers Ferry. He forded the Potomac on July 4, sweeping out a Union detachment holding the little railroad and canal junction at Point of Rocks, Maryland, and then recrossed the river.

The next day some of the Rangers returned to Fauquier County with full wagons, while Mosby and about 150 men skirmished from the Virginia side of the river with the Eighth Illinois Cavalry, which had occupied Point of Rocks. Mosby withdrew his main force toward Leesburg, leaving two squads to cause more problems in Maryland, and was soon tracking the Thirteenth New York and Second Massachusetts Cavalry under Maj. William H. Forbes. He caught up with them near Mount Zion Church on the Little River Turnpike. Forbes was captured in the engagement after trying unsuccessfully to skewer Mosby during the fierce, hand-to-hand fighting that left two-thirds of the Union force on the field as casualties. The Union troopers had been part of Lowell's brigade, leading the *Washington Star* to praise Mosby's bravery in defeating what had been an elite unit. The newspaper also reported that some two dozen of Mosby's men had surprised a group of picnickers at Falls Church, Virginia, not seven miles from the White House, danced with the women, and helped themselves to a meal. The picnickers likely knew that Rangers were in the area because on July 7, in response to a rumor that Mosby was moving on the Capital from Dranesville, pickets were alerted to watch the Chain Bridge above Washington.[1]

Mosby, however, was of little direct help to Early. His lieutenants had caught up with Early at Sharpsburg, Maryland, on July 6 and had told the general that Mosby was standing by for his orders. Mosby did cause some damage, but by then Early was already approaching Washington. Although Mosby's maneuvering had pulled some troops away from Washington, Early still could not penetrate the Capital's defenses and he withdrew on July 12. Early later charged that Mosby had not supported him during the raid, but there had been enmity between the two strong-willed commanders, and Mosby dismissed Early as an "old fraud." He said Early was "the first man who ever got the reputation of a hero by running from danger," alluding to Early's flight to Canada after the war, while Mosby, from his point of view, stayed in Virginia to help restore a democratic government.[2]

Whatever tensions existed between them after the war, Mosby did his best to cover Early's retreat into the Shenandoah Valley and his counterattack victory at Kernstown on July 24. Mosby's men got into a scrap with the Eighth Illinois Cavalry in Maryland, while Brig. Gen. John McCausland burned Chambersburg, Pennsylvania, on July 30. Events had reached a crisis, and on August 1, Grant appointed Sheridan to the command of the Army of the Shenandoah, and a new campaign for control of the Valley commenced.[3]

THE BERRYVILLE WAGON RAID

It may have been an exaggeration to say—as John Munson said—that a day hardly passed from August 1 to "midwinter that some of our men were not troubling Sheridan," but it was not much of one. Mosby so vexed "Little Phil" that within two weeks he was already calling on the Eighth Illinois Cavalry to find the Gray Ghost and "exterminate as many of Mosby's gang as they can." Sheridan, it might be said, was a man who understood provender, as a good quartermaster should, for a quartermaster is what he was when the war commenced. He had an intuitive understanding of supplies and the logistics required to concentrate and move them. Sheridan had a visceral fondness for wagons, especially when they were being used to haul foodstuffs and munitions to his men in the field. He had a reputation for keeping his soldiers well fed and clothed, and he was equally committed to depriving his enemy of complementary sustenance. Thus, he was much in accord with General Grant, who had previously ordered Hunter and his legions "to eat out Virginia clear and clean as far as they go, so that crows flying over it for the balance of this season will have to carry their provender with them." Hunter's successor now set out to do just that on August 10 as he began to move south from Harpers Ferry with 30,000 men to take on Early near Winchester. But Early fell back behind a fortified position between Strasburg and Cedar Creek, extending Sheridan's supply lines farther than he anticipated. The 525-wagon train bringing Sheridan's supplies left Bolivar Heights on August 12 under the protection of Brig. Gen. John Kenly's brigade, consisting of fewer than 1,000 home guards and militia. Badly organized, the slow-moving and lightly guarded wagon train stretched over five miles of road.[4]

Mosby, meanwhile, had slipped through Snicker's Gap with some 250 Rangers and a couple of light howitzers and was poised to strike. At dawn on the morning of August 13, Mosby's artillery opened fire from a mist-shrouded knoll near Buck Marsh Creek just north of Berryville, followed by a rush of horsemen into the rear of the train. "At no time in their history had the Rangers created more disturbance than followed around the wagon park and along the creek bottom during the next few minutes," according to Virgil Carrington Jones. Mosby suffered five casualties but killed six Union men and wounded nine others. He rounded up 200 prisoners, three dozen horses, 200 head of cattle, and 420 mules, then plundered and burned at least forty wagons. The enraged Sheridan, facing a reinforced Early before him and Mosby snapping at his heels, pulled back toward Halltown, pillaging the lush Valley as he went and stiffening the protective screen around his supply lines. Ramage called the Berryville Raid "Mosby's most strategic contribution in the war" on the grounds that he had forced Sheridan to divert seven times Mosby's own troop strength from his fighting force.[5]

Northern newspaper reaction to the raid embellished the Mosby Myth and rendered Sheridan something of a goat. The *Baltimore American* and the *New York Times* exaggerated the number of wagons destroyed and made the wagon guards appear to be bumbling cowards. Sheridan took exception particularly to a *New York Times* story that gave Mosby more credit for his opponent's retreat to Halltown than Sheridan thought he deserved and that blamed Sheridan for not blocking the passes through the Blue Ridge Mountains before the wagons moved south. Sheridan was so mortified that he tried to remove all war reporters from his district. But the Mosby Myth was not solely dependent on the press. A Berryville lad assisted Mosby during the raid and years later recalled that the Rangers "had for us all the glamour of Robin Hood and his merry men, all the courage and bravery of the ancient crusades, the unexpectedness of benevolent pirates and the stealth of Indians."[6]

A Confederate veteran made some sketches of the scene and commissioned three French military artists to produce oil paintings depicting the Berryville Raid. The three paintings, completed in 1868, now hang in the Museum of the Confederacy in Richmond. The first, by Jean-Adolphe Beaucé, depicts Mosby on horseback wrapped in his crimson-lined cape and bathed in golden light as he receives a scouting report of the wagon train's movements. The second canvas, by Henri Emmanuel Félix Philippoteaux, shows Mosby on the knoll near the howitzer as his men thunder into action. In 1899, Mosby sent a Ranger some photographic copies of the paintings, which were widely circulated in Europe and America. The final scene, painted by Charles

Edouard Armand-Dumaresq, shows Mosby on a barren ridge beneath a gray sky filled with smoke from the blazing wagons in the distance. His men file by waving plumed hats and herding wounded Union prisoners led by violin-playing Rangers. Williamson wrote of the painting:

> It is impossible to faithfully portray the reality of that scene as it appeared on that summer day. The long line of prisoners, mules, horses and cattle stretched out along the road. Our men, wild with excitement and elated with their success, gave vent to their feelings with shouts and yells and merry songs, the braying mules and lowing cattle joining in the chorus. The bright new captured uniforms of the Federal officers transformed our dusty rebel boys for the time into the holiday soldiers of peaceful days; and the citizens along our route, though well used to raids and the passing of armies through the country, gazed on the scene in mute astonishment, seemingly at a loss whether to stand or run on the approach of the cavalcade.[7]

REPRISAL AND RETRIBUTION

The cavalcade, however, brought on the wrath of Grant, who told Sheridan on August 16 to hang Mosby's men without trial if he caught them. He sent a more temperate order later. But Sheridan reported to Grant the next day that he had already hung one Ranger and shot six others even before he had received Grant's first instructions. Who these men might have been has never been determined. They were evidently not members of Mosby's command and might have been other partisans. The appearance of Sheridan in the Valley and Mosby's countermeasures had unleashed a new wave of brutality on both sides. Reprisal and retribution were now becoming commonplace. "The romantic notions of warfare that both sides believed in 1861 were meaningless three years later," Wert says. "The plumed hats and scarlet-lined capes worn by some of the Rangers were as outdated as the attitudes they symbolized. Northerners and Southerners had unleashed hellish furies which forever altered the nature of warfare."[8]

A plumed hat was a factor in a brutal skirmish that brought Mosby into bitter conflict with one of his greatest adversaries. On August 19, in retaliation for the ostensible bushwhacking of one of his pickets, Brig. Gen. George A. Custer ordered the burning of some houses near Berryville. Mosby's men cornered troopers of the Fifth Michigan Cavalry in the process of burning and looting a house and shot them. During the fighting a private was de-plumed when a Federal cavalryman he was pursuing fired a shot from his carbine that pierced the soldier's hat. The Rebel got off a fatal shot before the trooper could fire again. In his report on the incident, Mosby wrote: "Such was the indignation of our men at witnessing some of the finest residences in that portion of the State enveloped in flames, that no quarter was shown, and about 25 of them were shot to death for their villainy." The *New York Times* described the slayings as a massacre and proclaimed that Mosby had practically raised the black flag. The paper also claimed that Mosby's men had cut the throats of two soldiers and riddled others with bullets in an orgy of cruelty. Another story reported that all the Federal troopers had been hanged.[9]

Sheridan's next tactic was to organize his own predatory band to eliminate Mosby by fighting him with his own tactics. Armed with Spencer repeating rifles, and placed under the command of Richard Blazer, one hundred volunteers known as Blazer's Scouts set off in pursuit of Mosby. While resting on the east bank of the Shenandoah River on the afternoon of September 4, some seventy-five Rangers were surprised by Blazer's band and pushed into an open field where they managed a thirty-minute stand before being routed.[10]

"YOU ARE ALWAYS GETTING WOUNDED"

On September 14, while scouting near Centreville, Mosby and two Rangers were attacked by five cavalrymen from the Thirteenth New York. Two New Yorkers had pursued the trio for about a mile when Mosby turned and emptied the barrels of two Colt pistols at them. One man fell and was pinned under his horse, but fired a shot that shattered the handle of one of Mosby's weapons and lodged in his groin near an artery. His men took him to The Plains, where the wound was cleaned. The bullet was never removed. Mosby spent the next few weeks recuperating at his parents' residence. While he was recovering, Union cavalry under Brevet Maj. Gen. Alfred Torbert hanged two of Mosby's men and shot four other captives on September 23, 1864, at Front Royal in retaliation for the shooting of a popular cavalry officer by Rangers. Mosby later blamed General Custer, who was present at the executions but denied any responsibility for them, although his men were involved.[11]

During this period, Mosby posed for a photograph in Richmond. It is a strange photograph, with Mosby looking wan and emaciated in a capacious lieutenant colonel's jacket, and clutching the plumed hat on his lap. His eyes show none of their usual defiance, and his countenance appears almost seraphic. He hardly resembles the swaggering figure he had become in popular myth. Harold Holzer and Mark E. Neely Jr. address this central problem of rendering Mosby in art: "How does an artist limn a ghost? That was the question painters must have been asking themselves when they began to create portraits of the legendary 'Gray Ghost' of the Confederacy. . . . Photographs leave mixed testimony as to Mosby's appearance. A hatchet-faced hayseed in one, he looked like a neatly uniformed Virginia lawyer-turned-soldier in others. Such confusion about externals matches the internal complexity of the man."[12]

While he was in Richmond, Mosby took the opportunity to visit General Lee at his headquarters near Petersburg. "When he saw me hobbling up to him on crutches," Mosby recalled, "he came to meet me, and said, as he extended his hand, 'Colonel, I have never had but one fault to find with you—you are always getting wounded.' " Returning to Fauquier County a short time later, Mosby met three of his officers at Gordonsville and learned of the executions. He resumed command of his battalion on September 29. The first order of business was to disrupt the repair of the Manassas Gap Railroad, which would restore the supply route for Sheridan's army in the Shenandoah Valley. The Rangers struck first at Salem on October 4. After firing an ineffectual barrage from two howitzers, Mosby's men drove off a cavalry company guarding the railroad and captured about fifty infantrymen who had tried to form a rear guard. The Rangers attacked again on October 6 and 7. Next they clashed with three companies of the Eighth Illinois Cavalry along Goose Creek near Piedmont. Mosby's horse was shot out from under him and a trooper's horse trampled

Mosby's foot, badly bruising it. He needed crutches or a cane to walk, but he was back in action the next day.[13]

THE GREENBACK RAID

Keeping up the pressure, Mosby spread his forces through-out the Piedmont and the Shenandoah Valley, sent a unit into Maryland, and took eighty men north to attack a westbound train from Baltimore on the Baltimore & Ohio Railroad early on the morning of October 14 at a deep cut near Duffield's Station. The raiders removed a few rails, causing the locomotive and eight cars to derail and plow into an embankment. Mosby, still limp-ing, helped remove women and children from a car and then set fire to it. When German immigrants refused to obey orders to abandon another car—perhaps because they could not under-stand English—Mosby shouted, "Burn the Dutch if they won't come out!" The Rangers set fire to copies of the *New York Herald* and other newspapers taken from a vendor and threw them into the cars. They took horses, prisoners, and a paymaster's box con-taining $173,000, and rode away within an hour from what be-came known as the Greenback Raid. Other Rangers, meanwhile, burned five canal boats at White's Ford on the Potomac, cut tele-graph wires, and attacked troops near Adamstown.

Both raids caused a sensation in the Northern press and gave a much-needed boost to Confederate morale. *The Richmond Whig* crooned that the "indomitable and irrepressible Mosby is again in the saddle carrying destruction and consternation in his path" and severing the Baltimore & Ohio Railroad, "the great artery of communication" with the West. "If he has not yet won a Briga-dier's wreath upon his collar, the people have placed upon his brow one far more enduring." Mosby, however, wrote Lee that he hoped the general "will not believe the accounts published in the Northern papers, and copied in ours, of my robbery of pas-sengers on the railroad train I captured. So far from that, I strictly enjoined my officers and men that nothing of the kind would be permitted." Here, again, he is sensitive to his reputation.[14]

By October 19, Sheridan abandoned work on the Manassas Gap Railroad and ordered it closed. Mosby later claimed his at-tacks prevented Sheridan from capturing Richmond and gave the

Confederate government a reprieve of no less than six months. But Ramage concluded that Sheridan was really concerned with Early, and not Mosby, and had never seriously contemplated an advance on Richmond at the time. According to Ramage, Mosby's real accomplishment was to weaken Sheridan's command at crucial moments when he was engaging Early by requiring him to use thousands of troops to guard his supply lines. Ramage argues that, like "American forces in Vietnam, Sheridan fought a limited war against Mosby, a fight with one hand tied behind." Wert blames Sheridan for failing to follow Grant's strategic plan to advance on Charlottesville and Richmond after the Battle of Fisher's Hill on September 22. It was Sheridan, and not Mosby, he claims, who prolonged the war. Jones, however, is more charitable to Mosby's point of view and concludes that the detachments necessary to track Mosby "undoubtedly were largely responsible for prolonging the war until the spring of '65." Siepel, too, finds "some justification" to Mosby's claim. Ultimately, this must be an argument for the military historians who have to sift through the "what ifs." It is crucial to the Mosby Myth, however, that Mosby argued his case for the dubious honor of having prolonged the war.[15]

A SEVERE MERCY

With construction on the railroad abandoned, Mosby contemplated what to do about the executions of his men. Seven had died in Yankee custody within a month, and he was convinced that Custer was responsible. Mosby wrote Lee on October 29, proposing to hang an equal number of Custer's men whenever he captured them. Lee and Seddon approved, and on November 6, twenty-seven prisoners were lined up near Rectortown and ordered to draw lots. One of the condemned was a drummer boy. Mosby was in the vicinity but did not directly participate, and when he learned of the lad's fate, he ordered him spared. An eight-Ranger detail with no enthusiasm for their task took the prisoners to a wood near Berryville in the Shenandoah Valley, close to the Union lines. Three of the seven men selected for execution were hanged. Two were shot, but survived. Two managed to escape. Mosby reminded Sheridan in a letter that, since the slaying of his men at Front Royal, he had captured seven hundred prisoners and sent them all safely to Richmond. He did not mention to Sheridan that one of these was Brig. Gen. Alfred Napoleon Alexander Duffie, whom he had captured during a raid on October 25, and who had threatened in July to hang every Ranger he captured. Mosby told Sheridan he had ordered the seven men from the commands of Custer and Col. William Powell to be executed in retaliation, and that he would respond in kind to any further executions of his men. He sent copies of the letter to Richmond newspapers knowing they would be copied by the Northern papers.[16]

Years later, at the age of seventy-eight, Mosby reacted strongly to accounts of the hangings published in the *Washington Post* and *Harper's Weekly*. People had sent him copies of the articles, prompting him to write a former Ranger:

> I saw the headlines and then burned them. If I were a brute it might give pleasure to read them, but why should people think it would give me pleasure to talk, write, or read anything about my performing a disagreeable duty, I can't understand. . . . Three or four got away in a rain storm that night. If my motive had been revenge I would have ordered others to be executed in their place. I did not. I was really glad they got away as they carried the story to Sheridan's army which was the best way to stop the business. Revenge is never justifiable. . . . My object was to prevent the war from degenerating into a massacre. . . . It was really an act of mercy and there were no more such atrocities as Custer perpetrated at Front Royal. I have been abused a great deal but have never seen any criticism of my retaliation. It is very uncomplimentary to me to send me to read these newspaper accounts of a painful duty I performed. Because a man performs a painful duty, like whipping a child, it does not follow that it is a pleasure for him to be eternally reminded of it. If the recollection gives him pleasure then he is a brute.[17]

Such actions may be considered acts of mercy, but they are a severe mercy, and they are subject to the judgment of history. Mosby, at least in his own mind, was no brute, and the executions troubled him until the end of his life. That he took no pleasure in being reminded of his actions was, in his terms, the best evidence of his moral character. He was like a defense attorney building a case for an accused client: himself.

At the time of his writing to Sheridan, Mosby had about 800 men under his command. He next turned his attention to Blazer. He sent 110 men into the Shenandoah Valley, where the Rangers had trapped some 75 Scouts in a pasture near Myerstown, West Virginia, on November 18. A running battle ensued, and a Ranger overtook Blazer and clubbed him to the ground with the butt of his pistol. Blazer's force suffered fifty-five casualties and was thus no longer a nuisance to the Confederates. Mosby sent Blazer to Richmond, where he was locked up in the infamous Libby Prison until he was exchanged a few months later.[18]

On December 6, Mosby took the train to Petersburg and had dinner with the besieged Lee. As they partook of a leg of mutton, Mosby outlined a new organizational scheme that would place him in command of a regiment composed of two battalions. He proposed sending one battalion behind Union lines to the area between the Potomac and the Rappahannock Rivers. While they conferred, Grant was at his headquarters only about a mile away, prompting Mosby to recall in 1903 that he had "little dreamed then that I would ever sit down to dinner with Grant." Lee referred Mosby to Seddon, who approved the plan as of January 9, 1865. Mosby was promoted to colonel, retroactive to December 7, 1864. It is probably true, as a recent book claims, that Mosby "was and still is the best known non-general" of the Civil War.[19]

ONE CHANCE IN A THOUSAND

On December 21, the day after he returned to his command, Mosby attended the wedding of one of his Rangers near Rectortown. Mosby learned that six hundred troopers of the Thirteenth and Sixteenth New York Cavalries under Maj. Douglas Frazar were in the vicinity. He left the wedding with a Ranger to scout the Union position. Mosby recalled that he was more elegantly attired that evening than he had been at any time during the war. He wore a new uniform, a gray sack coat and gray trousers seamed with a yellow cord, and long cavalry boots. Two stars on his collar indicated the rank of lieutenant colonel. Over his uniform he wore a thick beaver-cloth coat and a cape lined in scarlet. He rode a fine sorrel and had an additional gray and scarlet cloak wrapped around his shoulders to ward off the chill winds. His hat bore an ostrich plume and a gold cord. Had the Gray Ghost been seen in this costume, he might have passed for the ghost of Jeb Stuart himself.

When they discovered the troopers building fires on the road to Rectortown and apparently making camp, they rode through a freezing drizzle to the home of Ludwell Lake, the father of one of his Rangers, and took supper with the family. As he recalled, "The lights shining through the windows tempted me, as I was cold and hungry, to stop where I knew we would be welcome." It was almost the last supper for the weary colonel. About nine o'clock they were interrupted by a group of Federal cavalrymen who came through the front door. He estimated later that as many as three hundred cavalrymen were surrounding the house. Mosby tried to cover the double stars on his collar and was preparing to bluff his way out of what looked like a desperate situation when a shot fired from the rear of the house narrowly missed Ludlow Lake and his daughter and struck him in the stomach. Mosby realized his only chance was to cause as much confusion as possible. "I am shot!" he shouted. In a moment the supper table had been overturned and the candles extinguished. Lake's daughter was screaming, and Lake, a corpulent man, "was dancing a hornpipe." Mosby staggered into a dark bedroom, removed and hid his bloody uniform coat, smeared his mouth with blood, and collapsed while the Federals stepped outside to stop the firing.

"During all this time I lay on the floor with the blood gushing from my wound," Mosby recalled. "In those few minutes it seemed to me that I lived my whole life over again; my mind traveled away from the scenes of death and carnage, in which I had been an actor for four years, to the peaceful home and wife and children I had left behind." When the soldiers returned with Major Frazar, Mosby told them he was a lieutenant with the Sixth Virginia Cavalry, and the family claimed he was a stranger. A doctor examined Mosby, said he was shot through the heart, and the soldiers left without noticing the uniform. A slave child no more than six years old was summoned and told to hitch two calves to an oxcart, on which Mosby was placed. He was then taken to another house about a mile and a half away as a precaution in case the soldiers returned. "It was a scene which beggared disbelief," Wert writes convincingly, "a young black boy hauling one of the most renowned and hunted Confederates in a cart, pulled by calves, down a farm lane through a sleet storm." Mosby, probably in shock, was nearly frozen when they arrived, his hair clotted with ice. Surgeons were summoned to remove the bullet. When Union troops became suspicious, they spread through the countryside looking for the mysterious Confederate officer and again came close to capturing him. Mosby, however, was kept well hidden and was taken to his parents' home near Lynchburg on January 3, 1865. His death was announced in the *Richmond Dispatch*, the *New York Herald*, the *New York Times*, and the *Baltimore American*, while other papers reported that he was mortally wounded. Sheridan celebrated New Year's Eve by writing one of his generals that Mosby had died in Charlottesville.[20]

Mosby said there were "nine hundred and ninety-nine chances out of a thousand against me. I took the single chance and won." He may have understated the odds. In wartime, soldiers face extraordinary risks, surviving or not surviving wounds by margins as slight as a mayfly's membranous wing. Mosby, although unlucky in the frequency of his woundings, was resilient and fated to survive. Had he been captured and identified on December 21, so close to the time of the hangings, he might have been lynched. "As I knew the feeling at the North against me and the great anxiety to either kill or capture me, I was sure I would be dragged away as a trophy, if they knew who their prisoner was," he wrote. What saved Mosby? Was it luck or, as his devoutly Catholic wife believed, divine intervention? Was Mosby immortal, or truly some sort of incorporeal being? Had the ghost metaphor become the man, or had the man simply become the metaphor? Could Mosby explain his own survival? Improbability becomes the very substance of myth. In his *Memoirs*, Mosby included an account of his near-capture that appeared in the *New York Herald* on December 31, 1864, and was copied by Southern newspapers. The article makes reference to Mosby's "magnificent cloak of gray, trimmed with English scarlet and gold clasps. This cloak had often been talked about by inhabitants of the Valley as belonging to Mosby, and was described by citizens as the richest article of the kind in either army." Here the cloak becomes an almost mystical mantle, inseparable from the powers of the man who wore it.[21]

Mosby stood before the assembled Confederate House of Representatives in Richmond on January 30, 1865. A resolution had been passed giving him a seat of honor, and delegates pressed forward to shake his hand. The Senate and the Virginia legislature received him with similar acclaim during the first days of February. He was the guest of Virginia governor William Smith and General Lee. Perhaps the most famous photograph of Mosby was taken at this time. He stands erect before a studio mural, his

left arm akimbo, his hand resting on a saber and scabbard. In his right hand are field glasses, their case secure in the crook of his right arm. Crossed bandoliers support two holstered pistols. His cavalry boots are polished, his colonel's uniform freshly pressed. The jaunty plume is just visible beneath the rear brim of his hat. His face is bearded, his eyes coldly defiant. William A. Tidwell suggests that the photograph may have been taken after the war. He points out that the uniform Mosby is wearing has the wrong markings on its collar and sleeves and, accordingly, may have been borrowed. The saber, not being a weapon Mosby favored, was also probably borrowed, he

A preening Mosby in Richmond near the end of the war, or shortly thereafter, already conscious of his postwar image. The binoculars hearken back to his days as a scout, while the ceremonial sword and the barely visible plume suggest the man of myth he had become. *American Heritage Engravings*

writes. Tidwell sees Mosby's countenance as "haughty, intelligent, and determined." Mosby also sat for heroic, aristocratic portraits by Edward Caledon Bruce and Louis Mathieu Didier Guillaume, who were both at work painting Lee, Jackson, Beauregard, and other Confederate icons even as the Confederacy was crumbling around them. The scarlet cape is prominent in both portraits.[22]

Later that year, the sculptor Edward Valentine produced a splendid bust of Mosby (see frontispiece) and sold plaster copies to art dealers. Ramage was much moved by the bust he saw at the Valentine Museum in Richmond while he was researching his Mosby biography. He thought the bust "stood out, as if it were alive, as if the spirit inside were about to take wing and fly away. It looks like an angry eagle, young and strong, thin and sharp-beaked, burning with an overwhelming passion to attack and vanquish some unseen antagonist." The bust has indeed a frightening intensity, particularly in the eyes. One reason is that Civil War photographers, following the conventions of portraiture of their time, asked subjects to avoid direct eye contact with the camera, which had the additional burden of requiring long exposures. Period photographs, Richard Brilliant explains, have a kind of "formal stillness, a heightened degree of self-composure that responds to the formality of the occasion." These formally composed images are what we expect to see when we visualize Civil War icons. Photographing Mosby, however, was like trying to photograph a dormant volcano or a clipper ship at anchor: its very essence was invisible in repose. Valentine's Mosby has the icy countenance of a predator. This is the Gray Ghost himself. "Yours I consider one of the most striking heads I have modelled," Valentine told him, and few would disagree.[23]

THE LINCOLN ASSASSINATION

It was the end of February before Mosby returned to his command. His Rangers had been active during his absence, but to little effect. On March 27, Mosby was put in nominal command of all that remained of the Confederate forces in Northern Virginia. But there were no regular forces left, and on April 9, Palm Sunday, General Lee surrendered at Appomattox. On that same day a Ranger detachment attempted to attack a wagon train near Burke's Station; the next day the Rangers were chased to a spot near Bull Run, where the men of Mosby's command fired their last shots of the war. Captured during the skirmish was Lt. Thomas F. Harney of the Confederate Torpedo Bureau, who had recently been assigned to Mosby's command. His presence in the command was the source of a later controversy associated with the Lincoln plot.[24]

Secretary of War Edwin M. Stanton had specifically excluded Mosby from the offer of a parole extended to Lee's men, but Grant interceded, and on April 11, General Winfield Scott Hancock's chief of staff, Brig. Gen. Charles H. Morgan, wrote Mosby proposing that he meet with Hancock to discuss terms. Hancock had replaced Sheridan as commander of the Middle Military Division on February 27. But Mosby had hopes of joining Johnston's army in North Carolina. While negotiations were taking place, Lincoln was shot by John Wilkes Booth at Ford's Theater in Washington on April 14 and died the next morning. Stanton sent Hancock the following message on the morning of April 19: "There is evidence that Mosby knew of Booth's plan, and was here in this city with him; also that some of the gang are endeavoring to escape by crossing the upper Potomac to get with Mosby or the secesh [secessionists] there."[25]

Was Mosby actually involved in the Lincoln murder conspiracy? Lewis Powell, alias Lewis Payne, a former Ranger and a deserter, had indeed broken into the residence of Secretary of State William Seward and slashed him with a bowie knife while Powell's friend Booth was murdering the president. In two interesting books, William A. Tidwell and his associates argue that the Confederate government had plotted to kidnap Lincoln and that when one attempt failed, it tried to send an explosives expert into Washington to blow up the White House. Harney, they allege, was sent to Mosby, who launched the raid as a diversion while Harney and an accomplice slipped into Washington. When Harney was captured, however, Booth, who had failed to kidnap Lincoln, decided to murder the president. Mosby was supposedly also responsible for getting the bombers out of the city and into safe territory, and may have been involved in earlier cloak-and-dagger operations.

Through a complex chain of events, Mosby, according to Tidwell, inherited the task of aiding the escape of Booth, who was following a predetermined route, possibly the one intended for Harney. Mosby's stalling response to Hancock was thereby an attempt to gain time to assess the confused situation in the wake of Lee's surrender and Lincoln's assassination. Hancock, who had brushed aside Stanton's claim of Mosby's involvement, agreed to a truce with the colonel until April 20. Booth, meanwhile, was telling people along his escape route that he was trying to find Mosby, and eventually he encountered a number of Mosby's men who, Tidwell suggests, may have been part of a security screen. Booth was finally cornered by Union cavalry and mortally wounded on April 26. Tidwell concludes that "the facts surrounding Colonel Mosby's involvement with Booth do not fit the romantic picture of the Gray Ghost, but they do fit the picture of a tough, talented, partisan leader who was willing to go to great effort to do his duty to his cause."

Tidwell and his associates push their circumstantial evidence to its limits, and their conclusion is far from proven. As in most conspiracy theories, everything is made to fit a central thesis that is impossible to refute, but which does not make it true. From arguing that Mosby was prepared to do anything to help the Confederate cause, Tidwell then jumps to the conclusion that "clearly he would not have been upset at the thought of killing a number of high officials in Washington if it could lead to victory." Wert, on the other hand, argues that Mosby's participation in such a secret plot "is out of character for the man and the officer. Neither he nor any of his men, who wrote rather voluminously about their exploits, ever hinted of any link to the Booth plots." Their silence is certainly no defense, however, because they would hardly boast after the war of their involvement in a plot to murder Lincoln. Nor is Mosby's character an entirely convincing defense.

But the best explanation lies within the Mosby Myth itself. Mosby had, after all, first gained notoriety by kidnapping a general and had attempted to capture the Union governor of Virginia. By the end of the war, Mosby had so flustered and befuddled the Federal government that it was natural for Stanton to credit reports that Mosby was with Booth in Washington. Mosby mentions the rumor in his *Memoirs* and quips that he "could prove an alibi by Hancock himself, as I was at that very time negotiating a truce with him."

The Lincoln assassination, like the Kennedy assassination and
many historical puzzles, can never be explained to everyone's
satisfaction. A rogue Catholic priest, whom Lincoln had defended
in a slander case in 1850, claimed in his memoirs that the Civil
War and the assassination were part of a papal plot with links to
Jefferson Davis. It is surprising that no one has tried to connect
Mosby, the husband and father of devout Roman Catholics, to
this putative conspiracy, later dredged up by the Ku Klux Klan
as a weapon of anti-Catholic hysteria. Were Booth and Powell
stooges of the Confederate Secret Service, Civil War-era Lee
Harvey Oswalds, and was Mosby a conduit for Jesuit hit men?
Fiction writers have found this sort of speculation fertile ground
to plow. And why not? Once a myth is unleashed, it has no fixed
boundaries. Anything becomes a possibility. If, indeed, Mosby,
or members of his disintegrating command at the end of the
war, really had some part in the Lincoln plot, their secret has
been interred with them. At an April 18 meeting with Brig. Gen.
George H. Chapman, who was second in command of Hancock's
cavalry, Mosby and his officers did express their regrets over
Lincoln's death. If that was a lie, it was a convincing one for
Hancock and the Union command.[26]

Mosby finally decided to disband his command rather than
surrender, and he assembled his men at noon in a field near Salem on April 21. It was a lugubrious scene, with a thick fog rolling over the countryside. Mosby rode before a line of horsemen
while company commanders read the colonel's farewell address:
"Soldiers, I have summoned you together for the last time. The
visions we have cherished of a free and independent country have
vanished, and that country is now the spoil of a conqueror. I disband your organization in preference to surrendering it to our
enemies."[27] On April 22, Hancock told Stanton that most of
Mosby's command had surrendered and Mosby had probably
fled. Hancock put a bounty on him and claimed that some of
Mosby's own men were trying to collect it.[28]

Mosby's whereabouts spawned many rumors. He was said
to be in exile or heading to Texas. One report had him in control
of Lynchburg with 1,000 guerrillas. Another had him proclaim-
ing himself an outlaw and heading a gang of desperados. Actually, Mosby had gone south with six men to Richmond, where he

learned of Johnston's surrender. He kept a low profile in Virginia while passions cooled and his eligibility for a parole was debated in Washington. Grant and Lee both intervened on his behalf. On June 17, Mosby was finally paroled at Lynchburg, where, a few days earlier, he had threatened to shoot his way out of a negotiating session with Union officers if they tried to arrest him. But Mosby continued to be harassed by the authorities and was arrested on several occasions. Pauline Mosby, without her husband's knowledge, made a personal appeal to Grant, who, on February 2, 1866, wrote an order permitting Mosby to travel anywhere he wished and to be exempt from military arrest.[29]

RENDING THE VEIL

Mosby was thirty-one years old when the Civil War ended and eighty-two years old when he died in 1916. Thus his postwar career lasted longer than half a century. Few notable Confederates lived longer. Stuart, Jackson, A. P. Hill, Patrick Cleburne, John Hunt Morgan, and Albert Sidney Johnston had died in the war. Lee had died in 1870, followed by George Pickett (1875), Braxton Bragg (1876), Nathan Bedford Forrest (1877), John Bell Hood (1879), Davis (1889), Joseph Johnston (1891), P. G. T. Beauregard and Kirby Smith (1893), Early (1894), Longstreet (1904), and Fitz Lee (1905). Joseph Wheeler, three years younger than Mosby, died in 1906, after serving as a major general in the Spanish-American War. Simon Buckner died in 1914. On the Union side, Mosby outlived his nemeses Custer (1876) and Sheridan (1888). Joshua Lawrence Chamberlain, a mythic hero comparable in some ways to Mosby, died in 1914. As a survivor, Mosby had an opportunity both to shape the Mosby Myth and to live long enough to compromise it. In fighting new battles after the war, according to Jones, "He tore away the veil of mystery that had made him famous. The reckless abandon with which he attacked and galloped away as a Partisan could not be repeated as a citizen."[30]

By September 1865, he had resumed his law practice, hanging out his shingle at the California Building in Warrenton. Having spent part of the war destroying railroads, he now took a more civil interest in their affairs and picked up some large fees as a railroad attorney. He also bought and sold real estate and acted as an agent for an insurance company. Ironically enough, shortly after Mosby arrived in Warrenton, someone stole his horse, but, according to a local newspaper, *The True Index,* "The sagacious animal preferring his rightful master took French leave of the thief and returned." Despite some minor brushes with the Federal authorities, he lived quietly, but seethed under Reconstruction rule along with most of his Virginian compatriots. In 1869, Mosby became involved in the Virginia gubernatorial contest, campaigning for the winning candidate of a conservative coalition bucking the Radical Republicans.[31]

In 1872 the presidential elections presented a choice between Grant, the incumbent, or Horace Greeley, the champion of the Liberal Republicans, who courted the Virginia conservatives and, by default, the Democrats. Mosby despised Greeley, but had "a very kindly feeling towards General Grant, not only on account of his magnanimous conduct at Appomattox, but also for his treatment of me at the close of hostilities." He also believed he shared with Grant the burden of regional opprobrium. "Grant was as much misunderstood in the South as I was in the North," he wrote. He came to support Grant, he said, because it seemed only logical. Southerners needed reconciliation, so it was pointless to protract quarrels already settled. He told a reporter for the *Richmond Enquirer* that an alliance with Grant was a way of giving Southerners "security for the future." On May 8, 1872, a meeting between the two wartime adversaries was arranged at the White House. The conference was cordial, and Mosby promised to support Grant against Greeley. He did not miss the opportunity to ask a favor in return, urging Grant to push forward a general amnesty bill to restore political rights guaranteed in the Fourteenth Amendment but denied to former Confederates. In a few days, Congress passed the bill, and Grant signed it.[32]

Mosby said that he crossed his Rubicon when he visited Grant, and he never recrossed it. (Julius Caesar had defied the Roman Senate by taking an army across the Rubicon, a small stream that formed the boundary between Italy and Cisalpine Gaul.) Once across the great divide, there was no turning back for Caesar or for Mosby. He campaigned hard for President Grant, who carried Virginia and won the election. Mosby actually had little effect on Grant's victory, having created considerable dissension, and he admitted that Grant gave him too much credit. His support for Grant did not extend to support for Grant's party in Virginia, however. Mosby knew he had to back Virginia conservatives to maintain any credibility with the state's voters. But to many in the South, Mosby was unforgiven, forever after a collaborator and a traitor because of his endorsement of Grant. He denied any venal motives and saw himself as a kind of people's tribune pleading the Southern cause in Washington, carrying on what Siepel calls "his private reconstruction of the South." Frequently, however, this meant patronage for Mosby's cronies, although not for Mosby himself. It was the same sort of high-minded spoils system that had served his Rangers well in the war. Mosby considered running for Congress but his foray into politics turned out badly, resulting in a street brawl, a near duel with squirrel rifles, and an arrest. He was accused of bringing his hit-and-run partisan warfare into the political arena.[33]

A pensive, postwar Mosby had resumed his law practice after disbanding his Rangers. His martial exploits already were the stuff of legend, which was enhanced by Mosby's penchant for controversy and conflict. *Library of Congress*

By the summer of 1876, Mosby faced a melancholy future. Pauline had given birth to five children after the war, but two had died, and on May 10, 1876, at the age of thirty-nine, Pauline also died. His law practice had suffered from his controversial political battles, and he was in debt. A year earlier he had written Grant that he could no longer visit the White House without causing the president political embarrassment. With Grant's term coming to an end in 1876, Mosby threw his support to the Republican candidate, Rutherford B. Hayes, and announced he was formally joining the Republican Party. In a letter published in the *New York*

Herald, he argued that sectionalism had been and remained the
bane of Southern politics and that a "solid South," blindly Democratic and antagonistic to the North, could only be inimical to
Southern interests. The phrase stuck for at least a century, but it
was not convincing in Virginia. In Warrenton, he almost squared
off in another duel, at twenty paces with double-barreled shot-
guns, against an opponent he claimed had called him a coward
and a traitor. One night, someone took a shot at him when he
emerged from a train at the Warrenton station. Leaving his children with relatives, Mosby accepted the victorious Hayes's appointment as United States Consul in Hong Kong. Sailing from
San Francisco shortly before Christmas, he arrived in China on
February 2, 1879.[34]

"A PARTICULARLY SHARP THORN"

True to form, he was in Hong Kong only a few weeks before
he was again causing a sensation. Mosby's superior in the State
Department was Frederick W. Seward, the son of Lincoln's secretary of state, William Seward. On the night of Lincoln's assassination, Lewis Powell, who had served in Mosby's command,
slashed William Seward with a bowie knife and fractured his son's
skull with a pistol butt. Fred Seward could not have been pleased
to have Mosby as one of his consuls, but the real problem was
that Mosby had taken it upon himself to flog the money chang-
ers in the diplomatic temple. Rather than accepting the position
as the sinecure it was intended to be, Mosby started checking the
books and found a pattern of corruption throughout the Consular Service in China. Ostensibly, consuls were expected to promote American commercial interests in the Far East. Because they
were poorly paid, they were given some latitude in the collection
of fees for consular services, such as issuing certificates for emi-
grants. There was a tacit understanding that their income was to
be generously supplemented by a system amounting to embezzle-
ment, bribery, and extortion. By publicly calling attention to these
outrages, Mosby had put Seward in an awkward position. His
cousin, George Seward, a former Consul General in Shanghai,
and then Minister to China, was being investigated by a Congressional committee for his own role in fraudulent schemes.[35]

Mosby was not alone in attempting to reform the Consular Service, but he was among the most vitriolic of its critics, equating consuls with pickpockets and other riffraff. Because Hayes had won election as a reformer, Mosby wisely urged that the Republicans clean their own stables instead of giving the Democrats a political opening. Soon Mosby was being smeared in the press as a troublemaker in what appeared to be a carefully choreographed counterattack directed by administration insiders. Mosby fought back: "I am in for the war and intend either to purge the public service of these scoundrels or go out myself." His tenacity won praise as well, and the *Philadelphia Times* charged that impeachment proceedings against George Seward "would have been dropped sure enough but for the accident of our getting one honest man into a Chinese consulate. Col. Mosby is that man and it seems he is to be made to suffer for his honesty." The *San Francisco Chronicle* hailed Mosby as "a particularly sharp thorn" in the side of an administration slow to live up to its promise of reform. As he had during the war, Mosby used the press to his advantage, taking his case to the *Washington Post*, the *New York Times*, and other major papers.[36]

The State Department faced a dilemma. If it got rid of Mosby, it ran the risk of unlimbering a loose cannon in another venue, perhaps Washington itself. Removing Mosby, too, would seem to give additional weight to his accusations, so officials tried to ignore him. With time on his hands, Mosby wrote letters to Hayes, Grant, and James A. Garfield, a rising star in Congress, revealing more irregularities and offering political advice. With Garfield's election as president in 1880, Mosby saw an opportunity to return home and asked for an appointment as assistant attorney general. After Garfield's assassination in 1881, Mosby's prospects were in the hands of Chester A. Arthur, who kept him in Hong Kong for the balance of his administration. By the time Mosby left office, however, he had provoked the resignation or replacement of several high officials.[37]

One of the strangest incidents in his remaining tenure in Hong Kong involved a summons on December 17, 1884, from a Chinese warlord, who invited the old colonel to take command of his army, augmented by hundreds of former Confederate soldiers, to fight the French in Indochina. Mosby declined, with the explanation

that there was a traditional friendship between the French and
the people of Virginia. Instead of riding into combat at the head
of a Chinese military detachment, Mosby proffered his resignation to the new Democratic president, Grover Cleveland, and
wrote to Grant, asking for assistance in finding him a job. On the
day before his death, Grant wrote railroad magnate Leland
Stanford, the newly elected senator from California, and asked
him to do something for the consul from Hong Kong. When
Mosby learned of Grant's death, he said: "I felt I had lost my best
friend." He departed Hong Kong on July 29, 1885, and upon his
arrival in San Francisco, he was handed a note from Stanford.
The next day Mosby accepted a job as an attorney for the Southern Pacific Railroad.[38]

RESURRECTION

Looking for opportunities to supplement his income, Mosby
agreed to lecture in New England on his war experiences. Late in
1886 he spoke to an enthusiastic crowd of about a thousand people
in Boston, dined with James Russell Lowell and Oliver Wendell
Holmes, and agreed to a seventeen-lecture tour. He realized that
while he might still be a pariah in his own state, his myth still
had currency in the North. The lectures led to a series of articles
for the *Boston Herald* and the *New York Sunday Mercury*, which
became the basis of *Mosby's War Reminiscences and Stuart's Cavalry Campaigns*, published in 1887 by Dodd, Mead & Company in
New York. He began writing his protracted defense of Jeb Stuart
about this time, placing two articles in *Belford's Monthly* in 1891
and articles in other newspapers.[39]

On January 16, 1895, Mosby attended his first and only gathering of his old command. Some 150 former Rangers assembled
in Alexandria, Virginia, and formed the John S. Mosby Camp,
Confederate Veterans. He gave an emotional speech, summon-
ing the spirit of Valhalla and alluding to perished hopes, but still
reminding the old Rangers they were now "citizens of a great
and united country" and within sight of its Capital. The war, he
said, was a great tragedy. He spoke of his service in China as an
exile, hinting at his unrequited love for his native state and wishing "that life's descending shadows had fallen upon me in the

midst of the friends and scenes I love best." He could never be indifferent, he said, to anything that concerned the honor and welfare of Virginia. "And I shall still feel, as I have always felt, that life cannot offer a more bitter cup than the one I drained when we parted at Salem." It was vintage Mosby, although he wrote years later that he had "no taste or toleration for [the] gush of such occasions." He told a former Ranger: "The gatherings in the South [are] in [no] sense reunions—they are nothing but political meetings where demagogues go to spout and keep alive for their own benefit the passions of the war."[40]

Returning to Virginia two years later to attend to family affairs after the death of his mother, he started to court President William McKinley, in the hope of securing another government appointment. But nothing suitable was offered, leaving him bitter and angry. On the afternoon of April 23, 1897, near the University of Virginia in Charlottesville, he was kicked in the head by a horse during a carriage ride. His skull was fractured and he lost an eye. Not for the first time, a premature obituary appeared in a Northern newspaper, the *New York World*, under the headline, "The Last of the Partisans." But he was not dead yet. Still, it was midsummer before the old colonel was able to return to San Francisco.[41]

"FIGHTING OLD CONFEDERATE"

Although Mosby had declined to take command of a Chinese army thirteen years earlier, he was more than ready to go into action against the Spanish in Cuba after the explosion of the battleship *Maine* in Havana harbor on February 15, 1898. He wrote the commanding general of the U.S. forces and asked for a commission, but he was told that he needed political endorsements first, which threw the one-eyed, sixty-four-year-old attorney into a rage. He told the *New York World* he was "surprised to hear that congressional influence was required to secure the privilege of fighting the battles of the country." He said he thought the homage he had received from both Lee and Grant should serve as sufficient testimonials to his military prowess. Apparently acting on his own initiative, Mosby organized "Mosby's Hussars" in Oakland, California, but the war ended before the light cavalry troop could ride into action. In any event, his time in California was coming to an end. In February 1901 he lost his job with the Southern Pacific Railroad. He again appealed to McKinley and finally received a government post. On August 3, Mosby was appointed special agent in the General Land Office of the U.S. Department of the Interior. The next month, McKinley was assassinated. Mosby's future was now in the hands of Theodore Roosevelt.[42]

Mosby arrived in Akron, Colorado, in November 1901 with a mandate to enforce an 1885 law that prohibited ranchers from placing fences on government lands. His job was simply to collect evidence of violations in parts of Colorado and Nebraska to submit to a federal attorney. Mosby, typically, took his responsibilities seriously, and began hassling his superiors to move prosecutions along faster than they were accustomed to moving them. As in China, it was not long before he picked up a whiff of corruption on the part of another agent and began making accusations and, accordingly, enemies. The whole enforcement issue was politically sensitive, with powerful cattle barons leveraging senators and judicial officials either to sponsor favorable legislation or to force prosecutors to scuttle cases detrimental to their interests.

Mosby managed to gain access to President Roosevelt in Washington, and the two blustering warhorses talked of calling out the cavalry to cut the barbed wire and bring down the fences. The press turned Mosby's visit into a circus. In Nebraska the *Lincoln Daily Star* accused him of thirsting for a bloodbath worthy of his guerrilla past. Even supporting newspapers framed the story in ludicrous terms. Roosevelt was praised in the *Detroit Free Press* for unleashing the "fighting old Confederate" to clean up the range, and the *Syracuse Sunday Herald* depicted Mosby as scalping corrupt officials and recalcitrant cattlemen. En route to Omaha to attend a grand jury hearing, Mosby was surrounded by reporters in a Chicago train station, where he accused both senators from Nebraska of aiding the cattle barons to protect their own financial interests. When he arrived in Omaha on November 27, 1902, he tried, mildly, to qualify his comments about the senators, but soon sensational stories were appearing in the *New York Times*, the *New York Herald*, the *Washington Post*, and the

Washington Evening Star, and the stories were being distributed nationally by the Associated Press. Undeterred, Mosby promised shocking revelations before the grand jury and predicted that numerous indictments would result.[43]

They did not result. Only one agent was indicted, and the grand jury failed to find merit in any of the land claims brought before it. Mosby was humiliated, ridiculed in the press, and banished to Alabama to round up trespassers on government woodlands. Eventually, the reform-minded Roosevelt did manage to get some convictions in his range wars, and a year after his removal to Alabama, Mosby received a letter from his former superior in the Land Office giving him most of the credit.[44]

Contentious to the end, the Gray Ghost in his later years would unleash his verbal artillery on everything from postcards and the Turkey Trot to college football and automobiles. Perhaps feeling the winds of modernism blowing against his ideals, he wrote a friend that it "seems to be my fate like Ulysses always to be drifting in a storm." © 1904 by Waldon Fawcett. *Library of Congress*

Mosby made no secret of his desire to leave Alabama and the Department of the Interior, and his friends tried to persuade Roosevelt to give him the Justice Department job he really wanted. Mosby finally had to resort to asking his brother-in-law, Charles W. Russell, to intervene. Russell, who headed the Justice Department's Bureau of Insular and Territorial Affairs, hired the seventy-year-old Mosby and set him up in a Washington office. He stayed on for six years, with little to do other than finish his book, *Stuart's Cavalry in the Gettysburg Campaign*, published in 1908, and give an occasional lecture. Chronically short of money, Mosby remained on the lecture circuit until near the end of his life. He journeyed as far as Toronto to address officers of the Royal Canadian Dragoons. As befitting a living myth, Mosby played himself in *All's Fair in Love and War*, a silent film based on his life. He had lived long enough to stride across the silver screen. Finally retired on July 1, 1910, as "superannuated," he said he felt like King Lear turned out to face the pitiless storm.[45]

THE LAST RIDE

All that was left was his *Memoirs*, and he spent his final days in Washington apartments writing and remembering. He published articles in *Munsey's*, *Leslie's Weekly*, the *New York Sunday Herald*, and the *Washington Post*. He sometimes received letters requesting autographs, which he duly provided, usually along with a suggestion that the writer purchase his books or arrange public lectures. Railing against the modern world, he condemned automobiles, football—which he said brought all the dignity of a cockfight to college campuses and was little more than another form of bullying—popular dances, postcards, and, probably, bicycles. He had been knocked to the pavement in Washington by a cyclist who pedaled off without bothering to attend to the half-blind old gentleman. He was often inconsistent in his views, both scolding those who kept the war alive and resenting those who did not. Piecing together stories he had collected from people who knew Mosby in his later years, or those who heard the stories from their elders, Virgil Carrington Jones described the old soldier's last days in *Ranger Mosby*, published in 1944:

> He had an abundance of personal dignity. But along with it were pronounced traits and peculiarities which tended to make enemies. He frequently was repellent on first acquaintance, yet interesting and kindly later. . . . A willingness to hurt others seemed to be an obsession. . . . He was to a rising generation a self-centered old man, best remembered to some by a red bandanna he carried in his pocket. They heard tales of his cunning and wondered if they were true.[46]

With the outbreak of the world war in Europe, he had spleen enough for one more fight and offered his services, "just in fun," to Britain's King George V. He received a courteous letter in reply. Mosby held forth on the war in an interview published in the *Philadelphia Bulletin* and reprinted in the *Fairfax Herald*. Blaming Germany for the war despite his friendship with Baron von

A Confederate battle flag and a spray of wildflowers adorn Mosby's grave in Warrenton Cemetery. Photograph by Paul Ashdown.

Massow, he predicted, incorrectly, that it would be over in six months. The Germans, he said, lacked the individual initiative of the Confederate soldier. "The German army is drilled like a great machine and when a regiment is broken up it cannot rally again." Mosby said that, if he were there "with 10,000 Cossacks and some of my old officers who served under me in our war, I'd break up all communication between the German army and Berlin, and I would run [Kaiser] William back to his capital in a hurry." The European war differed from the Civil War only in scale, he claimed, with communication the key to a quick victory. "I don't understand why they do not move with their cavalry. It vexes me, the slowness with which the allies operate. If I was there I would make William detach half of his army—that is, I would do it if I have as much sense now as I had during our war." But he was through with wars, and predicted, again incorrectly, that after the Great War it would be half a century before the European powers could fight again.[47]

John Mosby died on Memorial Day, May 30, 1916. He is buried on a hill in Warrenton, about ten miles beyond the citadels of "Mosby's Confederacy."

NOTES

1. Wert, *Mosby's Rangers*, 170–76; *Washington Star*, July 9, 1864; Ramage, *Gray Ghost*, 178.

2. Wert, *Mosby's Rangers*, 178–79; JSM to A. Monteiro, June 5, 1890, *Letters*, 64–65.

3. Wert, *Mosby's Rangers*, 184–88.

4. Munson, *Reminiscences*, 200; OR, Series 1, 43 (1): 776; OR, Series 1, 37 (2): 301; Jones, *Ranger Mosby*, 191–92.

5. Jones, *Ranger Mosby*, 197; Ramage, *Gray Ghost*, 191.

6. *Baltimore American*, August 19, 23, 1864; *New York Times*, August 19, 21, 22, 1864; Ramage, *Gray Ghost*, 192; Sam Moore, "Through the Shadow: A Boy's Memories," Clark County Historical Association Museum (Berryville, VA, n.d.), 114–15, 148–51, quoted by Wert, *Mosby's Rangers*, 193.

7. Holzer and Neely Jr., *Mine Eyes Have Seen the Glory*, 61–66; *Mosby's Memoirs*, 365; Williamson, *Mosby's Rangers*, 210.

8. OR, Series 1, 43 (1), 811; Wert, *Mosby's Rangers*, 196.

9. Williamson, *Mosby's Rangers*, 213–16, 416; *New York Times*, August 25, August 31, 1864.

10. Wert, *Mosby's Rangers*, 206–7; Ramage, *Gray Ghost*, 224–25.

11. Wert, *Mosby's Rangers*, 211–19.

12. Ibid., 209; Holzer and Neely Jr., *Mine Eyes Have Seen the Glory*, 59.

13. *Mosby's War Reminiscences*, 81; Wert, *Mosby's Rangers*, 220–27; *Mosby's Memoirs*, 320.

14. Wert, *Mosby's Rangers*, 232–35; Ramage, *Gray Ghost*, 206–8; Williamson, *Mosby's Rangers*, 264–66; *Richmond Whig*, October 18, 1864; JSM to Lee, November 6, 1864, quoted in Williamson, *Mosby's Rangers*, 420.

15. *Mosby's Memoirs*, 328; Mosby to Monteiro, February 19, 1895; *Letters*, 75–76; Ramage, *Gray Ghost*, 206–7, 242; Wert, *Mosby's Rangers*, 243; Jones, *Ranger Mosby*, 12; Siepel, *Rebel*, 127. See also Dennis E. Frye, " 'I Resolved to Play a Bold Game': John S. Mosby as a Factor in the 1864 Valley Campaign," in *Struggle for the Shenandoah: Essays on the 1864 Valley Campaign*, ed. Gary W. Gallagher (Kent, OH: Kent State University Press, 1991), 107–26.

16. Siepel, *Rebel*, 128; Jones, *Ranger Mosby*, 222–23; Williamson, *Mosby's Rangers*, 294–95; Wert, *Mosby's Rangers*, 238.

17. JSM to Landon Mason, March 29, 1912, *Letters*, 178–80.

18. Jones, *Ranger Mosby*, 230–31; Siepel, *Rebel*, 131; Ramage, *Gray Ghost*, 226–27; Williamson, *Mosby's Rangers*, 305–7.

19. JSM to Joseph Bryan, November 25, 1903, *Letters*, 124–25; Stephen J. Lang and Michael Caplanis, *Drawn to the Civil War* (Winston-Salem, NC: John F. Blair, 1999), 176; Ramage, *Gray Ghost*, 232.

20. *Mosby's Memoirs*, 334–52; Ramage, *Gray Ghost*, 233–37; Wert, *Mosby's Rangers*, 267; *Richmond Dispatch*, December 27, 1864; *New York Herald*, December 29, 1864; *Baltimore American*, December 28, 1864; *New York Times*, January 1, 1865; OR, Series 1, 43 (2): 838–40, 843–44.

21. *Mosby's Memoirs*, 339–41, 351–52.

22. *Richmond Whig*, February 1, 1865; Jones, *Ranger Mosby*, 253; Holzer and Neely Jr., *Mine Eyes Have Seen the Glory*, 57–69; JSM to PM, February 3, 1865, *Letters*, 36–37; William A. Tidwell, *April '65: Confederate Covert Action in the American Civil War* (Kent, OH: Kent State University Press, 1995), 166.

23. David Park, "Picturing the War: Visual Genres in Civil War News," *The Communication Review* 3, no. 4 (1999): 299–301; Richard Bril-

liant, *Portraiture* (Cambridge, MA: Harvard University Press, 1991), 10; Ramage, *Gray Ghost*, 337–38.

24. *Mosby's Memoirs*, 356; Williamson, *Mosby's Rangers*, 279; Ramage, *Gray Ghost*, 337.

25. Wert, *Mosby's Rangers*, 280–81; OR, Series 1, 46 (2): 838.

26. Wert, *Mosby's Rangers*, 283; Tidwell, *Come Retribution*; Tidwell, *April '65: Confederate Covert Action*, 196; *Mosby's Memoirs*, 23; Ramage, *Gray Ghost*, 264; Charles Chiniquy, *Fifty Years in the Church of Rome* (1886; reprint, Grand Rapids, MI: Baker Book House, 1958); Burke McCarty, *The Suppressed Truth about the Assassination of President Lincoln* (Philadelphia, 1924); *New York Times*, December 12, 1921, and December 12, 1922; Peterson, *Lincoln*, 92–93.

27. OR, Series 1, 46 (3): 1396.

28. Williamson, *Mosby's Rangers*, 398.

29. Jones, *Ranger Mosby*, 272–73; Ramage, *Gray Ghost*, 268–70.

30. Jones, *Ranger Mosby*, 309.

31. *New York Post*, November 19, 1867; Jones, *Ranger Mosby*, 286; Siepel, *Rebel*, 172–74; advertisements, *The True Index* (Warrenton, VA), December 9, 1865, September 1, 1866.

32. *Mosby's Memoirs*, 383; *Richmond Enquirer*, January 1873, n.d., quoted in *Mosby's Memoirs*, 387.

33. *Mosby's Memoirs*, 393–94; Ramage, *Gray Ghost*, 277–80; Siepel, *Rebel*, 183, 201.

34. Ramage, *Gray Ghost*, 280–84; *New York Herald*, August 12, 1876; Safire, *New Language of Politics*, 618–19.

35. Siepel, *Rebel*, 201–19.

36. Ibid., 220–26; *New York Sun*, October 7, 1879; *Philadelphia Times*, September 26, 1879; *San Francisco Chronicle*, n.d., circa March 1880, cited by Siepel, *Rebel*; *New York Times*, August 17, 1879; *Washington Post*, August 18, 1879.

37. Siepel, *Rebel*, 227–41.

38. Ibid., 241–44; Ramage, *Gray Ghost*, 298; *Mosby's Memoirs*, 399.

39. Jones, *Ranger Mosby*, 301; Ramage, *Gray Ghost*, 303–9; John S. Mosby, "Stuart's Cavalry in the Gettysburg Campaign," *Belford's Monthly* (October 1891): 149–63, and (November 1891): 261–75; JSM to Monteiro, August 7, 1894, *Letters*, 70.

40. JSM to Benton Chinn, June 6, 1906, JSM Papers, Fairfax County Public Library, quoted by Siepel, *Rebel*, 248; JSM to W. Ben Palmer, May 25, 1906, Albert G. Nalle Papers, Virginia Historical Society, Richmond, quoted by Siepel, *Rebel*, 281.

41. Siepel, *Rebel*, 250–51; Ramage, *Gray Ghost*, 304–5; *New York World*, n.d., JSM Scrapbooks, University of Virginia.

42. Siepel, *Rebel*, 252–56; *New York World*, May 6, 1898; *San Francisco Call*, May 13, June 24, and July 4, 1898, quoted by Siepel, *Rebel*; Ramage, *Gray Ghost*, 318.

43. Siepel, *Rebel*, 257–66; Ramage, *Gray Ghost*, 318–27; *New York Times*, November 28, 1902; *Washington Post*, November 27, 1902; *New York Herald*, November 29, 1902; *Lincoln Daily Star*, December 8, December 9, and December 27, 1902; *Omaha Evening Bee*, November 28, November 29,

1902; *Detroit Free Press* and *Syracuse Sunday Herald*, n.d., JSM Scrapbooks, University of Virginia.

44. Siepel, *Rebel*, 270–71; JSM to William McGee, November 30, 1902, *Letters*, 304–6.

45. Siepel, *Rebel*, 274–75; Spears, *Civil War on Screen*, 87; JSM to E. Leroy Sweetser, July 13, 1910, *Letters*, 166; J. H. Elmsley to JSM, December 16, 1913, *Letters*, 190–91.

46. Jones, *Ranger Mosby*, 305; JSM to Thomas Pinckney Bryan, December 7, 1909, *Letters*, 162–63; JSM to Spottswood Mosby, June 5, 1913, *Letters*, 187; JSM to Mosby Campbell, February 7, 1911, *Letters*, 176; JSM to Bettie Cocke, April 21, 1911, *Letters*, 177; JSM to Eben Swift, July 4, 1911, *Letters*, 177; JSM to Glen Walton Blodgett, August 7, 1914, JSM Papers, University of Virginia.

47. Siepel, *Rebel*, 287–88; *Fairfax Herald*, November 6, 1914; JSM to Spottswood Mosby, October 9, 1914, *Letters*, 197; JSM to Mosby Campbell, January 23, 1916, *Letters*, 240.

PART TWO

MYTHMAKERS

The real causes of war still remain out of range of our
rational thought; but the minds of nations at war are
invariably dominated by myths, which turn the conflict into melodrama and make it possible for each side
to feel that it is combatting some form of evil.
—Edmund Wilson, *Patriotic Gore* (1962)

I can now very well understand how the legendary
heroes of Greece were created.
—John S. Mosby, *Mosby's War Reminiscences and
Stuart's Cavalry Campaigns* (1887)

CHAPTER FOUR

THE IDEA OF A MYTH

Our task is to create a "usable past," for our
own living purposes.
—Herbert J. Muller, *The Uses of the Past: Profiles of
Former Societies* (1952)

PUTTING THE PAST into the service of the present, historians re-
write history to suit the new purposes of each generation, the
changes in social values, the transformation of a culture's funda-
mental mythology. Beginning in the 1890s, popular culture easily lionized the Rebel Mosby. At the turn of the century, when
race and the historical issue of slavery were more easily ignored,
the myth of the benevolent planter and contented slave was more
easily popularized, and the view of the South as simply "defending a way of life" was more generally acceptable. The view reso-
nated through popular culture in the classic novel *Gone With the
Wind* (1936), in which Southern defeat was a tragic end for a romanticized plantation aristocracy. And Mosby could be "sold" in
novels as a man of conviction, strength, and ingenuity—not so
different from other folk heroes who grew out of the frontier tradition. The prolific Ray Hogan, among others, found Mosby a
rich source for historical fiction. In fiction, Mosby was a man
whose individual heroics and defense of home atoned for potential condemnation that accompanied what later storytellers portrayed as a mere accident of history—that he only happened to
be a Confederate. More significant was the fact that he embodied
American ideals. By the 1950s, such casual indifference to the
implicit defense of slavery, even in television fiction, was becoming unacceptable. The short life of *The Gray Ghost* television series demonstrates how media cannot impose values—or perhaps
even suggest those that are at odds with the culture. In the late

1950s, it was the issue of equality and liberty that the Mosby story inevitably had to confront by elevating an ally of slavery to the role of hero.

A myth speaks to the culture in which it lives. It does not address mere historical facts, which are entwined with fiction in a braided rope of myth, made of hundreds of smaller threads, twisted together in a neat pattern to produce a single, unified strand. Washington and Lincoln, for example, stand out as icons in American culture and history, as symbols of heroism and liberty. The fairly straightforward ideals they represent at first glance, however, endure in spite of great complexity in their lives and the subsequent cultures that celebrate them. "Admittedly," writes Bernard Mayo, "the line between myth and reality, though often very broad, is sometimes narrow, and symbols in varying degree do have a basis in actualities. But this does not," he continues, "excuse the historian from his responsibility to separate fact from over-blown fancy to the utmost of his fallible abilities. Alas, while history does not repeat itself, historians repeat one another." For the historian entirely to jettison scholarship that elucidates the factual basis of the past "is abjectly to embrace the opposing concept of the poet, to whom myth is the supreme reality because, true or false, that is what people believe." And so there is a tension in cultural history between what was and what we believe.[1]

A myth, accordingly, may be very broad and ill defined, even vague, but it is inevitably a statement about that culture's values. In American mythology, a number of such stories waft through the society, then and now. And those story-myths commonly address a number of values, including:

1) *Individualism*, and Mosby fits this well as he is something of a rogue. He is distinctively individualistic, even to the point of contrarianism.

2) *The common man*, as a value, is idealized democracy, a system open to all. It is commonly known, too, as the Horatio Alger myth, and it is embedded in Mosby's self-created myth, apparent in his allusions to yeoman beginnings, and by his biographers, who point out that his educational lineage is very dissimilar from that of many other high-ranking military officers of the Civil War. He had had no formal military training or education. Mosby is in

this respect "self-made," fitting neatly into a genre of American mythology dedicated to ordinary people who rise to the top. Though not from "humble" beginnings, Mosby is still the doughty youngster who scraps his way to success in the American system—socially, economically, politically. In Mosby's case, he is also a bit of a brawler, a common man with an uncommon temper who, if he will not always rise to the top, at least will not be shoved to the bottom without a fight, as George Turpin was among the first to discover. This is also related to the value of individualism.

3) *The frontier tradition* is a continuously evolving set of values in American mythology. It is a tradition that embraces violence and conquest and that has shaped the nature and process of community building, economics, and ideology. Mosby exhibited both the savagery of the frontier existence and the civility of genteel society. Frontier themes were linked to his military exploits more fully after the war. The linking of the frontier and the military model of organization began after the Civil War, when large, competitive enterprises turned to what Richard Slotkin called the "military metaphor" as a model of organization. Some progressive writers and artists tied the metaphor to the frontier myth of the Indian-fighting regiment as an effective protagonist. Mosby's style of fighting—industrial efficiency and frontier savagery—may have been appreciated even more after the war. The theme also persists in the tradition of guerrilla warfare in American history, going back to Indian fighters.[2]

4) *Pragmatism* is itself a value that can be seen in the Mosby story, as he adapts to changing circumstances, both during the war as a guerrilla fighter and in his postwar career in law, politics, and government. Eventually, his political pragmatism was yet another paradox, as he later worked for the federal government that he had fought. He was a Rebel patriot.

5) *The rebel* is an American tradition evident in a variety of values, going back to the Puritan rebellion against English church and state authority and turning to the New World as a place of refuge. The Republic itself was born of rebellion. So there is a place for Mosby in this genre of myth in several respects. First, the value is manifest in the same way it is for all Confederates, who could have been denounced in history and popular culture as traitors, but instead were lionized for allegiance to their "Lost

Cause," for adhering to their beliefs. Second, he is a rebel against tradition in his casting off of conventional military tactics. And like the rebels of the Revolutionary War era, his tactics worked.

The historical Mosby embodied a range of American ideals and values. The Mosby Myth echoes and amplifies the importance of those same values.

THE GHOST IN THE MYTH

While not quite of the status of mythology, the Gray Ghost complements another tradition in American folklore, that of ghosts and haunts. His story does not reach the higher level of a cultural myth, but embraces stories and legends that are primarily entertaining, while often elevating the subject to the rank of a folk legend, perhaps even of myth. In American literature, a classic example of such folklore is Ichabod Crane's encounter with the Headless Horseman, as recounted by Washington Irving. But the genre exists contemporaneously—with great help, even promotion, from contemporary media—in other forms, such as UFOs, psychics, and other inexplicable (at least in empirical fashion) phenomena. The Mosby Myth is suggestive of such legends because of the fantastic proportions that his deeds assumed in the popular press, discussed in Chapter Five, and in the stories of the ghostly guerrilla fighter whom mothers used after the war to intimidate children at bedtime. Mosby is unusual among historical figures, not because of the exaggerations and legends that grew up around him, but because he became an expression of so many different myths and values.

"Myth" implies a ghost, a thing from the past that survives out of its original time and place. And a ghost in popular legend is often the spirit of someone who was at odds with the world around him or her, someone "unsettled." Ghosts may exist for any number of reasons, perhaps lingering to lament love unrequited or a painful tragedy or an injustice unresolved. Sometimes, the ghosts might even become active, moving furniture and closing doors. But usually they are simply present, nothing more or less, reminding people of unsettled issues or deeds of the past. Mosby worked hard to leave behind a myth—a ghost. In so doing, he left his past to his ghost, his myth, and unburdened himself of the national tragedy of which he was a part—perhaps even a prolonger. He left the burden to his ghost.

Declaring Mosby a ghost was a compliment to his skill at stealth, but it also could be seen as a declaration of the inevitable, for the Confederacy as well as for Mosby. Of course, Mosby did not die with the Confederacy. And the very existence of the ghost legend after the war served as a symbolic reminder of the spirit of the Confederacy, which survives to this day in various ways, from battlefield reenactments to organizations such as the United Daughters of the Confederacy. Ironically, the ghost—via the legend and the fascination of the audience—eventually possesses those who made the ghost the dispossessed. The Union conquered the Confederacy; a Southern ghost then captured the national imagination.[3]

The Mosby ghost was useful in another respect—it was irrational. The very idea of a ghost is irrational, not material, contrary to reason in an age of reason and logic. It was irrational in the same way that Mosby's tactics were "irrational" or unconventional. Mosby worked to promote the legal status of his Rangers, in order to avoid the stigma of the partisan as a mere robber and horse thief. He wanted to fit into a rational, legal system, and not be an outsider. And, at the same time, he was well aware of the dramatic value added by the irrational—the ghost—attached to his existence. But Mosby's ghost was more than a story or a bit of irrationality. It also reflected a dark side of the Mosby story, the part of him that executes prisoners, attacks trains with civilians on board, and thrills to battle. The ghost was the dark side of Mosby, the moral darkness that haunts any war. And the ghost is something unredeemed, incomplete, on the borders of life and death, of light and dark, suggestive of both moral and mortal ambiguity.

THE LIVING GHOST?

The Mosby Myth is based on a reality that is complex and burdened with nuance. For example, in comparison with that of Brig. Gen. Joshua Lawrence Chamberlain, famed for the defense of Little Round Top at Gettysburg and honored for the rest of his days, the Mosby story is much more problematic. Chamberlain was heroic in a gallant, moral fashion. He was on the winning side, fought for the "right" cause, and was himself a man of virtue. Mosby is not conducive to the same kind of myth because he fought on the losing side, which represented the immoral cause of slavery. Even though he did not advocate slavery, we are stuck with the fact that he fought on the side that defended the institution. Mosby's military fame was based on what many construed as basic banditry, and at times simply murder (the retaliatory executions), deeds that were never at issue in Chamberlain's career. Mosby was an enemy of the Union, but a hero to a region during the war. Accordingly, his individual characteristics are mythologized, as opposed to the consequences of his deeds. With Chamberlain, both character and consequences have been mythologized.[4]

Perhaps the most significant "fact" about Mosby is, ironically, that he was the Gray Ghost. And perhaps the ghostly Mosby came to be like the dead Confederacy: Its body had perished, but its existence had not. The ghosts of the Confederacy drifted in and out of the main roads of American consciousness, as the real Mosby moved in almost surreal fashion through a few counties in Virginia and Maryland. The Mosby ghost represents for the present something that is both dispossessed and dead—the Confederacy—and that at the same time takes possession of its dispossessors, as the tragedy of war and slavery still looms over the nation. The ghost confirms the death of someone or something. And so it does with Mosby, even in his own day, portending the inevitable death of that for which he fought. At the same time, the ghost haunts its killers, as Mosby himself haunted his antagonists and as the cause for which he fought haunted later generations. Renee L. Bergland makes a similar argument in more depth, and in the context of Native Americans and the national psyche, in her insightful book, *The National Uncanny: Indian Ghosts and American Subjects.*

Mosby and the endurance of the irrational—the ghost—also survive as a metaphoric assault on the manifestations of modernity. He attacked railroads and telegraph lines, both symbols of national unity, progress, and even religious revivalism. Jeffrey Sconce has explained how the telegraph and other forms of communications technology also created paranormal cultural anxieties among populations when they were first introduced. Electricity was impalpable, inexplicable, and mysterious. By disrupting relatively new forms of electronic communication, Mosby was tampering with a tenuous psychic balance inherent in communications systems. He was a "ghost" who was invading the "ghostly" telegraph. In twentieth-century imaginations, he also was symbolically attacking modernism, which represented the advantages of the North over the South. Of course, Sherman and others did the same things. But in Mosby's case, it was a man on a horse attacking the Iron Horse, pitting the central symbol of the traditional frontier against the central symbol of the conquest of the frontier. The plumed hat was as quaint in modern warfare as the sabers he so disdained. Thus, he straddled the two eras, wearing the plume, a symbol of tradition and romance and chivalry, but unhesitatingly using pistols rather than sabers. Later in life, he continued the assault on modernism, especially as it emerged in the first decade of the twentieth century.[5]

THE MAN AND THE MYTH

After the First World War, the West was a popular theme that offered relief from emerging modernism. The West and the frontier had been "closed" just long enough so that its perils were no longer an obstacle, and its conquest recent enough so that it was still fresh in the national memory. Hence, Mosby died (1916) at about the right time. Many were reacting to modernism, including the horror of war, by turning to traditions, myths, and symbols of certainty. Fundamentalist Christianity was organizing and being heard; nativist politicians pushed to exclude foreigners; and men such as Henry Ford and Thomas Edison became national heroes as much for their success story, from mythically appropriate modest beginnings, as for their actual achievements. Mosby was a symbol of the civilized warrior, and his guerrilla tactics represented controlled savagery among the civilized, recalling the frontier conflicts of the previous century. He fought for a civilized society, the Southern one in general and the Virginia one in particular. But his style of fighting was, at the outset of the war, outside the rules of civilized warfare.

It was not the savagery of frontier battle or even particularly brutal by modern standards. Instead, it seemed savage at the time, and Mosby worked to create the aura of chivalric savagery, perhaps reflecting his desire to fight the most effective war possible and at the same time remain within the contemporary boundaries of legal, civilized warfare. While Custer was mythologized later for fighting the frontier and its savagery, symbolized by the Indians, Mosby's myth was being built on bringing savagery, in the form of tactics associated with Indians, back to civilization. What the myths surrounding the two men have in common is the frontier. Like Custer's "last stand," Mosby's story became an adaptation of the Western, a way of romanticizing the primitive, whatever the outcome. In both stories, the protagonist loses. Mosby wins the battle but loses the war, while Custer loses the battle but his side wins the war. Both men offer critical raw material for legend-making: attractive, even dashing, individualists, acting on their own with appropriately scant deference to authority. Both are, ultimately, involved in tragedy (personal for Custer and regional for Mosby) and make their marks in history with blood.

Another factor in the flowering of the Mosby Myth was, of course, Mosby himself. He lived a long and active life, and his myth also had the benefit of a comparatively high survival rate among his Rangers. Mosby not only had more years to work on creating and sustaining his story, but the low casualty rate among his men meant a higher proportion of them survived to tell and embellish stories of the Rangers. A number of the men did live for a long time, with the last one dying in 1939. Mosby's skill in using the press and molding an image for himself during the Civil War is evident as he stayed attuned to press reports on his activities and campaigned for keeping the Partisan Ranger Act so that legally he was not just the leader of an outlaw gang. Later on, he worked in his memoirs and articles to create a story that confirmed the facts of an extraordinary life that fit ideals so typically American. He had the considerable advantage, too, of erudition and wit. His writing could be as engaging and unpredictable as his military exploits.

Another advantage for Mosby was the changing nature of the press in the nineteenth century and its growing reliance on fact-based stories rather than opinion-oriented politics. Mosby provided both the exciting story and the "numbers"—of enemy prisoners and casualties, of horses seized, munitions and supplies plundered. But perhaps most significant for the development of the Mosby Myth in the press is that the values of a culture are necessarily embedded in the press. So an emerging story, legend, or myth is molded to fit those values. Mosby can be an outlaw during the Civil War and a heroic figure by the turn of the century, as the standards for judging him are shifted from wartime values dealing immediately with life and death, victory and defeat to the more subtle, deeper, and more profound cultural values of individualism, success, and loyalty.

DISTILLING THE MYTH

When a piece of folklore finds its way into the popular press as a "story," it is refined, as certain details are emphasized or exaggerated, while others are diminished or omitted. Whether in print, video, or audio, media help create a consensus about the "true" version of a story by validating it via repetition. In this way, the press confirms a story's or myth's legitimacy, preserves it, and sets limits for it. As Jack Lule explains, news and myth both "offer and repeat stories. They draw stories from real life. They tell stories that confront issues of social, public life. And they use these stories to instruct and inform. They are moral tales. . . . They present portrayals of heroes and villians, of models to emulate and outcasts to denigrate." In Mosby's case, an example of such press-imposed limits could be seen in reports on the number of men who were under his command. The Civil War-era stories vary widely, even wildly, with as few as thirty or forty and as many as eight hundred Rangers reported as being in action. But the myth was given boundaries, and the significant fact about the Mosby Myth is that he consistently took on and defeated larger forces. Television and radio may further narrow a myth with the selectivity of material that is dictated by the limitations of their formats: Print media thrive on a myriad of facts. Audio and video media are driven less by fact and more by form. Television had to narrow the frame for the Mosby story, to take it away from the broader, complex story of the Civil War and force it into the more limited frame of the individual, a stock Western character of daring and conviction. A good television episode, with perhaps a slight deferential nod toward history, simply provided yet another vehicle for traveling a well-worn road of the television-drama formula.[6]

Because a myth exists primarily as a story, it may be driven by faith rather than logic, be based on ideals rather than realities. As a myth is employed to coordinate and organize reality and values, it can exaggerate what actually happened to the point of having almost no relation to a real historical event. Or it can simplify history to the point of fictionalizing it. But the myth, if it is to function for the culture, must reflect in some fashion "true" values of that culture. And so the Mosby Myth could be true to ideals or values while not adhering to historical fact. The historical story of his war exploits became a springboard for the greater truth embedded in cultural myths—the value of individualism, the rewards of ingenuity, the righteousness of conviction. A myth is as changeable as the people and society in which it exists.[7]

A VERY CIVIL WAR: TELEVISION AND WAR

History, for the television industry, has been quite useful, although perhaps not in the fashion that Herbert Muller, in the epigraph to this chapter, had in mind. History can generate stories and profits, but the history employed by television must conform to cultural values and myths. *The Gray Ghost* may have attempted to do so, but the inherent tension between the emerging civil rights movement of the 1950s and the history of slaveholding was too complex to address in a simple video-narrative.

Media, of course, use history to sell entertainment, and media history is to a great extent the history of popular myth and fantasy. Media reflect popular images by selling what people want to believe about the past. There is, according to Dan Nimmo and James E. Combs, a variety of historical fantasy on television, including "fiction fantasy." Mosby's story was a fiction fantasy that combined historical individuals and events, but fictionalized them with dramatizations. They cite a show about a fictional trial of Custer exemplifying this type of program, which "speaks to that ambivalence and to uncertainties about a central myth, the West.

Was the conquest of the West a heroic drama conducted by fear-less men, such as Custer, or was it a brutal savaging of indig-enous peoples for purposes of greed conducted by raging villains, such as Custer?" Such shows, they point out, are not "mythically adequate" because they fail to resolve the issue.[8]

And so it was for *The Gray Ghost*, which celebrated the Ameri-can individual, the martial spirit, and ingenuity, but could not reconcile those myths and values with an implicit defense of sla-very and an assault on federalism, a form of government that had demonstrated itself so magnificently worthy in saving the world, democracy, and America in the previous decade. *The Gray Ghost* was subsumed in the Western myth. Within its simple nar-rative, television offered a comfortable and useful structure for the producers and consumers of the stories, and one that has been commercially successful. How can a medium so wedded to logi-cal structure address the illogical, the irrational, the mayhem of war? Ken Burns demonstrated how it can be done, but his Civil War epic was not in conventional television-drama format. In addition, television has an audience to which it must appeal, and much of that audience is in the South. As with television audi-ences everywhere, the expectation and demand are not for nu-ance, but for entertainment. So television was left in a quandary when it came to creating a story about a Southern soldier: How does one create a protagonist who is "good" but defends an in-stitution that is evil? Television's stories about the Civil War, as well as other wars, often show it as a rational, conflicted, roman-ticized testing ground of men and national values. Television war generally has been an affirmation of American virtues. This genre has supported and continues to support any number of myths.[9] Let us cite four.

The Garden Myth. As in *Gone With the Wind* and its ripoffs, the idea is that war shattered the idyllic innocence of the South. Sla-very was idealized in the "mammy" figure. Suffering was blood-less and soldiers were dashing. The Mosby Myth is an extension of this basic myth, related to the Garden Myth that celebrates the Edenic rural life over "dirty" urban existence. The Mosby Myth celebrates an imagined triumph of country over city. Mosby sym-bolized the rural life, and in legend inverted reality by having the country bleed the city, rather than vice versa, which was so commonly the pattern and one protested by the populists of the postwar era.

In fact, the railroads and their shipping rates were a catalyst to the early populist movements among Western and Midwestern farmers. In Mosby and his Rangers, later generations found an uncommon reversal of the railroads robbing the people along their tracks. Instead, these men came out of the woods and fields to plunder the railroads joyfully in the cause of an agrarian, Jeffersonian way of life. The "bad guys" for many in the post-Civil War generations were not in gray uniforms, but in tuxedos. Many of the so-called robber barons of the Gilded Age built their fortunes on railroads. And so the stories of Mosby and his Rangers literally wrecking and pillaging the railroads were an ironic play on justice—even if administered a few decades before the fact. And even better, Mosby conquered the Iron Horse, that ultimate symbol of urban intrusion, using actual horses, which are critical to any story or picture—mythic or otherwise—of conquering the American frontier.[10]

Innocence. This is related to the Garden Myth, but focuses more on the people who inhabit the Garden. In this version, various psychopaths and criminals have been presented as people who were driven to their outlawry by a society that did not understand them, or by a society in which the individuals had been done an injustice and thus were driven to crime. A short-lived television network series, *The Legend of Jesse James*, which ran in 1965–66, even framed that murderous psychopath as a basically misunderstood man. It recast the Robin Hood myth in the American West, with Jesse James and his brother Frank robbing trains in order to repay people who had been wronged by the railroads. It was a very 1960s approach to the story. Novels, films and other television series treated a host of characters in such a fashion—bounty hunters, vigilantes, and killers alike. Clint Eastwood became a popular icon in the era with his low-budget "spaghetti westerns," whose protagonist was often an antisocial drifter, operating on the edge of the law, looking for money or revenge or both. But right and wrong, innocence and guilt were never serious themes in such shows. Charles Bronson's character in the *Death Wish* movies a few years later turned a killer-vigilante into a hero, an innocent man wronged by society. The Mosby Myth uses this theme in showing Mosby as a man fighting for his principles. The nuances and complexities of the issue of slavery and of state versus federal primacy are sublimated to simpler ideas.[11]

Southern Aristocracy. The plantation owners were granted the fiction of noble lineage. It is a mythology that ignores the hard reality of the kind of people it took to carve a profitable plantation out of near wilderness and to run a gang-labor farm. Mosby casts himself in the role of the aristocratic warrior, his appearance alone being evidence of such a mind-set. His flamboyant attire was noted consistently in press reports along with his "gentlemanly" and "gallant" manner.

The Nature of War. War is sanitized so people die neatly and quickly. Killing is meaningful and purposeful. *The Gray Ghost* presents war as an opportunity to frame man's more noble virtues—loyalty, bravery, gallantry, and even a sense of justice.

THE WARRIOR'S SPIRIT

The Mosby Myth's endurance can be credited to other themes in American history, too, including military history. Mosby was part of the so-called ranger mystique that emerged in the press and popular culture of the late nineteenth century, in legends based on the success of Mosby and other guerrilla fighters. He and his ilk were both pragmatic and savage, and Mosby was a particularly good exemplar of these traits that are so common and so strong in American myth. He was a ranger in a "transitional" war, one that began as a traditional conflict and ended as the first modern one. But Mosby also drew on another American value, and was among those American icons who had what Slotkin calls an "intuitive affinity for capitalism," meaning that he had a good sense for profit and plunder. Mosby himself did not even partake of the loot on many occasions, thus linking his immediate purpose and subsequent legend to a higher cause, even though it came to be the one romanticized as the "Lost Cause." His style of fighting—savage and "profitable"—became an important part of the general ranger mystique that was expressed so vividly in the "New Frontier" theme of the Kennedy administration of the early 1960s. The Green Berets of that era were a military elite, professional soldiers drawing on the tactics and style of frontier rangers from as far back as the French and Indian Wars, the Revolution's Swamp Fox, and, of course, Mosby.[12]

The first rangers in the New World were militia groups who protected settlements in open, isolated countryside. The first organized colonial ranger company was formed in New England in 1675 by Capt. Benjamin Church, who adapted his tactics from the Indians who were menacing the frontier settlements. The most famous unit of the colonial period was Rogers' Rangers, under Maj. Robert Rogers, which fought during the French and Indian War. Ethan Allen led an irregular body of militia popularly known as the Green Mountain Boys before and during the Revolution. The earlier rangers, first fighting Indians on the frontier and later the British, linked Mosby's Rangers to a tradition of guerrilla warfare that in many ways was peculiarly American, especially in its contending with a frontier area and an indigenous population that conducted war by a different set of rules.

The first American edition of the standard European reference work on irregular warfare, *The Partisan, or the Art of Making War in Detachment*, was published in Philadelphia in 1776 and dedicated to George Washington. During the American Revolution, Francis Marion formed a ranger company in 1780 and fought the British in South Carolina. The Swamp Fox usually struck the British forces at night and then disappeared into Low Country marshes. He became one of the great heroes of the Revolution and was exceeded in fame only by Washington. It was Parson Weems's mythmaking biography of Marion that had been Mosby's favorite boyhood reading. Robert E. Lee's father, Gen. "Lighthorse Harry" Lee, had led a partisan force in Washington's army. During the War of 1812, ranger units were commanded by Andrew Jackson and were used as scouts by Gen. Zachary Taylor during the Mexican War. During the Civil War, more than four hundred units, almost all of them Confederate, were called rangers, although most were rangers in name only. Mosby's Rangers was the most successful of these small-unit commands.[13]

During the Second World War a ranger battalion was organized under the command of Brig. Gen. William O. Darby. Darby's

Rangers participated in the disastrous Dieppe raid in Normandy, saw their first major action in North Africa, and invaded Sicily and the Italian peninsula with General Patton. Other ranger units made raids in Norway and France and served in the D-Day invasion and the Battle of the Bulge. In the Pacific, a ranger battalion took part in the Philippines invasion in 1944. A ranger-style unit called Merrill's Marauders, under Maj. Gen. Frank D. Merrill, fought behind Japanese lines in Burma. A ranger company saw action in Korea and then was nearly annihilated. This unit was succeeded by airborne ranger companies and small marauder units. In Vietnam, Special Forces, Long Range Reconnaissance Patrol units, or "lurps," and ranger units operated throughout the conflict and continue to play a role in American military tactics today.

By the late 1960s it was especially problematic to project a heroic image of a guerrilla fighter because of Vietnam and the nature of Vietcong warfare. Such tactics were the style of the enemy, noted for its "dishonest" tactics (such as mingling with the civilian population). The Vietcong were not savages in the noble tradition of the American frontier, but savages in an unsavory, primitive way, exemplified by the use of sharpened "pungi" sticks, placed in camouflaged pits along trails and tipped with feces. The popular image of war was that of the massive assault, the D-Day style of invasion. This form of warfare is not only easy to depict in film, but it also makes it easy to tell good guys from bad guys and what the score is, something often very difficult in Vietnam. The American military usually behaved in "massive-assault" fashion in Vietnam, while the Vietnamese guerrilla fighter behaved in a way that was antithetical to the behavior of the idealized American warrior. Ranger historian Maj. John Lock distinguishes between the modern rangers, beginning with Darby, and the earlier ones: "Though not 'formally' trained in accordance with the standards prescribed by today's prestigious U.S. Army Ranger School, the early deeds of Rogers, Marion, and Mosby easily meet the standards and intent of today's modern Ranger. In actuality, they do more than meet the standards. They *are* the standard." Mosby was one of the first inductees into the Army's Ranger Hall of Fame in 1992.[14]

INDUSTRIAL-ERA MOSBY

Mosby also exemplified a new style of leadership that could adapt itself to the irregularities of war, favoring practical improvisation over traditional military regularity. Mosby's "new" approach has even been carried into the twenty-first century, with a chapter in Tom Wheeler's *Leadership Lessons from the Civil War* devoted to the Ranger leader's tactics: "Lesson Nine: If You Can't Win . . . Change the Rules." The events highlighted are the capture of Stoughton and the Miskel's Farm skirmish. Wheeler states, "The Information Age is one huge reformation of the rules. . . . The electronic era seems to be saying, 'If it ain't broke, break it!' The other guy wrote the old rules. Win by writing your own rules." (Wheeler, it should be noted, is the president of the Cellular Telecommunications Industry Association. He represents an industry that promotes mobility and a kind of decentralized, guerrilla approach to communications, a "reformation of the rules.") Mosby did not equip his Rangers with cellular phones, but he did develop unorthodox means to keep them within a communications system.[15]

Paradoxically, Mosby represented both the industrial efficiency of the Gilded Age and the tenacious hold that the Agrarian Myth has always had on the American imagination. The paradox could be seen in the early twentieth century with a reactionary response to industrialism and urbanism, which came in the context of a society that basked in the economic fruits of industrialism. The cost of goods declined, as general economic well-being increased in the post-First World War nation, as immigration surged, filling factories with cheap labor and cities with slums. Xenophobia surged, too, as cities came to be increasingly viewed as centers of sin and evil. Certain ethnic groups were seen as biologically and socially inferior, as groups that might cause the general society to "regress," using the language of the day, in the direction of savagery. The Mosby Myth could accommodate both sides of such a culture. Mosby appealed to the "scientific management" aspects of modernism because he was efficient.[16]

In industrial terms, the investment of only a few hundred men in Mosby's operation brought a very high return for Lee and the South, as Mosby's Rangers suffered few casualties and inflicted many, drew little on the Confederate supplies as they lived off the land, but carried off vast amounts of Union armaments, supplies, and horses. But the Mosby paradox resides in the fact that his corporate efficiency was in the context of his "anticorporate" activity. He was attacking not only a foreign invader, from the Southern point of view, but he was battling the giant corporation. He was living off the agricultural land and looting the industrial North's supply lines. He was not only defending the agrarian South, but also the myth of individualism in the face of an increasingly corporate culture. And to the end of his life, Mosby could not resolve the paradox. He selectively participated in Civil War reunions, rituals, and symbols of reconciliation. As Mosby neared the end of his life, the Gray Ghost myth was still lively and youthful and continues to be so. Mosby spent his final years working on his *Memoirs* and publishing articles in newspapers. He was seen on the streets of Washington—irony enough that the Gray Ghost of the Confederacy should spend his last days there—reminding people of his presence and making a few final raids on modern sensibilities.

NOTES

1. See Merrill D. Peterson, *Lincoln in American Memory* (New York: Oxford University Press, 1994); Karal Ann Marling, *George Washington Slept Here: Colonial Revivals and American Culture, 1876–1986* (Cambridge, MA: Harvard University Press, 1988); Mayo, *Myths and Men*, 41.

2. Richard Slotkin, *Gunfighter Nation: The Myth of the Frontier in Twentieth-Century America* (New York: Atheneum, 1992), 89–90.

3. On the role of ghosts in the cultural imagination, see Renee L. Bergland, *The National Uncanny: Indian Ghosts and American Subjects* (Hanover, NH: University Press of New England, 2000).

4. John J. Pullen, *Joshua Chamberlain* (Mechanicsburg, PA: Stackpole Books, 1999).

5. See Jeffrey Sconce, *Haunted Media: Electronic Presence from Telegraphy to Television* (Durham, NC: Duke University Press, 2000); see also Daniel J. Czitrom, *Media and the American Mind* (Chapel Hill: University of North Carolina Press, 1982), 1–29.

6. Jack Lule, *Daily News, Eternal Stories: The Mythological Role of Journalism* (New York: Guilford Press, 2001), 21.

7. For a fuller discussion on the problem of duality in myth, see Slotkin, *Gunfighter Nation*, 13–14.

8. Dan Nimmo and James E. Combs, *Mediated Political Realities* (New York: Longman, 1983), 72–84.

9. On American myth, see James Oliver Robertson, *American Myth, American Reality* (New York: Hill and Wang, 1980); Nicholas Cords and Patrick Gerster, eds., *Myth and the American Experience*, 2 vols. (New York: Glencoe Press, 1973).

10. Cullen, *Civil War in Popular Culture*, 69, looks at *Gone With the Wind* in terms of race, class, and gender.

11. Alex McNeil, *Total Television*, 3d edition (New York: Penguin Books, 1991), 432.

12. Slotkin, *Gunfighter Nation*, 449, 455–59.

13. See John D. Lock, *To Fight with Intrepidity: The Complete History of the U.S. Army Rangers, 1622 to Present* (New York: Pocket Books, 1998).

14. Stanley Karnow, *Vietnam: A History* (1983; reprint, New York: Penguin Books, 1984), 416; Lock, *To Fight with Intrepidity*, xvi.

15. Tom Wheeler, "Lesson Nine: If You Can't Win . . . Change the Rules," *Leadership Lessons from the Civil War: Winning Strategies for Today's Managers* (New York: Doubleday, 2000), 183.

16. Slotkin, *Gunfighter Nation*, 90–91, discusses the idea of military efficiency's being linked to ideas of industrial management.

CHAPTER FIVE

BOHEMIAN FABLES
Mosby in the Press

As stories, myth and news have always been
matters for interpretation.
—Jack Lule, *Daily News, Eternal Stories: The Mythological
Role of Journalism* (2001)

"ALL HISTORIC DOUBTS about my own existence have, I believe,
been settled," Mosby wrote in response to stories that he was
nothing but a tall tale. He added, however, that "the fables published by the Bohemians who followed the army made an impression that still lives in popular recollection." He was right,
but Mosby worked harder than any "bohemian," a general term
then for journalists, to create a myth and a legacy. He understood
the press, how it worked, and the importance of public opinion.
Mosby operated on the edges—of the Confederacy and the Union,
of legal rangers and mere partisan bandits, of new war tactics
and old. He fought for a communications-poor South that
had only a fraction of the rail and telegraph lines of the North,
which was communications-rich by comparison. He was on
the physical edge of the prosperous North, plundering its railroads, cutting its telegraph lines, and "capturing"—in fact and
in word—its newspapers.[1]

The lively adjectives that peppered the press accounts of his
exploits were not unique to Mosby, as such colorful writing could
be found regularly in news from the period. Even though the
coverage of Mosby was not stylistically unusual, it is important
because the press stories were the earliest network and foundation for his myth. Newspaper coverage was important, too, for
what Ramage called the "multiplier effect" of tying down enemy
troops and resources disproportionate to the small number of the

Rangers. But, more significant for this study, the press was central to creating for Mosby a myth that would emerge rather quickly during the war and evolve during the next century. The myth was grounded in "documented" exploits, given the credibility of time, place, casualties, and the testimony of witnesses. His myth's origins are in the popular press and culture of the nineteenth and twentieth centuries. This source has served his myth very well. It helps the myth remain vital in the culture by making the Mosby legend both malleable to and congruent with the values of society.[2]

AN ERA OF TRANSITION

Newspapers in the early Republic and the early nineteenth century were opinion peddlers, journals allied in spirit, and often by economic support, with politicians and political parties. Newspaper content was tilted toward ideas and political opinion more than facts or "news." This balance began to change in the 1830s as innovative editors, particularly in New York City, and new technology combined to create a market for information both timely and factual. Publishers began to invest in newsgathering in unprecedented fashion. The telegraph, with its first line opened between New York and Washington, DC, in 1844, made the transmission of information faster and increased its cost, at least for the immediate future. But it was a major factor in pushing newspapers toward a style of newswriting that emphasized facts over the earlier narrative form. The relatively high cost of transmitting stories via telegraph and the limited access to information conduits resulted in the formation of news associations that enabled newspapers to pool resources and share telegraph time.

The first such venture was the New York Associated Press in 1849. The Southern Associated Press and the Press Association of Confederate States emerged during the Civil War to fulfill the same function for Southern states. With about 50,000 miles of lines at the beginning of the war, the telegraph had become critical in news transmission and in shaping the nature of news. The telegraph and press associations made news more objective and balanced than the traditional narrative news story. The telegraph's expense meant that sending only the facts critical to a story would be more economical. And, because breakdowns were common in the early years of the telegraph, it was wise to send the most important information first—which became the standard for modern newswriting, the so-called inverted pyramid, with the most important facts opening a story. The press associations serving a number of clients needed to offer a product that was not tailored to particular publications' and editors' points of view, from a perspective that could be shared by all clients. That perspective was a factual one, leaving opinions and interpretations to the clients' newspapers.[3]

It was an era of transition, with flamboyant and innovative editors, including Horace Greeley of the *New York Tribune* and James Gordon Bennett of the *New York Herald*, selling a profitable package of opinion and news. This transition was important to the creation of the Mosby Myth for a number of reasons. First, the press was demonstrably factual, and this gave credibility to stories of Mosby's exploits, particularly when the same story would appear in a number of publications, with more or less the same account. Repetition is critical in verifying legends as can be seen in such incredible contemporary ones as Bigfoot and UFOs. Lacking evidence, the purveyors of the fantastic turn to one another to validate their claims. They offer an accumulation of stories—not material evidence—as a foundation for the reality of their tales. Second, the press of the Civil War still represented a strong tradition of opinion and storytelling, with serialized fiction as common fare. And Mosby was a good story.

The Civil War press was also becoming a visual press, as publishers began adopting new technologies that made possible the use of photographs, illustrations, and maps. New publications such as *Harper's Weekly* and *Frank Leslie's Illustrated Newspaper* were providing the Northern public with battle images that made the war seem a palpable reality. *Leslie's*, initially the more sensational of the two, featured stories with shocking illustrations. *Harper's* at first took a more sober and cautious approach to the war, but soon bowed to competitive pressures by stealing many of its rival's best artists. Mosby was a good subject for illustrators who desired to take artistic liberties while re-creating his exploits. The illustration that appeared on the first page of *Harper's*

Weekly on September 5, 1863, showed Mosby's men looting wagons and guzzling captured spirits like a band of debauched highwaymen. Because Mosby's tactics depended on what could be construed as pilferage, kidnapping, arson, trainwrecking, ambushing, rustling, retaliatory hanging, six-gun shootouts, spying, and general mayhem, it was not difficult for artists to imagine grisly scenes that would curdle the milk on the breakfast tables of indignant Northern readers.[4]

DEAD AGAIN

The press fed the Mosby legend in many respects, but perhaps at the time nothing embellished it so well as stories about his death. He died and came back to life with great regularity in the press, which was fitting for the Gray Ghost. The *New York Herald* reported him "dead and buried." A few days later, a story headlined "Death of the Notorious Pirate of the Valley" verified Mosby's demise, citing a story in the *Richmond Dispatch*, which may well have picked it up from Union papers to begin with, and so completed the circle of misinformation. Within a few days, the paper reported Mosby's survival, even retaining the language of the *Richmond Dispatch* about the "gallant" Mosby. "But, if we are to believe the rebel stories, Mosby is not yet dead. He may possibly recover; 'the devil takes care of his own.' " Even with that resurrection, the *New York Times* still reported the next day that Mosby had been killed.[5]

Such reports were an odd complement to descriptions of Mosby attired in elegant cape and plumed hat, the romantic image enhanced by death or near death—stories that became eerie in their own right simply by happening again and again. The *Richmond Dispatch* depicted him as flirting with danger and having fun. "The waggish Mosby, with part of his gang, on Sunday night, encamped two and a half miles from Upton's Hill, almost within range of the guns on the Washington fortifications. On Sunday afternoon he stopped a funeral procession, on its way from Lewinsville to Washington, and stole horses attached to the hearse. He afterwards visited Falls Church, and amused himself by taking observations of our new contraband farms."[6]

Stopping the funeral procession becomes symbolic as Mosby appeared in press reports to have interrupted his own journey to the grave time and again. He personified the romanticized cavalier warrior, traveling the land and engaging in martial exploits, all in good humor in the face of death. Even at the end of the war, and in the Northern press, a grudging admiration seems to seep through a *New York Times* report that Mosby did not recognize Lee's surrender (AP story) and was "determined to fight so long as he has a man left."[7]

ATROCITIES AND COWARDICE

Press coverage in the North was often ambivalent about Mosby—guerrilla fighter or horse thief, soldier or killer, ranger tactician or coward? The *New York Tribune* occasionally romanticized Mosby and at other times was steadfast in its conviction that he was little more than a common criminal. At the end of the war it grouped him with notorious partisans accused of using the conflict as a cover for murder and robbery, "preying alike upon friend and foe, if indeed they have any friends among the Southern people, who must necessarily be the greatest sufferers by their predatory raids." Mosby, unlike his men, refused to surrender, the *Herald* reported, and opined that Grant should declare Mosby an outlaw and pursue him and his kind and "get rid of them." A few days later, the newspaper attempted to belittle Mosby further by reprinting a story from the *Richmond Whig* reporting that, upon the disbanding of the Rangers, Mosby had opted to flee to the West, leaving behind his wife: "It is not known whether he seeks the Western country with belligerent intentions, or . . . some sequestered spot where taxation is unknown."[8]

Earlier in the war, the *New York Times* had reported that the "heartless outrage" continued with Mosby's hanging of three more prisoners in retaliation for executions of his own men by Custer. And worse, the reporter noted that Mosby "boasted" of having spies and getting supplies from Alexandria twice a week. He was described as a "pompous somebody," admittedly of "rather pleasing address." And so, even in damning Mosby for his war crimes, the press still saw him as a dashing fellow. He was an outlaw, but such a colorful one. The *Times* later called attention to the outlaw aspect of the Rangers with a report of a Mosby officer bragging about shooting a forage master and a Negro. The paper charged Mosby's band with hanging three men, and doing so with the bodies barely off the ground: "A species of refined cruelty not often practiced by people claiming to be civilized." Perhaps those words—"refined cruelty"—hint at the fascination with war and violence generally and with Mosby in particular. It may imply that "cruelty" is for savages, for the uncivilized, but at the same time those words acknowledge that war and violence might also be amenable to refinement.

A few months earlier, the *Times* had defended the hanging of Mosby's men because the Rangers were mere murderers who reportedly had killed four Union cavalrymen riding in advance of the wagon train, then "rifled the persons" of three of the Union soldiers, and fled without molesting the wagon train. Mosby's mode of warfare was decried, with one *Times* headline damning it thoroughly: "Massacre by Mosby—Rebel Treachery—Cowardly Cruelty." The story, out of Berryville, condemned Mosby and his men for dressing as civilians and Union soldiers in the course of attacks on pickets and other troops: "Reports were being made of outrages perpetrated by the bushwackers under Mosby. Men were everywhere fired at, . . . and several wanton murders were reported. . . . Ten men were murdered on the ground after surrendering, nearly all of whom were shot through the head. . . . Some of the fiends, appalled at the bloody agonies, did not shoot their prisoners until ordered to shoot the d- -n Yankee son of a b - - - h by their officers." That report was followed a few days later by another atrocity story, which stated that Mosby hanged thirty Union soldiers. Mosby had never hanged any such number of prisoners, but his notoriety, like his harassing of supply lines, had a multiplier effect on his own outlaw reputation in some quarters.[9]

Even in the South, Mosby was admittedly a pirate, called so by the *Richmond Dispatch*, and that paper's description of him as a "daring and distinguished guerrilla chief" was reprinted in the *New York Herald*. So the Southern admiration of Mosby, the myth building, made its way northward through the common practice of reprinting stories from other newspapers. Just as the Union and Confederate soldiers traded tobacco and coffee, the newspapers swapped news, adding another layer to the incestuous nature of the war. A sketch of Mosby, apparently penned by the *Herald* reporter and attached to the *Dispatch* report, lashed out at a presumably dead Mosby: "Like Morgan, Anderson and other guerrillas of like character, Mosby has met with a dog's death. His career, like theirs, has been short and inglorious. He added nothing to the cause of the rebellion by his conquests. He has only served to disgrace the country and degrade the profession of arms." It embellished the image of a self-interested outlaw by reporting he had been in Richmond on December 1 "nursing his wounds and begging for promotion."[10]

FACTS OF ACCOMPLISHMENT

The press of the Civil War era may have best served the emerging Mosby legend by giving it a foundation in fact—or just in the presumption of fact. Newspapers of the era were more than ever in the business of printing facts, due to the limits and the nature of technology. Ironically, the rush for facts often meant grasping at anything, including "facts" that were not true, and so the press often became a republisher of rumors. Newspapers then apparently were not in the habit of printing corrections or retractions when stories proved false. This journalism, too, was guerrillalike —brief "raids" on the truth, followed by exaggeration, bombast, and then sober moralizing and finger-wagging.

War is a crisis that provides the opportunity for sensational stories of tragedy, heroism, grief, and triumph. And it was a crisis that could be presented in the starkest empirical terms: the number of dead, the miles won or lost, the name of a city or region conquered. So in a reversal of the fable of the emperor without clothing, it was a "ghost" adorned with the very visible spoils of war. The *Richmond Dispatch* detailed, in June 1863, Mosby's attack on a train from Alexandria, and his capturing 200 to 300 soldiers and destroying the locomotive before being overpowered "by a heavy force of the enemy." The Rangers scattered, but Mosby and his men were said to have returned to charge the Yankees two more times. The estimate of the number captured well illustrates the press as a mythmaker: 200 to 300? It is a generous

range. But it is "factual" in that it has hard numbers, and it implies Mosby's military prowess in that he simply captured so
many soldiers it was hard to count them all.

About two months later, "the daring scout Mosby" was credited with capturing 40 Union soldiers. The reporter speculated
that Mosby was "doing much good," but "it is feared his usefulness may be spoiled by too rapid promotion." Mosby's forces were
reckoned at improbably high numbers at times, as high as 400 to
even 800 men. At other times, the size of his force was given incredibly wide margins of error, with a story in 1864 estimating
Mosby's force attacking a wagon train at 25 to 150 men. The range
is almost ridiculous, in light of what might be expected of a force
of 25 men versus 150 men in a military action. It borders on being
an admission of ignorance about what is going on, but nevertheless knowing that a good story is in the making, whatever the
dreary facts.[11]

Mosby's accomplishments—or outrages, if one were of Union
sympathy—were easy to enumerate. Even if the numbers were
wrong, they still provided a foundation for a myth. Actually, rumors and exaggerations are what one would expect in the absence of reliable information. People wanted to know about the
war. In more contemporary terms, there was a market for war
news. It was not—and is not—an "either/or" proposition, in
which a stark dichotomy exists between fact and falsehood. Instead, truth and rumor blend in whatever quantity necessary to
produce a newspaper, and truth becomes a matter of degree of
correctness or incorrectness.

The *New York Herald* understood early on that Mosby was
uncommon in terms of military strategy, reporting that "all is
quiet in the [Shenandoah] valley—that is, in common military
parlance; but we may be sure that the enemy is very much dis-
quieted by such men as Mosby . . . and ere long we will hear of
another lot of wagon, &c, turned over to the Confederate government, and more prisoners gobbled up, though we may be sure
that Mosby will not go to any extra trouble to catch prisoners
since the murder of his men." After Lee surrendered at Appomattox, the *New York Times* reported from the War Department in
Washington, "nearly all" of Mosby's men had surrendered, but
Mosby had not, and that some of his men were hunting for him

for a reward. Mosby was elevated even to being a rebel among rebels.[12]

Mosby was good for the press in another way, and that was by capturing correspondents—the ultimate manipulation of the press. He allowed newspapers to report on the deed and so provide evidence of their own heroic proximity to the action. The *New York Herald* reported that two more of its own correspondents had been captured, and the "inevitable and inscrutable Mosby manages to break through our lines occasionally." And when one of the captured correspondents was paroled and described his ordeal in the *Herald*, he noted the good life of his captors, well clothed in captured Union uniforms, in good health and spirits, their deference to their leader, who "looks no bandit chief. . . . He evinces no physical tokens signalling the audacious and successful partisan leader he is. . . . He acted and spoke as a gentleman, with no show of vulgarity or bullying cruelty or lurking sneers at his victims." He was, in others words, the very picture of the romanticized bandit, Robin Hood, with his Merry Men. The *Herald* even picked up an item from the *Richmond Examiner*, which crowned Mosby "our prince of guerrillas."[13]

PUBLICITY STRATEGIST

Mosby was a versatile and adaptable fighter, not only in his comprehension of the advantages of pistols over swords, but also in his understanding of the significance of communications and transportation systems and of the role of the press in shaping opinion about him. He disrupted enemy communications with attacks on railroads and wagon trains, by cutting telegraph lines, and by snatching vedettes and pickets. At the same time, he improved the communications and information system for the Confederacy with scouting and behind-the-lines activity. He became, in effect, a master propagandist, promoting the embellishment of his feats as he closely studied captured Union papers for information, and extending the Confederate lines of communication as he disrupted the flow of information for the Union. Newspapers and communications were at the heart of the "multiplier effect," which basically meant successful propaganda.

Though military historians may debate the real effect of Mosby's raids, he surely helped Confederate morale by repeatedly showing how a smaller force could defeat a large one. It was, in microcosm, the problem the whole South faced—defeating the larger, stronger opponent. The attacks on a communications system were never decisive, because communications could be restored or rerouted. Mosby may have made both North and South more cognizant of the importance of communications in modern warfare. Ultimately, however, the guerrillas were too few in number to make a substantial difference. But Mosby's lesson was not lost on later generations, who learned to go after communications systems first, as U.S. forces did in the Gulf War. Such tactics put communications at the center, whereas for the Confederates, it was simply peripheral.

All the activity involving communications for immediate military purposes had several consequences for Mosby and his legacy. First, it gave him experience in dealing with the press and developing an image, something he did not forget in his postwar years as he took his causes to the public. Second, by the end of the Civil War, there was a historical record to serve as the foundation for the Mosby Myth, a record that supposedly was more or less unbiased, or at least balanced one bias against another. The 1860s newspaper Mosby is basically the same one who appears in the next century in film, novels, and television.

WHEN MOSBY REALLY DIED

By the time of Mosby's actual death in 1916, the building of his national myth was under way. The subsequent efforts of novelists and television scriptwriters further exaggerated his exploits. Newspaper obituaries depicted the Mosby that began with his war adventures, an image that he confirmed in his *Memoirs*. The obituaries emphasized Mosby's daring and bravery, with almost as much attention to his efforts at reconciliation. He "dared death over fifty years" and was given credit for neutralizing as many as 15,000 Federal troops in the Shenandoah Valley. His capture of Stoughton was reportedly accomplished while Mosby and his Rangers were surrounded by 17,000 Federal troops. If that were not enough, another obituary stated that he was "famous as a cavalry leader the world over," which was probably true in light of the fact that he was at one point offered a field command of a Chinese army. The *New York Tribune*, declaring Mosby the "last of the partisans," elevated the romance of his wartime accomplishments, describing Mosby as "a gallant knight, quick to sacrifice himself without stint where he deemed that loyalty called for self-sacrifice." He was nothing less than Arthurian. The obituary emphasized the nobility of the Ranger who "always insisted that plunder was not the object of his raids and [that] he himself never accepted plunder." That was, at least in part, a questionable declaration. Mosby did not share in the plunder, but that loot was the very point of many of his raids—as provisions for his Rangers, as "payment" for the men, and for the general cause of the South.[14]

According to the *New Orleans Times-Picayune*, Mosby was a "Bogey Man," with "daredevil bravery" and "native shrewdness." And so the Gray Ghost materialized in Mosby's obituaries. It was the resurrection of a bogey man, not just a clever cavalry officer. From gallant knighthood to armed apparition, he had become a "military genius" whose mere "300 men kept occupied 30,000 of the Federal forces." Mosby had already begun to sound like a dime-novel hero in his *New York Times* obituary: "Entire brigades were sent after him and a big price was placed on his head, but he was always able to give his pursuers the slip, and when he slipped, as a rule, he carried something with him, but Mosby was never caught and the reward was never won."[15]

A few Southern newspapers grasped the greater potential and context of the Mosby Myth. The *Nashville Banner* understood the paradox of the mythical "American man" who was at once both common and uncommon, in the tradition of such figures as Andrew Jackson and Abraham Lincoln—individuals of ordinary background—who rose to the highest position in the land and who took the idea of democracy a step further in their own times. The *Banner* stated that Mosby was "in a class all to himself," one "who attained . . . nation-wide fame and whose deeds will live in history," yet "his title was never more than that of colonel." There was an apparent apology for Mosby, who, the paper pointed out,

"was not a guerrilla, but he fought after the manner of the guerrillas and was greatest of all the partisan rangers." Mosby was
compared to the Swamp Fox, Francis Marion of the Revolutionary War, and yet he put "to shame a later aggregation of supposed soldiers who assumed the name [of 'rough riders']." But
lest the accomplishments of an anti-Union hero be too celebrated,
the newspaper concluded with praise for Mosby's role in reconciliation, who in his old age "had a place in the hearts of his former
friends and foes alike." The *Richmond Virginian* pointed out the
legacy and heritage of Mosby: "With the bitterness of the war all
gone, there remains to Americans, North and South, a precious
heritage of valor, of self-sacrifice, of sturdy, unflagging never-
give-up spirit, a heritage which, in future days of possible stress,
will prove an inspiration unto us." And so perhaps this is where
the ultimate paradox of his myth resided. He could be at once a
rebel and a reconciler.[16]

NOTES

1. *Mosby's War Reminiscences*, 117. See Louis M. Starr, *Bohemian Brigade: Civil War Newsmen in Action* (New York: Alfred A. Knopf, 1954);
and James M. Perry, *A Bohemian Brigade: The Civil War Correspondents*
(New York: John Wiley & Sons, 2000).

2. Ramage, *Gray Ghost*, 4.

3. Brayton Harris, *Blue and Gray in Black and White: Newspapers in
the Civil War* (Dulles, VA: Batsford Brassey, 1999), 6–8.

4. Park, "Picturing the War," 287–321.

5. *New York Herald*, December 28, 29, 30, 31, 1864; *New York Times*,
January 1, 1865.

6. *Richmond Dispatch*, August 27, 1863.

7. *New York Times*, April 14, 1865.

8. *New York Herald*, May 1, 4, 1865.

9. *New York Times*, November 10, 12, 1864, and August 19, 25, 31,
1864.

10. *New York Herald*, December 30, 1864.

11. *Richmond Dispatch*, June 3, 1863, August 11, 1863, and the *New
York Times*, January 11, 1864, all reported the Mosby attacking force at
about 400 men, which was probably an exaggeration. The *Charleston
Mercury* reported on September 3, 1863, that the number of men was
800; *New York Times*, August 21, 1864.

12. *New York Herald*, October 15, 1864; *New York Times*, April 23, 1865.

13. *New York Herald*, November 2, 1863, January 30, 1864, and September 10, 1864.

14. *Louisville Courier-Journal*, May 31, 1916; *Atlanta Constitution*, May 31, 1916; *Washington Post*, May 31, 1916; *New York Tribune*, May 31, 1916.

15. *New Orleans Times-Picayune*, May 31, 1916; *New York Tribune*, May 31, 1916; *New York Times*, May 31, 1916.

16. *Nashville Banner*, May 31, 1916; *Richmond Virginian*, May 31, 1916.

CHAPTER SIX

MOSBY IN POPULAR
LITERATURE AND BIOGRAPHY

It isn't necessary that any history should be written;
let the story tellers invent it all.
—John S. Mosby, to a newspaper reporter (1904)

MYTHS FLOWER IN the garden of popular culture, first sprouting
in the form of tall tales, journalistic accounts, sketches, letters,
memoirs, and speeches, and then bearing fruit in plays, reenactments, memorials, novels, poetry, biographies, and the visual arts,
including comic books, juvenilia, film, and television. Mosby is
well represented in popular culture. The historian Robert A.
Lively examined more than five hundred Civil War novels published between the time of the war and the 1957 publication of
his classic study, *Fiction Fights the Civil War*. He concludes that
fictional history, in general, is "reasonably good history, a substantial stimulus to the scholar's search for truth." For the most
part, mass-market Civil War novels are well constructed and re-
sponsive to popular emotional needs for unambiguous heroes and
for characters who confront real human problems in the wake of
historical events. He bemoans, however, a lack of scholarly interest in popular literature:

> Scholars are unwise when they ignore the general reader's at-
> tention to fictional history. The statistics of Civil War novel pro-
> duction reveal a widespread fascination with the era which
> wants encouragement rather than frustration, a partial intimacy
> with national folklore which invites exploitation rather than
> sterilization through the use of the over-disciplined fact. Per-
> ception of kinship with the past waits in a large audience for
> the historian's nurturing, and his chores will be lighter if he

appreciates the quality of the social myths he documents. Even when these myths are impassioned distortions of the public memory, they may serve the scholar's ends.[1]

Although the increased interest in popular culture studies in universities after the publication of Lively's book has, to a degree, redressed this situation, it was not until 1986 that a comprehensive annotated bibliography of Civil War fiction, Albert J. Menendez's *Civil War Novels: An Annotated Bibliography*, became available. Alice Fahs's *The Imagined Civil War: Popular Literature of the North and South, 1861–1865*, appeared only in 2001. Jim Cullen points out in his important book *The Civil War in Popular Culture* that popular works, such as Margaret Mitchell's *Gone With the Wind* and Ken Burns's public television series *The Civil War*, undoubtedly do more to shape people's acquaintance with the past than shelves of scholarly volumes intended to serve readers who have both the time and the ability to profit from a serious study of historical events. Cullen, too, calls our attention to the fact that the way history is presented addresses social myths in different periods.[2]

Mosby recognized that he had no patent on his own past. He sometimes dismissed the stories that had grown up about him as harmless fabrications, but he also spent most of his postwar life insisting on the accuracy of his version of events he thought important. He knew another story existed that was coeval with his own truth. If we are ever to understand Mosby, we must acknowledge the need multiple generations have had to invent him. We always have to approach him with the same stealth and cunning he employed to penetrate the conventional forces arrayed against him. He is a peculiar kind of figure for literary interpretation because, as he has told us, his own existence during the war was questioned. It served his own interests to be thought of as ubiquitous, incorporeal, and evasive. And, because he could not be captured by conventional strategies, it served the interests of his opponents and the recording press to either deny his presence or exaggerate his power. In this sense, the postwar popular literature about Mosby became fictions of a fiction. The literature, however, also reinforces the importance of stories as a way of understanding the past.

"BLOODY WILD–BOAR"

Mosby's first appearance as a popular literary figure probably occurred during the spring of 1864 when a play, *The Guerilla, or Mosby in 500 Sutler Wagons*, was staged in Alexandria. Mosby's friend Frank Stringfellow claimed he snuck into the city to see a packed performance and returned to Fauquier County with published copies of the melodrama for Mosby. Stringfellow said he enjoyed the performance, but his qualifications as a theater critic are undocumented. Soon, a dime novel, *Jack Mosby, the Guerilla*, depicted Mosby as a black-bearded sadist who tortures prisoners, persuades his sweetheart to seduce Union soldiers and lure them into a trap, and tries to burn New York City by igniting a phosphorous-soaked bed at the Astor House. On the night of November 25–26, 1864, a group of Confederate saboteurs actually did attempt to burn the city of New York, although Mosby was not implicated in the plot. One of the arsonists, Robert Cobb Kennedy, was captured, tried, convicted, and executed. Ironically, his defense attorney was none other than Edwin H. Stoughton, the general Mosby had captured earlier in the war. The primary audience for these literary fictions was probably the soldiers themselves. Plays were written and staged soon after battles. Printers discovered that cheap books could also be produced and distributed quickly. Erastus Beadle, a dime novel publisher, claimed to have sold more than four million copies in army camps.[3]

It was partly to refute such blather that Virginia novelist John Esten Cooke included Mosby in *Surry of Eagle's-Nest*, a novel based on his own war experiences as one of Stuart's staff officers, and *Wearing of the Gray*, a memoir, with sketches and portraits of Confederate heroes. Both volumes were highly popular after the war and well into the next century, and probably did much to sustain Mosby's wartime reputation in both the South and the North by including him among the primary figures of interest. Cooke tried to present his Confederates in a manner acceptable to Northern readers, who provided a more lucrative literary market, and some of his sketches first appeared in the *New York World* and the *Southern Illustrated News*. As a fiction writer, according to Edmund Wilson, Cooke wrote absurdly nostalgic, sentimental melodramas of little literary merit, although his nonfiction was more realistic.

The Mosby of *Surry of Eagle's-Nest* is a noble, jovial, and compassionate gentleman who attributes his "bloody wild-boar" image in the Northern press to Union generals who make him out to be a bandit to excuse their ineptitude in fighting him as a legitimate soldier. In *Wearing of the Gray*, Cooke makes explicit reference to the Mosby of the dime novels, defends the legitimacy of his partisan command, and dismisses "any imputations upon the character of this officer, or upon the nature of the warfare which he carried on, as absurd." Mosby later told a reporter that Cooke's stories were all myths. "It isn't necessary that any history should be written; let the story tellers invent it all," he said.[4]

MAGNOLIAS AND "OLE MARSTER"

Clarke Venable's adventure novel *Mosby's Night Hawk* (1931) involves a young Virginian who serves with Mosby and becomes a "night hawk," a scout known for his nocturnal rides. Although the novel contains some truly appalling literary racism, complete with happy, superstitious, loyal, groveling slaves who speak in comic dialect, *Mosby's Night Hawk* stays closer to the historical record than most of the other novels in which Mosby appears as a character. Mosby is described as "a myth with substance" and "a force without substance," suggesting the complexity of elusive tactics. Edna Hoffman Evans's *Sunstar and Pepper*, a horse-and-boy historical novel, was published in 1947. While standing in front of his Magnolia Hill plantation in Virginia one day in 1862, sixteen-year-old Potter "Pepper" Pepperill spots Jeb Stuart, and joins the cavalry as a scout and courier. The action roughly spans the period between June 1862 and May 1863. Pepper and Mosby, who is portrayed as a kind of wise and gentle elder brother to him, scout behind enemy lines. As in most Civil War juvenilia, the emphasis is on reconciliation, the growing awareness of both sides that peace is better than war and sectional differences less important than building a stronger country. Mosby is the noble citizen-soldier, a virtuous hero young readers can embrace as a role model. "He's a soldier and gentleman, and I believe he really hates this war," Pepper thinks. The novel panders to all the stereotypical images of the plantation culture, including slaves who love the South and "ole Marster."[5]

Mosby also appears as a character in two novels published in 1948, Jere Hungerford Wheelwright's *Gentlemen, Hush!* and Garald Lagard's swashbuckling *Scarlet Cockerel*, a kind of *Captain Blood* meets *Gone With the Wind*. Wheelwright's story turns on the adventures of three teenaged Confederates toward the end of the war and during the early Reconstruction era. Mosby appears as a crafty defense attorney who gains an acquittal for one of the boys who is wrongly accused of murder. This enlarges the Mosby Myth by emphasizing Mosby's postwar legal career as well as his military fame. *Scarlet Cockerel* is part maritime adventure, part horse opera, but a skillfully told tale. Lane Byrn is a young medical student returning to his Virginia plantation, at his father's behest, just as the war begins. He becomes embroiled in a gunrunning plot on the schooner *Whisper* and is befriended by its master, Captain Selmo. Also aboard the *Whisper* is the beautiful daughter of a Federal army officer. A romance ensues, Selmo and Byrn eventually join Mosby's Partisans, and Byrn becomes the rooster-feathered Scarlet Cockerel.

In the *Scarlet Cockerel*, Mosby is a laconic, ruthless romantic, magnificently adorned in his scarlet-lined cavalry cape and ostrich-plumed slouch hat, but most notable are the "color and deep chill of his eyes. They were blue, hard as midwinter ice and as cold." His importance to the Confederate cause is magnified, so much so that Byrn says the Yankees would rather capture Mosby than Davis. Actual historical events such as the Berryhill Raid and the capture of Stoughton are accurately recounted, but Lagard acknowledges that he took liberties with the chronology in structuring his narrative. Mosby's antipathy toward Custer is emphasized, and the battle sequences are vivid and convincingly sanguinary. For historical accuracy, Mosby's men make a little too much use of cutlery, including a battle-ax Mosby occasionally wields in combat, although there is ample pistolry as well. Selmo dies in a final bloodbath just before the Partisans disband at the end of the war, and the Scarlet Cockerel is reunited with his lover as he tries to save the life of the Union officer who was his rival for her affections. *Scarlet Cockerel* is a good action yarn for a post-Second World War audience seeking a Lost Cause adventure story with a whiff of seabreeze-and-magnolias and a celebration of individual heroism. The formula also fits the theme of most Civil War romantic fiction, in which, as Wilson explains, two lovers are divided by their loyalties to different flags.[6]

RAY HOGAN

No novelist has done more to gild the Mosby Myth than Ray Hogan, who was born in 1908 in Willow Springs, Missouri, where his father was the local marshal. In 1914 his father bought a hotel in Albuquerque, New Mexico, and Hogan picked up the plots for many of his later novels by listening to stories told by travelers. Hogan was in his fifth decade before he published his first novel. By writing on average more than two thousand words per day, he eventually produced more than a hundred Western novels and nonfiction books, hundreds of magazine articles, and film and television scripts.[7]

Hogan had already written a dozen Westerns when he began a series of books about Mosby in 1960, probably to draw on the popularity of *The Gray Ghost* television series. Mosby was an ideal subject for a Western writer because the raider's irregular cavalry tactics, rustling, retributive hanging, horse stealing, trainwrecking, sharpshooting, robbery, and kidnapping could be props for stories set in Virginia as readily as in Texas. Indians could be converted to Yankees, and bushwhackers, spies, incompetent generals, deserters, and crooked sutlers could be substituted for black-hatted gunmen. Mosby had the advantage of acting like a Western bandit while being portrayed as a courageous fighter for Southern independence. Because he was dealing with a historical figure, Hogan established some guidelines for his Mosby books as a preface to his first Mosby novel, *The Ghost Raider*:

> The incredible exploits of John Singleton Mosby, Major, Forty-third Battalion, CSA, were so numerous that many have not been recorded in history books covering the great and terrible struggle of the Civil War. The man's remarkable penchant for the daring and the impossible has perverted truth to legend and, conversely, legend to truth, the result of which has birthed an heroic character replete with all the virtues of the idealistic American fighting for what he believes right.

> This work is fiction. Some of the names, places and events
> mentioned herein will be recognized as actual. It is merely so
> for the sake of clarification and continuity in a story that could
> have happened to the fabulous Ranger.

So here we have in place all the architecture of mythmaking. As a historical figure, Mosby cannot be contained by actual events, because his "incredible exploits" are too numerous to have been recorded. His ability to do the impossible has so "perverted truth" that he has become more legend than man, and, what is more, he has become a heroic embodiment of American chivalric virtues, an idealist who fights for his beliefs. As a storyteller, Hogan proposes to use actual events merely for narrative convenience, and what he invents is what *could have happened* to Mosby. He thus captures the *essential* Mosby by way of *myth*, not history.

The Ghost Raider begins with a meeting between Lee, Stuart, and Mosby shortly before Gettysburg. Lee orders Mosby to undertake a secret mission to determine the size and disposition of Hooker's forces. Intelligence has reported that Hooker is recruiting teamsters to deliver two hundred forage wagons to his army. Equally vital is Mosby's rescue of a captured Confederate officer, Maj. Curtis Sanford, who has mapped the area that Lt. Gen. Richard Ewell must penetrate during the first wave of the invasion. But Mosby blames Sanford for the death of his close friend, Tom Ballenger, and of his friend's entire company. Lee reminds Mosby that a court of inquiry has exonerated Sanford. Mosby obeys reluctantly and declines Stuart's offer of troops for the mission, promising that he can complete his assignment with just nineteen men. He proposes to slip into Hooker's camp and rescue Sanford with two men and to send the rest of his command to disrupt the railroad Hooker is using to supply his troops from depots in Washington. For all he must accomplish, he has just two days.

Hogan's plot develops with suitable melodramatic charm. Mosby plucks the sullen Sanford from the stockade, eludes capture, destroys wagons, and blows up a troop train. After commandeering an ambulance and escaping pursuing troops in a running gun battle, Mosby delivers Sanford to Lee and warns the commander about the size of Hooker's force. Sanford gives

Lee false information and presumably seals the fate of Lee's army. Historical inaccuracies confuse the story. Mosby's and Stuart's actual roles in the Gettysburg campaign are ignored. And Stuart, eyes alight and gazing north, has the last word in the novel by giving Mosby the location of the coming battle. That location, of course, was fortuitous and it was not actually known in advance of the campaign. Another gaffe occurs when Mosby recalls that Lee once threatened to shoot him if he ever again referred to a bugle as a horn. Hogan has confused his Lees—it was Fitzhugh Lee who had threatened him on that ground—and misquotes his source. Fitz Lee had threatened to have him arrested, not shot. Hogan has Mosby learning his military tactics from a sergeant named Grumble Jones, who was actually Mosby's commanding officer in the Washington Mounted Rifles, and later a general.[8]

The next novel, *Raider's Revenge*, begins during the Loudoun Heights Raid. The premise is that the raid fails because a spy has alerted Major Cole to the coming attack, and Mosby walks into a trap. Mosby fears the spy will compromise Stuart's spring offensive, and so he sends a sergeant into Harpers Ferry to stop him before he can reveal the plans. The sergeant eventually finds the traitor, a captain in Mosby's battalion, and kills him. The novel unravels with improbable escapes, a goofy love story, weak characters, and contrived dialogue.[9]

In his third Mosby novel, *Rebel Raid*, Hogan returns to the beginning of the war, when the real Mosby was on picket duty. He promotes Mosby to first lieutenant and gives him his Partisan command in September 1861. His first big mission occurs when Jefferson Davis orders him to slip into Washington and rescue Mary Dulane, a spy who has been captured by the chief of the Federal Secret Service. Mosby manages to join the Secret Service, posing, incredibly, as a Union scout named John Singleton— probably not the best cover he could have selected. His first assignment is to protect Lincoln, and he prevents an assassin from shooting him. Mosby realizes the Confederacy might be better served if Lincoln were dead, but he balks at outright murder. He foils a counterplot to murder Davis and rescues Mary Dulane, managing to have saved two presidents within a few days. Hogan exploits Mosby's mythic prowess as a phantom who might appear within Union lines at any time. *Rebel Raid* takes Mosby far

beyond plausible historical fiction. A number of ahistorical howl-
ers slip into the novel. For example, Maj. Gen. William S.
Rosecrans becomes "Rosencrantz," perhaps awaiting relief from
Guildenstern or Hamlet on the assumption that a little
Shakespeare never hurt anyone, even in a Western.[10]

Hogan again slips his historical moorings in the next novel
in the series, *Rebel in Yankee Blue*. He tries to justify his speculative approach to Civil War history in another wily author's note
at the beginning of the novel: "There is a basis for this story but
since there is no written proof, it must be considered fiction,
couched in fact." Fiction, indeed, because the novel begins with
Mosby conferring with Lee on Seminary Ridge on the third day
of the Battle of Gettysburg. Mosby had just returned from a ride
around Meade's army on the morning of July 3 before the ill-
fated Pickett's charge. The real Mosby was returning to Virginia
at the time with cattle and horses he had taken during a raid at
Mercersburg, Pennsylvania. If there is no written proof, it is because it never happened, nor does it really matter, because Hogan
is writing myth history and not factual history.

Mosby's mission is to get into Meade's camp and learn what
his plans are so Lee can retreat safely into Virginia. Difficult problems do not bother Mosby, apparently because, as he tells Stuart,
he learned in law school that there is always an answer to a knotty
problem. The real Mosby, however, was expelled from the university and studied law in a jail cell. Hogan again exaggerates
Mosby's importance, claiming that he was very likely at that time
the most feared soldier in the war. Once inside the Union camp,
Mosby and four Rangers learn Vicksburg has fallen and must get
this news to Lee so he can escape before Grant's army arrives.
Grant, of course, would have required air transport to arrive in
time to menace the Army of Northern Virginia. Mosby sneaks
into a root cellar under Meade's headquarters and overhears the
commanding general's plans to block Lee's move through the
mountain passes. Mosby delays him long enough for Lee to cross
the Potomac. *Rebel in Yankee Blue* enhances the myth that Mosby
might have been anywhere at all critical moments.[11]

Hell to Hallelujah, on the other hand, is a fine action yarn that
draws on Hogan's mastery of the Western genre. After the Battle
of the Wilderness, Lee sends Mosby to blow up a bridge to cut

Grant's army off from its supplies. Mosby takes a munitions expert and another man through enemy territory, blows the bridge, and returns. Along the way he wipes out a group of marauders who are preying on civilians and encounters a Union officer who was a friend before the war. All the moral issues of the war are rolled out in this adventure tale. Mosby defends himself against charges that he is as bad as the outlaws he kills. He justifies his actions by showing mercy to captives and aiding Union women, while the central dilemma of partisan warfare is intelligently vetted. He chides a Union officer for believing what is published in Northern newspapers: "You might look deeper for the facts, Colonel. I am a soldier fighting for what I believe is right." But what is right to Mosby is very wrong from the Union point of view, and Mosby is told he will hang if captured. Hogan's action scenes are polished, however, and *Hell to Hallelujah* occasionally becomes the six-shooter equivalent of *For Whom the Bell Tolls*, Hemingway's superb novel of the Spanish Civil War.

Night Raider presents Mosby as a more complex figure. The story begins during the winter of 1863 with Mosby planning a raid on Hooker's supply wagons at Occaquan Creek. Stuart is eager to find out if the supplies are coming from a forward depot at Fairfax, because such a base could be a clue to Hooker's movements. But first Mosby has to determine whether Mason Key, a young Pennsylvanian in his command, is a spy. And he is puzzled by the lack of intelligence from Micah Reynolds, Stuart's agent in Fairfax. After seizing a wagon train and then holding off two hundred Federal cavalrymen through a series of tricky maneuvers, Mosby and a few men slip into town to meet Reynolds, whom he finds perplexingly reticent and nervous. He turns out to be an impostor—the real Micah Reynolds is in a Federal jail. Mosby captures Stoughton after he escapes a trap set by the impostor and leaves the depot rigged with explosives. Key pursues an escaping officer, and Mosby, assuming Key is about to betray the Rangers, pursues him. He learns Key is loyal and also finds and frees the real Reynolds. Then Mosby becomes separated from the Rangers and has to effect an escape from Union cavalry by hiding in a flooded ditch, sprinting across a valley, mounting a horse, and disappearing into a thicket with pursuers close on his heels. After rescuing his command from another Yankee column,

Mosby reaches Stuart, who tells Mosby his raid could affect the outcome of the war—which, of course, it did not.

Hogan's fanciful recounting of the events surrounding Mosby's capture of Stoughton is no more historical than one of his Western melodramas, as he turns Mosby into a Confederate cowboy transposed to the Virginia countryside. The artist who drew the cover art for the British edition of the novel portrays Mosby as a Jack Palance-style gunfighter with a ten-gallon hat. In the novel, Grant issues his standing order for the hanging of captured Rangers more than a year too early—and long before he was even in command of the army—and the author also plays fast and loose with Custer and the Front Royal hangings. Hogan does allow Mosby, in quiet moments, to reflect on the meaning of the war and his own service in the Southern cause. And Hogan does occasionally explicate the details of the partisan enterprise and portray the mythical Mosby as an intelligent, humane, and often-conflicted citizen soldier.[12]

Hogan's *Rebel Ghost* begins on May 12, 1864, with Mosby dodging cannonballs on a low ridge near Spotsylvania Court House. Still mourning Jeb Stuart, who had been mortally wounded at Yellow Tavern, Mosby and his Rangers have rejoined Lee after a scouting mission and have been thrown into the battle. Lee sends Mosby to find Breckinridge in the Shenandoah Valley and direct him to move his brigades to block Grant's drive on Richmond. Mosby and a Ranger scout, Hob Lovan, set out to slip through the Union lines. Again, a spy figures in the story. Jasper Denning, a spy on Lee's staff, poses as a sutler to obtain information from Union lines, but he is actually a Federal secret agent and captures Mosby and Lovan soon after they leave Lee's camp. The Rangers escape, and eventually reach Breckinridge. Along the way, Mosby and Lovan destroy an entire town by blowing up a warehouse full of gunpowder and capturing a battery of cannon. They also manage to free a couple of thousand Confederates from a Yankee prison.

Rebel Ghost is among the least plausible of Hogan's Mosby novels. As usual, Hogan invents historical events and tampers with the chronology. Stuart, for example, died in Richmond on the very day that Mosby supposedly was in the front lines at Spotsylvania, so if he was in mourning for his commander, he would have had to have been telepathic. During the Spotsylvania campaign, Mosby was raiding in the mountains, and it is improbable that Lee would have summoned the redoubtable Rangers for infantry duty. The Mosby of *Rebel Ghost* is part commando, part John Wayne, garroting and knifing sentries, fording rivers and creeks, leaping onto galloping horses from high bluffs, firing his pistols from horseback at pursuing cavalry, and rescuing hapless women and children from outlaws. Hogan also reinforces another aspect of the Mosby Myth: Mosby fights because he believes that the war will serve some beneficial purpose, regardless of its outcome. This simplistic Darwinian rationalization subtly undergirds the thematic structure of many of Hogan's Western novels. The frontier struggles strengthen and purify people and are necessary to build a strong nation.

Book jacket art and promotional teasers written by publishers are an often overlooked key to the framing of historical myths. The publisher of a paperback edition of *Rebel Ghost* took particular liberties. Mosby is depicted on horseback in a white uniform, brandishing a saber as he rides through a spectral mist. Above the image is a brief text: "Major John Mosby was a savior to the South—and a menace to the North." The back cover copy reads:

> General Grant has just declared that every Confederate soldier be hung or shot without a trial. Only a few will be able to survive the massacre, the rest will perish along with the South's independence.
>
> Major John Mosby . . . is the most cunning and ruthless soldier around. Considered a savage by the Union troops, he succeeded in eluding the enemy from the start. Now Mosby is taken prisoner during a sneak attack. Forced to face the most perilous battle of his life, Mosby must free himself from his captors and return to the safety of his own troops.

Other than the fact that the promotional copy has little to do with the plot and implicates Grant in a plan to exterminate the entire Confederate army, it seems to have cast Mosby simultaneously as a "savior" and a bloodthirsty war criminal primarily interested in saving his own neck.[13]

With the end of the Civil War Centennial, and the syndicated reruns of *The Gray Ghost* gradually disappearing from television screens, Hogan was writing more Western novels, but his fans could still enjoy *Mosby's Last Raid*, the final one in his original Mosby series. The book opens in the late summer of 1864 shortly after the Berryville Raid. Mosby, still recovering from a wound, is preparing to destroy a bridge over the Shenandoah River to sever Sheridan's supply lines. Mosby fears a spy has been alerting Sheridan's forces to his movements. He realizes that his command is no longer composed of hand-picked partisans and that some Rangers are little more than cutthroat mercenaries who would turn him in for the price on his head. Mosby succeeds in blowing up the bridge but narrowly escapes a Yankee trap. He receives orders from General Lee to contact Dr. Evan Davis, a Confederate agent, in Rectortown, which is within Union lines. Mosby and a scout, Al Guff, find Davis, who tells Mosby that Sheridan is planning to rebuild the Manassas Gap Railroad in order to move supplies to Charlottesville. With a well-supplied force in Charlottesville, Grant would then be able to move against Lee from three directions and force him back on Richmond.

Concealing his plans to prevent the spy from notifying Sheridan, Mosby scatters the workmen who are repairing the railroad, destroys tracks and trains, and spreads panic and confusion among Sheridan's troops. He rescues two of his men who have been betrayed by the spy, Lige Camber, and captured by Union soldiers. Mosby and his men shoot their way to freedom and Camber is trampled to death by horses. Faced with new orders from Lee that would put him in administrative charge of all Confederate forces remaining in Northern Virginia and away from his command, Mosby plans one final raid. He learns that a train carrying an army payroll has left Baltimore and will reach Harpers Ferry at midnight. The Rangers derail the train, escape with the payroll, and return to "Mosby's Confederacy." The story is based, loosely, on the Greenback Raid. *Mosby's Last Raid* is a rather dark novel, with Mosby in a philosophical, almost fatalistic, mood in comparison to the sometimes swaggering character of the previous books. Mosby's internal security problems were real enough, but Hogan's spy hunt and Wild West daredevilry is a fanciful detour in an otherwise well-plotted adventure.[14]

Mosby's actual achievements would seem to be more than enough grist for the novelist's mill without the necessity for turning him into an almost supernatural paladin, but such is the artifice of the Mosby Myth. Hogan's novels are full of boisterous adventure and just enough history to satisfy the Civil War dilettante. The novels introduced Mosby to a wider audience and gave him the cachet of an action hero. Hogan was still writing well into his nineties and ought to be regarded as a national treasure. Battered copies of Hogan paperbacks are still piled high on the shelves of secondhand bookstores and provide a lot of entertainment for pocket change.

THE SCARLET RAIDER

Given Mosby's reputation for battlefield heroics and his horse-opera adventures in prime-time television, it is surprising he has not appeared in more books for young readers. An exception is an interesting novel by Joseph B. Icenhower that appeared in 1961, just in time for the Civil War Centennial and shortly after the cancellation of *The Gray Ghost* on television. Icenhower, a highly decorated retired Navy rear admiral and former World War II submarine commander, had written several sea stories and nonfiction books about submarine warfare before he took on the Civil War and John Mosby. *The Scarlet Raider* was one of the Chilton Company's literary yarns for school libraries and summer camp booklists.

The story begins with fifteen-year-old Tim Morgan smuggling medical supplies through Yankee lines near Fairfax, Virginia, shortly before Gettysburg. Tim's father is a wounded veteran. Now he and Tim provide Mosby with needed supplies and vital information. Tim dreams that Mosby himself will come to collect the supplies, and Tim's father knows that every Virginia youngster reveres the gallant raider. They hear the sound of horses outside their cabin, a knock on the door, and there stands the raider himself in his scarlet-lined cape and gray slouch hat with the famous ostrich plume and wearing the two studded Colt pistols in their holsters.

Tim tells Mosby he has been threatened by a Union corporal, Bull Ruffing, who wants him to smuggle contraband for profit. Mosby warns him to be careful and gives him some stolen Yan-

kee silver to swap for more supplies. He also gives Tim an undated appointment as a trooper in his command to protect the
boy in the event he is captured as a spy. Tim then has a confrontation with Ruffing and is saved by a kindly Irish sergeant, pre-
dictably named Murphy, from New York, who discovers the
contraband and warns Tim never to return to Fairfax. Tim then
joins Mosby's Rangers, gets a magnificent horse named Midnight
(his previous horse had, of course, been named Nellie), special
training from Sgt. Hank Slaughter, and is ready for action. He
and Slaughter sneak across the Potomac to scout Union defenses
near Seneca Falls, where Stuart is expected to move into Maryland on his raid during the Gettysburg campaign. Although Sergeant Slaughter is injured, Tim gets the information back to
Mosby, who takes out the batteries defending the crossing after a
sharp engagement. Tim, a hero, is mentioned in dispatches to Lee,
and he becomes perhaps the youngest corporal in the Confederate Army.

After another battle, Tim befriends the kindly Irish sergeant
who has been wounded and taken prisoner. Assigned to help
bring the wounded Union and Confederate soldiers to Rebel lines,
Tim's unit is captured by Ruffing, by now a deserter, and a gang
of bushwhackers. Assisted by the daughter of a Union sympathizer, Tim is able to escape and distribute weapons to the Rangers and Murphy. The bushwhackers are killed, and Ruffing is
wounded. Mosby arrives, allows Murphy to return Ruffing to his
unit for trial, and, with a nod and a wink, orders Tim to thank the
young woman who helped him. They are in love, of course, and
know the war will not last forever.

The main theme of this Centennial-year novel is honor among
enemies. A model of gallant compassion, Mosby never gives way
to hatred. In the end, it is the ability of both sides to work together that wins the day. Ruffing and his venal bushwhackers
are portrayed in sharp contrast to the elegant Partisans, who are
wrongly branded as bushwhackers by their opponents. The ge-
nial and wise Irish sergeant, a stereotype in many Civil War novels, is rewarded for his earlier kindness to Tim, who grows from
boy to man within a matter of months. The novel follows the familiar character-building formula.[15]

GRAY VICTORY

Robert Skimin's *Gray Victory*, published in 1988, is the most interesting and original novel to feature Mosby. Skimin is a retired Army officer, aviator, and paratrooper who was the first aviator attached to the Green Berets. *Gray Victory* is in the alternative history genre made popular by such writers as Harry Turtledove and William Sanders. Alternative history is a cross between historical fiction and science fiction. Sanders's *The Wild Blue and the Gray*, for example, takes place in an alternate world. In 1916 the Confederacy is allied with the Indian Nations of Oklahoma, and a Cherokee becomes a pilot in the Confederate Air Force fighting against the Germans. In Turtledove's *Guns of the South: A Novel of the Civil War*, South African white supremacists from the twenty-first century use a time-travel machine to supply the Confederacy with AK-47 rifles to change the outcome of the war. *Gray Victory* is set in 1866. The Confederacy has achieved its independence because Johnston remains in command at Atlanta and keeps Sherman out of the city until the 1864 elections. (The historical Davis had relieved Johnston of command on July 17, 1864.) This leads to Lincoln's election defeat by McClellan, who immediately declares a cease-fire.[16]

Mosby is appointed chief of military intelligence in the regular Confederate States Army. His main duty is to monitor a black liberation movement called Abraham. Unknown to Mosby, however, Abraham is being infiltrated by a group of radical Northern abolitionists in a paramilitary operation called Amistad headed by Thomas Wentworth Higginson, who had commanded a regiment of black soldiers in the war. Higginson recruits Salmon Brown, an embittered son of John Brown, to head Amistad, which, Higginson hopes, will assassinate Confederate leaders, provoke an insurrection, and prompt the Federal army to restore the Union. Joining Brown is a New Orleans octoroon known only as Verita, a Sorbonne-educated Marxist and abolitionist. McClellan gets wind of the plot and appoints Gen. John Rawlins, Grant's wartime adjutant, as his special agent to coordinate intelligence operations with Mosby and prevent the resumption of war.

Meanwhile, Edward A. Pollard, the editor of the anti-Davis *Richmond Examiner*, accuses Davis of covering up Stuart's alleged responsibility for the Confederate defeat at Gettysburg three years earlier. Davis, who will soon face Joseph Johnston in a presidential election with Lee as Davis's running mate (evidently, the Confederate Constitution has been amended to permit Davis to run for a second term), convenes a rigged court of inquiry to let Stuart take the blame for Gettysburg. Gen. Braxton Bragg is appointed to head the court. Stuart asks Mosby to be his counsel at the hearing; and although Mosby is reluctant, he realizes he has a stake in the trial's outcome.

Mosby knows the origins of Stuart's ride through the Army of the Potomac and the cavalryman's subsequent tardiness at Gettysburg. In fact, he thinks to himself, "*John Singleton Mosby had instigated the whole damn thing.*" The real Mosby had indeed suggested Stuart's route through the Federal lines before the Battle of Gettysburg and had felt responsible when Stuart was accused of leaving Lee without sufficient cavalry. (Ramage, however, notes that the idea was already in the wind before Mosby conferred with Stuart on June 22, 1863.) What follows is a clever parody of high courtroom drama as various principals in the battle take the stand to vet the Gettysburg controversy. Mosby himself becomes a witness. Many who testify seem slightly deranged. A dazed Hooker sobs and denies he was fired from command. Major Von Borcke, Stuart's wartime chief of staff, sounds like a Teutonic Falstaff recalling a romp with Prince Hal and almost destroys Mosby's defense as he sweats and trembles on the witness stand. Longstreet breaks into a rhapsody about seeing the ghosts of the fallen and discredits Lee's generalship.[17]

In the final courtroom melodrama, Lee testifies, exonerates Stuart and Longstreet, and reiterates his own responsibility for the defeat at Gettysburg. Assassins strike the courtroom, Mosby knocks Davis to the floor to save him from a pistol shot, Stuart is mortally wounded as he takes a bullet intended for Lee, and Rawlins is killed protecting Davis and Mosby. Generals, cabinet ministers, journalists, and spectators are caught in the crossfire, and the assassins are slaughtered or captured. Stuart dies, cradled in Lee's embrace, as Lee says, "He took my bullet," meaning, perhaps, the "bullet" for Gettysburg as well.

Numerous aspects of the Mosby Myth are represented in Skimin's novel. Mosby is a crafty yet highly principled attorney.

He is a man of reason, a scholar, pragmatic, moral, and capable of rhetorical brilliance. He theorizes, collects information, looks for plausible explanations. His peacetime methods differ from his wartime exploits only in a matter of degree: "That was the way it was with intelligence—the dashing around behind the lines, the daring stuff, that was only a particle of it. The rest was slow and mechanical. In peacetime it was *all* slow and mechanical." He is magnanimous and virtuous, especially in contrast to the other characters in the novel.

Skimin also emphasizes Mosby's romantic appeal. In the novel, Mosby is a widower who is pursued by Spring Blakely, John Breckinridge's niece. Mosby is suitably gallant and lusty, fairly standard fare for the popular, bodice-ripping Southern novel. But Blakely also serves as Mosby's conscience on the racial issue. Here the myth shows Mosby as the Good Master who is kind to his slaves, but who gradually comes to see that even benevolent bondage is morally indefensible. In order to win Blakely's approval, he frees his slaves, telling her, "Many of us have to get our own houses in order before we'll be able to solve our country's problems. This is my personal start." But he still vows to oppose Abraham on the grounds that it is seditious. He advises one of the leaders of the movement, "If we're going to sort all of this out, we are going to need some strong Negro leaders with sense in their heads and patience in their hearts." Mosby has a final confrontation with Verita, who has been sentenced to be hanged, and tries to get her to reveal the names of other revolutionaries. He argues that her methods are wrong because racial justice can only be obtained gradually. She spurns his appeals and declares: "Mosby, I'll be alive a thousand years after you are ashes."

This exchange is interesting because Skimin depicts Mosby as a pragmatic moderate, a putative anticommunist and a defender of establishment values. Although he had been a rebel himself, he is now a proponent of social order and an opponent of revolution. This stance also means he must attempt to preserve the delicate peace between the North and South. Late in the novel Mosby tells Grant: "I know how it is with the press and the politicians. It's a popular thing to talk about charging across the Potomac and finishing the job with those damned slavers. I know that, sir, but a man like you can stop it." A U.S. congressman reciprocates by telling Mosby, "As long as we have people like you to talk with, maybe some common sense will prevail." But as soon as Mosby leaves the room, Grant and the congressman agree that the only course of action is to fight again to the finish. Thus the "gray victory" of the title: The South has won the victory, but the victory is gray and unresolved.[18]

MOSBY MISCELLANEA

Mosby has been sighted in a number of literary haunts, raiding readers' sensibilities in various guises—a historical memory, a guerrilla professor-philosopher, an assassin, and even as a cat. Mosby makes a cameo appearance in F. Scott Fitzgerald's famous novel *Tender Is the Night*. Fitzgerald's father, Edward Fitzgerald, spent his childhood near Rockville, Maryland. During the Civil War he had helped Confederate spies cross the Potomac and assisted one of Mosby's Rangers in escaping from Union-controlled territory. Fitzgerald, the great novelist and short story writer of the Jazz Age and the Lost Generation, grew up hearing tales of his father's adventures. In the novel, Dick Diver sits in a Paris restaurant and reflects on the war: "Momentarily, he sat again on his father's knee, riding with Mosby while the old loyalties and devotions fought on around him." In the novel, Mosby represents an idealized past, according to critic John Limon, a "beautiful history" of a dignified war remote from the emptiness of the Lost Generation.[19]

In 1968, Saul Bellow, who won the Nobel Prize for Literature in 1976, published *Mosby's Memoirs and Other Stories*. In the title story, a university professor writes his memoirs while living on a mountain in Mexico. Willis Mosby is a kind of fanatic who is a master of "logical tightness." He is a man afflicted with intellectual pride, for whom the act of writing his life story becomes a kind of spiritual unraveling. He was like John Mosby, "because his mode of discourse was so upsetting to the academic community." He was "invited to no television programs because he was like the Guerrilla Mosby of the Civil War. When he galloped in, all were slaughtered." J. O. Tate, in a foreword to a new edition of John Mosby's *Memoirs*, found Bellow's story "essentially unrelated to the allusion insisted upon," and takes exception to the suggestion that Mosby was something of a butcher. But this judgment seems to miss the intentionally ironic texture of the story. Willis Mosby is, perhaps unintentionally, a kind of philosophical Gray Ghost who becomes, like John Mosby, an emotional prisoner of a past that both defines and condemns him. For both the professor and the colonel, their "doom was to live to the end as Mosby."[20]

Mosby made an oblique appearance in a popular children's story by Beppie Noyes. The story originated when a gray cat took up residence during the construction of the John F. Kennedy Center for the Performing Arts in Washington. The cat sometimes appeared on stage during performances, attacked rats in the basement, and foiled pursuers. Soon the cat was being called "The Gray Ghost," and then "Mosby," which gave Noyes her story and her title: Mosby, the Kennedy Center Cat, first published in 1978. Noyes, at the age of eighty, signed copies of a new edition at the Kennedy Center in 1998. Mosby, the nimble cat and chief ratter, is a parody of his namesake. He evades and outwits the Washington establishment and becomes a popular hero because of his stealth, independence, guile, and toughness. Mosby himself was sometimes called "The Panther of the Valley," so it is not surprising he found his way into cat fiction. The heroes of children's stories often, like children, are small and must overcome challenging situations. The Mosby Myth fits the formula and has enduring appeal.[21]

The popular historical novelist Harold Coyle made reference to Mosby in Until the End (1986), the conclusion to his Civil War saga. His Mosby is as much a menace to residents of the Northern Virginia counties he ostensibly defends as he is to the Union armies. The best-selling historical novelist John Jakes featured Mosby in a sprawling Civil War epic titled On Secret Service, published in 2000. The complex plot involves Pinkerton agents, spies, and political and military figures, and it culminates in the Lincoln assassination. Jakes used Tidwell's Come Retribution and other speculative sources as grist for his story. Mosby is aware of the failed mission, supposedly authorized by Davis, to kidnap Lincoln and of a new plan to blow up Lincoln and his entire cabinet at the White House. Cooperating with the Richmond authorities,

Mosby assigns one of his men, who had previously found Mosby "unreliable; potentially violent, if not deranged," to help implement the plot by murdering an informer. When the soldier declines and asks Mosby, "What have we come down to, sir?" Mosby replies: "I try not to ask myself that question, Lieutenant." The moral ambivalence of the war and its corrupting influence on both sides is a continuing theme of the novel, which reached a much larger audience than any of the previous ones involving Mosby. Like Skimin and Hogan, Jakes finds Mosby a useful character for a cloak-and-dagger tale.[22]

FROM CATS TO COWBOYS AND BEYOND

If we look at the entire body of the Mosby literature, several points can be made. First, Mosby is a remarkably protean figure for fiction writers. He can be plotted as a cowboy hero, a spy, a villain, a metaphor, or a cat. He can be invoked on the boulevards of Paris or the mountains of Mexico. He can be an arsonist, a train robber, a kidnapper, a bomber, a torturer, and even a ratkiller. Or he can be a friend to children, a rescuer of distressed damsels, a patriot, a defense attorney, a savior, a lover, and even a prototypical Cold Warrior. Next, he shows no signs of going away. He has continued to appear in popular fiction from the time of the Civil War to the beginning of the twenty-first century. He became a more significant figure during the Civil War literary renaissance in the period leading up to the Centennial. Perhaps Mosby's particular kind of fighting failed to arouse the interest of writers until grander themes and larger figures had been exhausted, or until Mosby's legacy in the South had had time to emerge from the morass of politics.

The historian Arthur M. Schlesinger Jr. has commented that because literature is closer to myth than to history, it "may fertilize the historical mind and serve to stretch and enrich historical understanding." No fiction writer, however, has come close to plumbing the depths of Mosby as a complex historical character. He is almost always one-dimensional, and never fully human, being cut to fit the needs of a specific narrative storyline. He has eluded fiction writers as he eluded the Union army. Worse, he is usually made ridiculous, capable of comic-book heroics and near-

supernatural powers in the tall-tale tradition. He is typically
"Mosbyman" rather than Mosby the man. Like the Union officers, the modern-day fiction writers are not quick enough or clever
enough to capture the Gray Ghost. Hogan, because he wrote more
about him than any other author, has actually come closest in
some of his best passages to validating Mosby as a morally conscious, rational human being, with believable human fears and
desires. Still, he is seldom fully a character in any of the novels,
but rather a rip cord to be yanked whenever a plot needs sudden
and rapid inflation. Mosby in real life lived in a mental universe
conflated by classical mythology and the detritus of daily existence. He could summon the *Aeneid* or a subpoena, depending on
the task at hand. Only Fitzgerald and Bellow have brought Mosby
to the borders of higher literary respectability—but only as a footnote. As a popular literary myth, he has yet to achieve the legitimacy he sought throughout the war, and he remains a partisan.
He always knew that if he wanted to be a character in his own
creation myth, he was going to have to write the story himself.[23]

MOSBY AS MEMOIRIST

Mosby's tale unfolded in his *Mosby's War Reminiscences and
Stuart's Cavalry Campaigns* (1887), *Stuart's Cavalry in the Gettysburg
Campaign* (1908), and *The Memoirs of Colonel John S. Mosby* (1917).
David J. Eicher finds *Stuart's Cavalry* persuasive and supported
by at least one subsequent study, while Ramage finds it disorganized, aggressive, and tendentious. Ramage locates Mosby's best
writing in the *Reminiscences* and notes that the *Memoirs* are un-
finished and fragmented, but still useful for historians. Eicher finds
"amazing errors" in the *Memoirs*, "an occasionally suspicious
source," but judges it more valuable than the *Reminiscences*. Siepel
evaluates *Stuart's Cavalry* as "heavy going for non-scholars, and
dismissed today even by scholars—not as trivial, certainly, but
as a case of heart running far in advance of head." Tate puts
Mosby's Memoirs "on the short shelf of the best memoirs of the
most American of wars."

Jones emphasizes the practical value of the *Memoirs*, suggesting that the book gave American soldiers in the Great War a timely
look at the value of partisan tactics, and claims that the U.S. Army

later found the work to be a valuable guidebook to fighting a guerrilla war. He sees the eyewitness accounts of Confederate officers in action as an invaluable addition to the historical record. Jones notes some errors that he suggests are the result of Mosby's writing the book in old age, and out of financial exigency. He praises its human touch, its adversarial logic, and its literary grounding in the classics. Wilson values the *Memoirs* and the *Reminiscences* for their erudition, humor, narrative and anecdotal structure, and authenticity, and for Mosby's awareness of the roots of his own mythology. He notes that the *Reminiscences*, because they are based on lectures intended to amuse audiences, read "almost like the imaginary adventures of some character of the Conan Doyle era—Raffles or Brigadier Gerard."[24]

These comments reflect the proper concerns and perspectives of different kinds of observers. For historians, however, sources must be judged for their reliability. A journalist-turned-biographer such as Jones views his quarry as the subject of an extended newspaper feature story. Mosby has all the requisite personality quirks of any small-town eccentric ripe for a write-up by a good reporter. He is colorful, quotable, something of an anachronism, a fountain of anecdotes—some of them credible—controversial, heroic, and a little dangerous. He is also "timely," one of the essential news values, in the narrative Jones created. Mosby's own story becomes important, then, because of its functional consequence. In a preface to the 1957 edition of Mosby's memoirs, Jones writes: "The public has at last awakened to the value of the personal memoirs of Colonel John Singleton Mosby." By this he means, in the journalistic sense, that Mosby is timely and thus newsworthy, an assessment that the pragmatic Mosby likely would have appreciated. Wilson reads Mosby as an idiosyncratic literary and cultural critic. He is less concerned with Civil War history than he is with the mythology that encloses it. Each writer has his own Mosby to contend with—and they are not necessarily the same Mosby.

MOSBY IN MEMOIR AND BIOGRAPHY

Beginning with John Esten Cooke, Mosby has been the subject of numerous memoirs and biographies, all of which have

168   THE MOSBY MYTH

shaped the Mosby Myth. At the end of the war, John Scott gained
Mosby's approval to write an authorized biography, *Partisan Life
with Col. John S. Mosby*. Scott had unrestricted access to Mosby
and even lived with his family while writing the book, which
was published in 1867. According to Ramage, Scott's book exaggerates Mosby's achievements and contains errors in chronology
and dates, but still has the virtue of independent judgment despite Mosby's involvement. Eicher sees Scott's account of Mosby's
shooting Turpin as an attempt to turn a rather sordid event into
high adventure and holds that the cumulative effect of the early
material is to mythologize Mosby rather than explain him. John
Marshall Crawford, a former private in Mosby's command, published *Mosby and His Men*, also in 1867, but this book, too, contains factual errors and embellishments, according to Ramage.

James J. Williamson, a Marylander who joined Mosby's command in 1863, published *Mosby's Rangers* in 1896 and an expanded
second edition in 1909. Williamson's personal narrative draws
upon a diary he kept during the war and includes many photographs, sketches, and illustrations, excerpts from other works,
poems, correspondence, reports, maps, and newspaper accounts.
Williamson takes liberties by inventing dialogue, but Ramage
judges the book more accurate and reliable than some previous
eyewitness accounts. Other memoirs include John W. Munson's
Reminiscences of a Mosby Guerrilla (1906), parts of which were first
published in *Munsey's Magazine* in 1904; Monteiro's *War Reminiscences by a Surgeon of Mosby's Command* (1906); and John Alexander's *Mosby's Men* (1907).[25]

In 1912, Alexander Hunter, a former Confederate soldier who
knew Mosby but did not serve in his command, published *The
Women of the Debatable Land*, which included a chapter on the Gray
Ghost. Wert considered Hunter a more objective source than many
Rangers who wrote about Mosby. According to Hunter, Mosby
was self-centered, cold, stoical, and without "human sympathy,"
but a great and underappreciated military genius. Don C. Seitz,
a biographer of Joseph Pulitzer, included Mosby in his 1925 book,
*Uncommon Americans: Pencil Portraits of Men and Women Who Have
Broken the Rules*. Mosby appeared in the company of Israel
Putnam, Nathan Bedford Forrest, Ethan Allen, Davy Crockett,
Tecumseh, and Susan B. Anthony. The years between 1900 and

1920, during which many of the memoirs appeared, were a turning point in Confederate remembrance. The New South was coming of age a half-century after the end of the war. In 1912 a Southerner, Woodrow Wilson, had been elected president. In 1913 veterans had gathered at Gettysburg to commemorate the fiftieth anniversary of the battle, and the ceremonies became an important symbol of reunion. Social tensions were declining, and, as Gaines M. Foster has written in his *Ghosts of the Confederacy*, "Defused and diminished by so many diverse meanings and uses, the Confederate tradition lost much if not all of its cultural power." Mosby died in 1916, and his story as he told it, and as his men remembered it, was achieving a kind of closure. It would be the task of another generation to assemble the larger story from the shards of memory.[26]

Accordingly, it was not until *Ranger Mosby* that the great partisan had his first real biographer. Virgil Carrington Jones was born in Charlottesville in 1906. After graduating from Washington and Lee University in 1930, he became a journalist, working for the *Huntsville Times* in Alabama, the *Richmond Times-Dispatch*, the *Washington Evening Star*, and the *Wall Street Journal*. His story of how he came to write *Ranger Mosby*, told in a preface of January 1944, itself becomes a kind of myth, with Jones (appropriately christened Virgil) casting himself in the role of an epic bard who composes his own *Aeneid*. Another journalist's remark in 1938 that Mosby was a forgotten American hero set Jones on a six-year search for the historical Mosby, a story he tells us he knew, in bits, from his childhood in Trevilians, Virginia. It was a story learned early in the century during Confederate reunions, conversations in a corner store, and around a great-aunt's stove. Jones was also able to obtain information from Mosby's children as well as the last-known surviving member of Mosby's Rangers, John Mason Lawrence, who died on October 17, 1939. Writing the book in Washington during the Second World War, Jones drew inspiration by reading about the commandos fighting in Europe and seeing them as modern incarnations of Mosby's Rangers. He pushed this thesis hard throughout the war. In an article published in the *Richmond Times-Dispatch* in 1942, Jones wrote: "The Commandos now preying on Nazi-occupied territory stir memories of the frail, stoop-shouldered Virginian who expanded and gave romance to this type of warfare on the American continent more than three-quarters of a century ago."[27]

He specifically cites British raids at Dieppe in occupied France, and in Libya against Gen. Erwin Rommel, the Desert Fox, as inspired by Mosby's raids in Northern Virginia. In a speech he gave at the University of Virginia in 1944, Jones said that the modern commandos "are following in the footsteps of Mosby. . . . I am confident that our Allied raiders of today who have heard of Mosby and his success go about their dangerous business with him in their minds. A prominent commando leader once intimated as much. There, in the thoughts of the 1944 version of his unbeatable Rangers, the indomitable spirit of this little Confederate lives again in the ranks of American history."[28]

In *Ranger Mosby*, Jones had emphasized Mosby's war years, devoting only about 15 percent of his book to the rest of Mosby's life. While richly documented, *Ranger Mosby* is really a narrative biography relying on imaginary conversations and highly descriptive characterizations. Eicher judges the book as "serviceable" and "respectable though it takes liberties for the sake of the story" and concludes that it "stands up rather well." Ramage says the book "endures as a well-written classic." In 1956, Jones published a broader study of partisan warfare, including Mosby's command, in his *Gray Ghosts and Rebel Raiders*. Jones again gives a dramatic account of how he came to write *Ranger Mosby*. He had gradually come to the conclusion that the guerrillas in general had been overlooked, and he determined to write "a justification of Confederate independent warfare." But because he was an unknown student of the war, he first approached the Virginia journalist and historian Douglas Southall Freeman, author of epic biographies of Lee and his commanders. As a custodian of Southern history, Freeman was in a position to scoff at Jones's thesis, but he gave the project his benediction. Jones later gained the support of another popular Civil War historian, Bruce Catton, who wrote a generous foreword to *Gray Ghosts and Rebel Raiders*. The book inspired *The Gray Ghost* television series, which considerably embellished the Mosby Myth. Both of Jones's books, as well as the television series, supported by Jones's speeches and newspaper writing, give us a Mosby who fit the times in which the books were written and the series was broadcast. His daring exploits during the Civil War are given a contemporary context: Mosby matters because of the applicability of his tactics during the Second World War and, potentially, the Cold War.[29]

Jonathan Daniels, a press secretary to Franklin D. Roosevelt and editor of the Raleigh, North Carolina, *News and Observer*, wrote a lively biography of Mosby for young readers in 1959. *Mosby, Gray Ghost of the Confederacy*, emphasized Mosby's heroic military achievements. The book, issued by the J. B. Lippincott Co., joined biographies for young people of other historical figures such as Admiral David Farragut, scientist Louis Agassiz, the painters Picasso, Dürer, and Botticelli, and Mary, Queen of Scots, on the publisher's list. *Mosby* was one of a number of books about the South and Southern history that Daniels wrote between 1938 and 1973, a period of historical reevaluation and reassertion, even for liberals such as Daniels.

Anecdotal stories about Mosby also occasionally appeared in memoirs, especially with the approach of the Civil War Centennial. J. Bryan III, a former Richmond journalist, wrote an amusing memoir, *The Sword over the Mantel: The Civil War and I*, in 1960. Bryan discusses how he was "completely conditioned, so soaked in The War that even then I was becoming unsure whether a certain story was one I had read or one I had heard." This is a good insight into the formation of a myth. He recalls, "whether in memory or imagination," his grandfather telling him about his service with "the Colonel" during the war. "Who was the colonel, Grandfather?" he asked. "Who? *Who*? Almighty God! To think that—He was Colonel Mosby, you miserable young idiot!" In 1965, *John Mosby, Rebel Raider of the Civil War*, another young-adult biography, was published. The story, by Anne Welsh Guy, emphasizes Mosby's frontier boyhood and Civil War service and portrays him as a gallant Virginian admired by both North and South in a reunited country.[30]

Almost half of Siepel's biography, which appeared in 1983, is devoted to an account of Mosby's life after the war. Siepel tries to separate Mosby from Confederate mythology and present him as a complex American figure in the context of his times. His Mosby, therefore, is as much tragic as heroic, more the rebel-in-full than simply the Rebel of the violent lustrum of the war. In an introduction to the book, former senator Eugene McCarthy, himself a political maverick, claims Mosby would be remembered as a national rather than a regional hero had he fought on the winning side—a dubious claim given that Mosby's contrarianism was the essence of his fame and that for most of his lifetime he was more welcome in the North than in the South. Siepel, according to McCarthy, presents Mosby as a case study of a recurring type of maverick American political figure. Wert praises Siepel's account of Mosby's postwar career, but finds "hardly anything new or refreshing" in his report of the war years. He says the relationship between Mosby and the Rangers is not well developed.[31]

Wert tries to rectify this lack in his *Mosby's Rangers* (1990). While primarily a study of Mosby's command, the book does provide insight into Mosby as a commander. Ramage credits Wert for revising Mosby's claims that he prolonged the war by harrying Sheridan, which also undercuts Jones's thesis about Mosby's effectiveness. Eicher contends Wert "overinterprets his material, and his predilection for the Mosby legend tarnishes much of his commentary. His contention that Mosby's Rangers constituted the 'most famous command of the Civil War' is patently ridiculous." But he also praises Wert's style and insights into the true nature of guerrilla warfare and the men who fought as Rangers. Robert C. Reinders, reviewing the book for the *Milwaukee Journal*, judges *Mosby's Rangers* to be "excellent military history," but says it lacks "social analysis." Wert does, however, provide a good deal of analysis about the communities that sustained the partisans. Hugh C. Keen and Horace Mewborn provide additional insights into the Rangers in their *43rd Battalion Virginia Cavalry: Mosby's Command*, published in 1993.[32]

Susan Provost Beller, a children's librarian from Vermont, wrote *Mosby and His Rangers: Adventures of the Gray Ghost*, a brief, balanced account of Mosby's command as an adventure story for younger readers, published in 1992. She relies primarily on Mosby's own words and the memoirs of those who served with him. Beller reminds her readers that history is a collection of stories, but not the entire story. She tries to separate the Gray Ghost myth from the reality of guerrilla fighting and to explain how Mosby "passed from Southern hero into Southern legend, a sweet memory for a nation defeated in an otherwise bitter war."[33]

Ramage's excellent, comprehensive biography, *Gray Ghost: The Life of Col. John Singleton Mosby*, appeared in 1999, thirteen years after his *Rebel Raider: The Life of General John Hunt Morgan*. The two books provide definitive and contrasting histories of the Confederacy's two most prominent raiders. Ramage is the first biographer to devote any attention to Mosby as a cultural as well as a military figure. He offers a scholarly, balanced assessment of Mosby's war record that is well grounded in the available facts. He also provides psychological explanations that give insight into Mosby's personality and the impact of his military tactics. Ramage's biography created new interest in Mosby at the end of the twentieth century.[34]

While Ramage, Wert, and Siepel all attempt to demythologize Mosby by separating the man from the myth, especially in terms of military history, Mosby presents an almost impossible challenge to the historian. Breaking down a myth requires more than separating fact from fiction. To a large degree, a myth exists independently of its subject and begins to take on a life of its own. The historical Mosby becomes just an exceptional mortal man, while the Mosby Myth actually grows with every effort to deracinate it. Each new volume published on Lincoln or Hitler or Lee or Hemingway or Elvis Presley or Lawrence of Arabia, for example, seems to stoke the myth that is being deconstructed. Ultimately, there is only so much we can ever know about a human life. The unknowns become more mysterious as we try to plumb the depths of the human psyche. Where biography ends, literature and legend begin, as expressed in Hogan's declaration that his stories are about what *could have happened* to Mosby. Thanks to the good efforts of historians and biographers, we now have as full a record of the life of John Singleton Mosby as we are ever likely to have. The Gray Ghost, however, remains what he has always been: a fictional character.

This problem was further illustrated during a famous television debate between the writer James Agee and the distinguished historian Allan Nevins on March 29, 1953. Agee had written the script for the *Omnibus* television series called *Abraham Lincoln— The Early Years*. Agee, the artist, had invented and dramatized incidents from Lincoln's life to which Nevins, the historian, took

strong exception. "He has tampered with the truth. He has taken
a myth . . . and presented it to a great American audience as if it
were verified truth," Nevins complained. Failing to persuade
Nevins of the artistic virtue of his attempt to present a mythical
Lincoln who was larger than history, Agee finally conceded he
was "entirely guilty," but went on to say that it has been "defi-
nitely proved that there is no Santa Claus, but of course there is a
Santa Claus. There are two kinds of truth."[35] If there are two kinds
of truth, there are, indeed, two Abraham Lincolns and two John
Mosbys.

NOTES

1. Robert A. Lively, *Fiction Fights the Civil War* (Chapel Hill: University of North Carolina Press, 1957), 190–91.

2. Albert J. Menendez, *Civil War Novels: An Annotated Bibliography*
(New York: Garland, 1986); Alice Fahs, *The Imagined Civil War: Popular
Literature of the North and South, 1861–1865* (Chapel Hill: University of
North Carolina Press, 2001); Cullen, *Civil War in Popular Culture*, 2–3.

3. *Confederate Scout: Virginia's Frank Stringfellow*, ed. James Dudley
Peavey (privately published, 1956), 50; Cooke, *Wearing of the Gray*, 102;
Nat Brandt, *The Man Who Tried to Burn New York* (Syracuse, NY: Syra-
cuse University Press, 1986); Russel Nye, *The Unembarrassed Muse* (New
York: Dial Press, 1970), 43, 147.

4. John Esten Cooke, *Surry of Eagle's-Nest* (1866, reprint, Ridgewood,
NJ: Gregg Press, 1968); Wilson, *Patriotic Gore*, 192–96, 315; Thomas E.
Dasher, "John Esten Cooke," *Antebellum Writers in New York and the South*,
ed. Joel Myerson, *Dictionary of Literary Biography* (Detroit: Gale Research,
1979), 3:64–70; Cooke, *Wearing of the Gray*, 102–15; John O. Beaty, *John
Esten Cooke, Virginian* (1922; reprint, Port Washington, NY: Kennikat
Press, 1965), 91–100; unidentified newspaper, n.d., JSM Scrapbooks, Uni-
versity of Virginia.

5. Clarke Venable, *Mosby's Night Hawk* (Chicago: Reilly & Lee, 1931);
Edna Hoffman Evans, *Sunstar and Pepper* (Chapel Hill: University of
North Carolina Press, 1947).

6. Jere Hungerford Wheelwright, *Gentlemen, Hush!* (New York:
Charles Scribner's Sons, 1948); Garald Lagard, *Scarlet Cockerel* (New York:
William Morrow, 1948); Wilson, *Patriotic Gore*, 327.

7. "(Robert) Ray Hogan," *Encyclopedia of Frontier and Western Fiction*, ed. Jon Tuska and Vicki Piekarski (New York: McGraw-Hill, 1983),
179.

8. Ray Hogan, *The Ghost Raider* (New York: Pyramid Publications,
1960).

9. Ray Hogan, *Raider's Revenge* (New York: Pyramid Publications,
1960).

10. Ray Hogan, *Rebel Raid* (New York: Berkeley, 1961; reprint, Bath, England: Chivers Press, 1988).

11. Ray Hogan, *Rebel in Yankee Blue* (New York: Avon, 1962).

12. Ray Hogan, *Hell to Hallelujah* (New York: Macfadden, 1962); idem, *Night Raider* (New York: Avon, 1964; reprint, Bath, England: Chivers Press, 1992).

13. Ray Hogan, *Rebel Ghost* (New York: Macfadden, 1964; reprint, Toronto: PaperJacks, 1987).

14. Ray Hogan, *Mosby's Last Raid* (New York: Macfadden, 1966).

15. Joseph B. Icenhower, *The Scarlet Raider* (Philadelphia and New York: Chilton Book Co., 1961).

16. William Sanders, *The Wild Blue and the Gray* (New York: Warner Books, 1991); Harry Turtledove, *Guns of the South: A Novel of the Civil War* (New York: Ballantine Books, 1993).

17. Ramage, *Gray Ghost*, 94.

18. Robert Skimin, *Gray Victory* (New York: St. Martin's Press, 1988).

19. Andre Le Vot, *F. Scott Fitzgerald* (New York: Doubleday, 1983), 5; John Limon, *Writing after War* (New York: Oxford University Press, 1994), 113–14.

20. Saul Bellow, *Mosby's Memoirs and Other Stories* (New York: Viking Press, 1968); Robert R. Dutton, *Saul Bellow* (Boston: Twayne Publishers, 1982), 172–73; J. O. Tate, foreword, *Mosby's Memoirs*, xii–xiii; Ellen Pifer, *Saul Bellow against the Grain* (Philadelphia: University of Pennsylvania Press, 1990), 81–95, 176.

21. Beppie Noyes, *Mosby, the Kennedy Center Cat* (Washington, DC: Acropolis Books, 1978).

22. Harold Coyle, *Until the End* (New York: Simon & Schuster, 1996); John Jakes, *On Secret Service* (New York: E. P. Dutton, 2000).

23. Schlesinger is quoted in Michael Kammen, *A Season of Youth* (New York: Alfred A. Knopf, 1978), 152.

24. David J. Eicher, *The Civil War in Books: An Analytical Bibliography* (Urbana: University of Illinois Press, 1997), 30–31, 101; Ramage, *Gray Ghost*, 403; Siepel, *Rebel*, 248; Tate, Foreword, *Mosby's Memoirs*, xxi; Wilson, *Patriotic Gore*, 307–19.

25. Ramage, *Gray Ghost*, 404; Eicher, *Civil War in Books*, 101; J. Marshall Crawford, *Mosby and His Men* (New York: G. W. Carleton & Co., 1867); Jones, Preface, *The Memoirs of Colonel John S. Mosby*, ed. Charles Wells Russell (1917; reprint, Bloomington: Indiana University Press, 1959), v–xv; John W. Munson, *Recollections of a Mosby Guerrilla* (1906; reprint, Washington, DC: Zenger Publishing Co., 1983); Monteiro, *War Reminiscences by the Surgeon of Mosby's Command*; Alexander, *Mosby's Men*.

26. Hunter, *Women of the Debatable Land*, 39–50; Don C. Seitz, *Uncommon Americans: Pencil Portraits of Men and Women Who Have Broken the Rules* (Indianapolis: Bobbs-Merrill, 1925); Gaines M. Foster, *Ghosts of the Confederacy* (New York: Oxford University Press, 1987), 193–97.

27. Jones, "The Way Mosby Used to Do It," *Richmond Times-Dispatch*, November 22, 1942; Thomas J. Evans and James M. Moyer, *Mosby's Confederacy: A Guide to the Roads and Sites of Colonel John Singleton Mosby* (Shippensburg, PA: White Mane Publishers, 1991), 31.

28. Jones, "Ranger Mosby in Albemarle," *Papers of the Albemarle County Historical Society* (Charlottesville, VA), 5 (June 1945): 46.

29. Eicher, *Civil War in Books*, 101; Ramage, *Gray Ghost*, 405; Jones, Preface, and Catton, Foreword, *Gray Ghosts and Rebel Rangers*.

30. Jonathan Daniels, *Mosby, Gray Ghost of the Confederacy* (Philadelphia: J. B. Lippincott, 1957); J. Bryan III, *The Sword over the Mantel: The Civil War and I* (New York: McGraw-Hill, 1960), 26–27; Anne Welsh Guy, *John Mosby, Rebel Raider of the Civil War* (New York: Abelard-Schuman, 1965).

31. Eugene J. McCarthy, Introduction, Siepel, *Rebel*, xiii–xv; Wert, review of Siepel's *Rebel: The Life and Times of John Singleton Mosby, Civil War Times Illustrated* (April 1984): 54.

32. Ramage, *Gray Ghost*, 405; Eicher, *Civil War in Books*, 376; Robert C. Reinders, "They Were the Civil War's Green Berets," *Milwaukee Journal*, October 7, 1990; Hugh C. Keen and Horace Mewborn, *43rd Battalion Virginia Cavalry: Mosby's Command* (Lynchburg, VA: H. E. Howard, 1993).

33. Susan Provost Beller, *Mosby and His Rangers: Adventures of the Gray Ghost* (Cincinnati: Betterway Books, 1992), 88.

34. Ramage, *Gray Ghost*, 6.

35. Laurence Bergreen, *James Agee: A Life* (New York: E. P. Dutton, 1984), 373–74.

CHAPTER SEVEN

MOSBY ON TELEVISION AND IN POPULAR ART

I told them that, to my knowledge, Mosby never used
a tent as a guerrilla leader and, had he done so, I was
sure he never would have put his name on it.
—Virgil Carrington Jones, letter (1976)

CBS hasn't any more courage than a dead chicken.
—Jack DeWitt, chief writer, *The Gray Ghost* (1978)

THE GRAY GHOST was the first television series to focus on the
military aspects of the Civil War. Appropriately, it concerned cavalry, the type of military unit most familiar to both cinema and
television audiences. The series, which was in production before
the 1957–58 season, was based loosely on many of Mosby's actual exploits during the war. Although it was a commercial success, *The Gray Ghost* reveals how sensitive an issue that war
remained almost a century after it was fought. By making the
audience confront history as well as the mythology of the conflict at a time when Americans were worried about civil rights
and national security, the series provoked controversy. The fact
that the series *looked* like a Western, and was written and produced by veteran Western filmmakers, often former journalists,
who were attempting to create conventional, noncontroversial,
and commercially attractive entertainment, provided little cover.

THE CIVIL WAR AS POSTWAR WESTERN

The content of a new medium is usually, at least at first, a
cautious adaptation of all media that have preceded it. The first
Civil War films were inspired by the literary and theatrical

conventions of the precinema era. Although some of the first silent films, such as D. W. Griffith's controversial *Birth of a Nation*
(1915), emphasized conflict, most, including the three films about
Mosby, avoided broader issues and simply viewed the Civil War
as bad for both sides. The healing of divisions took priority over
battles. Although initially popular as melodrama early in the
twentieth century, Civil War films had limited midcentury appeal and usually lost money. They were costly to produce, and,
with a few exceptions, were sentimental, banal, and formulaic.
Early television writers were cautious about developing Civil War
stories into television drama. When such programs were attempted on television, they usually created the impression that
the Civil War was practically free of ideology with no enduring
sectional differences. And yet the Civil War did offer a treasury
of dramatic stories, which, if told well and adapted to the limitations of the television screen, held the promise of vibrant and
rewarding entertainment. As William C. Davis puts it, "The natural affinity of film for a story like this has never been questioned.
The biggest event in our history belongs on the biggest canvas
humans can devise."[1]

Some stories vaguely connected to the Civil War had appeared
on television as early as 1946, but in a Western context. Richard
West identifies 139 Western series presented on television from
1946 to 1978. Most of these series simply skipped the war and
marginalized controversy by focusing on Civil War veterans.
Writers could always mine the mother lode of epic narrative,
drawing on tales of wandering "veterans" from Ulysses to Ingmar
Bergman's chess-playing knight in the classic Swedish film *The
Seventh Seal*. Westerns usually were set in the period between 1865
and 1890 rather than in the earlier periods of frontier history. Stories taking place before the war would have had to confront slavery, while stories set during the war required expensive battle
scenes and would have had to confront messy ideological issues.
Those set after the war, however, could emphasize reconciliation
and renewal, often conforming to a national narrative of progress
splayed across a Western landscape, or they could explore themes
of alienation and exile.[2]

As scriptwriters worked to develop plots and characters to
fit that quarter-century time frame, the Civil War, safely contained

in a previous era, was a narrative bank from which they could make frequent withdrawals. Like all wars, the Civil War produced a rootless population well schooled in the use of weaponry, a talent "that could not find a market in a peaceful and law-abiding milieu. . . . Such men—frequently Southerners—drifted westward like their fathers who had emigrated a generation before, hoping for a fresh start." Moreover, the West had been fiercely contested ground during the Civil War, spawning unprecedented savagery, much of it perpetrated by mounted marauders operating beyond the control of either army. The Wild West was a direct result of the Civil War. The desperados of the 1870s and 1880s usually had learned their grisly trade from these irregular units.

The Civil War never really ended in the West, spilling over from the battlefields to the frontier. Westerns were full of characters continuing the vengeance and vandalism they had wrought during the conflict, as well as others who continued fighting against them. It was not always necessary for these characters to be situated within the traditional Western genre. The Western, at any rate, is a loose genre about a territory vast in time and space, with the idea of the frontier as a common element. Some doughty and deranged characters emerged in series, including *The Restless Gun* (NBC, 1957–1959), *Have Gun, Will Travel* (CBS, 1957–1963), *Maverick* (ABC, 1957–1961), *The Rifleman* (ABC, 1958–1963), *Yancy Derringer* (CBS, 1958–59), *Bronco* (ABC, 1958–1962), *MacKenzie's Raiders* (Syndicated, 1958–59), *The Rough Riders* (ABC, 1958–59), *The Rebel* (ABC, 1959–1961), and *The Legend of Jesse James* (ABC, 1965–66). The Civil War was merely a point of departure. The war motivated the characters, many of whom obviously suffered from what veterans of later conflicts would call shell shock, post-traumatic stress syndrome, or simply insanity. Directors occasionally used stock footage of Civil War battles borrowed from the Hollywood movie vaults when a character was recalling the war.[3]

With the exception of *The Gray Ghost*, then, the Civil War as midcentury television text was predominantly a Western genre dealing with the aftermath of sectional rivalry and the struggle of the combatants to override the landscape of traumatic memory. But as writers sought ways to integrate the postbellum anguish of these characters into the standard romantic frontier tradition, themes dwelling on repentance, reconciliation, and healing gradually gave way to more conventional morality plays staged in frontier cattle towns. The Western landscape became mythic and moral rather than place- or time-bound. Stories migrated from the present to the past as the television formula exploited contemporary historical concerns for subject matter. By removing these issues to an older time, they could be placed within a system of concrete values. That vaguely defined "older time" became the mythical realm of television.[4]

That the historical concerns of midcentury America could be projected on a sagebrush landscape indicates a "synchronization between qualities inherent within the genre and values relevant to American life at the time." Paula S. Fass observed that television introduces audiences to the "facts and fantasies of American society." Individual programs, especially those reflecting public concerns, can be viewed as unique social texts as well as keys to relevant values. For the historian, she contended, television programs can provide a focus for studying the slow process by which common images evolve within a recognizable context. At their best, television programs can at once stabilize public images and symbols and give them temporal elasticity. These representations are the most effective kinds of public symbols and the most useful as cultural documents because they parallel the historical process itself.[5]

THE GRAY GHOST

Programs at the margins of a genre are significant keys to public opinion and historical meaning during a period of social tension, when "temporal elasticity" is stretched to its limits. *The Gray Ghost* was the *exception* to the displaced Civil War veteran narrative in the Western genre. Jones's *Ranger Mosby* and *Gray Ghosts and Rebel Raiders* came to the attention of a producer, Lindsley Parsons, the former editor and publisher of the *San Marino News* in California. Parsons had written his first Western screenplay in 1933 at the age of twenty-eight. He went on to produce low-budget gangster, action, and Western films, including *Sierra Passage* (1951), *Torpedo Alley* (1953), *Jack Slade* (1953), *Cry Vengeance* (1954), *Dragon Wells Massacre* (1957), and *Oregon Pas-*

sage (1957). Parsons told CBS executive Tom Moore that Mosby had commercial potential within the Western genre. "He and I were talking about various kinds of folk heroes and this seemed like a good idea," Moore recalled.

Tod Andrews, a well-established stage, screen, and television actor born in New York City on November 10, 1914, while Mosby was still alive, was an inspired choice to play Mosby. After appearing in four motion pictures, Andrews had toured as the lead role in the popular Broadway play *Mr. Roberts*, taking over from Henry Fonda in 1951. Ironically enough, he had had a small part in 1941 in the famous film *They Died With Their Boots On*, which starred Errol Flynn in the role of Custer. Andrews had the advantage of somewhat resembling Mosby, whom he played in *The Gray Ghost* with understated, Fondaesque charm. CBS hired Jones as a historical consultant, and he and Andrews made several visits to Mosby's Confederacy so that Andrews could become familiar with the historical setting for Mosby's adventures. Parsons advised Jones that the first thirty-nine scripts would make use of some fiction, but that later scripts could adhere more closely to history. He told Jones he could review each script for accuracy before it went into production. Jones said the pilot film used to sell the series "wasn't too bad, except one scene that showed Mosby seated in a tent, with his name on a placard attached to the outside. I told them that, to my knowledge, Mosby never used a tent as a guerrilla leader and, had he done so, I was

Tod Andrews played a dapper John Mosby in the short-lived television series *The Gray Ghost*. The soft-spoken Andrews portrayed Mosby as a gentlemanly Southern patriot, cunning but never ruthless. The historical Mosby's preference for the pistol gave Andrews the prop he needed to bridge the gap between Virginia soldier and Wild West cowboy, a staple of 1950s television fare. *Photofest*

sure he never would have put his name on it." The scene remained in the pilot, but adjustments were made in future episodes.[6]

Jones incurred some risk in agreeing to serve as a consultant to the show. He was cited in the credits after each episode, but it was not often clear that the stories were "inspired by," rather than "based on," the life of John Mosby. Historians might well have assumed that if Jones had vetted each episode, then he was not much of a stickler for historical accuracy. Although some critics dismissed *The Gray Ghost* as just another Western "with lots of galloping horses, gunplay, and derring-do," the program did have distinctive attributes. There was at least an attempt at historical accuracy that was rare for the genre. Jones recalled a script about a campaign involving both Grant and Stuart that

> showed Mosby standing beside a sutler's wagon and saying to one of his men on the other side, John, throw me a peach. I pointed out that any such action would have had to take place between March 12, 1864, when Grant took over as Chief of the Armies of the United States, and May 11, 1864, when Stuart was fatally wounded at Yellow Tavern. This would involve a season when peaches could not have existed, for there was no refrigeration by which they could have been retained through the winter. I suggested that the reference be to an apple or turnip, either of which could have been kept in a root cellar.

As a cavalry unit, Mosby's Rangers were familiar to a television audience accustomed to Westerns. The frontier was simply returned from the West to western Virginia where it began. By concentrating on small-unit action in a geographically limited but highly strategic theater of the war, the so-called Mosby's Confederacy, scriptwriters could invent combat situations both appropriately realistic and cinematically feasible. The strategic context of the war could be inferred from Mosby's tactics. Chief writer Jack DeWitt's scripts gave the series the texture of documentary while preserving the drama of the invented narrative.

The colorful DeWitt was born in Morrilton, Arkansas, in 1900. As an infant he was taken to England by his mother. DeWitt, according to a close friend, claimed to have been expelled from both Cambridge and the Sorbonne and to have fought in the French Foreign Legion, but he was inclined to tell tall tales. He became a journalist and worked for a time for Reuters. In the 1940s he began writing fiction, and in 1962 he joined General Motors in Santa Barbara, California, while continuing to write screenplays. Among his script credits are *Bells of San Fernando* (1947), *Young Daniel Boone* (1950), *Gun Belt* (1953), *Sitting Bull* (1954), *Rumble on the Docks* (1956), *Oregon Passage* (1957), *Wolf Larsen* (1958), *Jack of Diamonds* (1967), and *A Man Called Horse* (1970), *The Return of a Man Called Horse* (1976), and *Triumphs of a Man Called Horse* (1983).[7]

At the outset, however, CBS could not find national sponsors. Neither Moore nor Parsons apparently considered that *The Gray Ghost* would be viewed as anything other than a Western action series. Moore said: "There was some apprehension that a favorable Confederate was not in keeping with the times. A few years before, CBS had taken *Amos 'n' Andy* off the air. We tried to sell it to all the networks but they all had the same apprehension." CBS Television Sales, Inc., an autonomous unit of CBS, put the series out for syndication or sale to individual television stations. CBS touted the series as "Epic in scope, universal in appeal" and boasted of regional sponsors. At this point, Moore and Parsons were surprised to find they had a hot property. The program appealed to audiences in many regions, especially in the South. By June 1958 it was the third most popular syndicated program, based on a weighted survey of the top twenty-two national markets. As many as 21 million viewers may have been exposed to the series during its first year. "We made money on it," Moore said.[8] The *New York Times* quipped:

> The only time Mosby came close to being licked was in the Battle of Madison Avenue, before the series went on the air. . . . The pilot film was exhibited to TV executives in all parts of the nation. Only Boston objected.
>
> This business of portraying a rebel as a hero, the station asserted, was downright subversive. Meanwhile, the series was quickly signed elsewhere. . . . Even Boston capitulated.[9]

The pilot film rather grandly established the purposes of the series, opening with a dramatic voice-over to battle scenes culled from old movies and excerpts from upcoming episodes. As transcribed from a scratchy copy of the pilot, here is the text of the introductory remarks:

As in all times of great national stress, great heroes were born but none more colorful than John Singleton Mosby, the man most mentioned by Gen. Robert E. Lee in his official reports. Not a professional soldier, he was a lawyer from the University of Virginia whose natural qualities of leadership rallied reckless men to his side. From Texas, Tennessee, Virginia they came, raw backwoodsmen and college lads, farmers and city clerks, all eager to fight. Mosby's Rangers they were called and the country rocked to their exploits. For Col. John Mosby used fighting tactics unheard of then at West Point, but a technique which has played a part in every war since. Guerrilla warfare, a never-ending series of raids, fires, kidnappings, and train wrecks, earned Mosby the name of the Gray Ghost. He was a resourceful master of espionage and counterespionage who could use a beautiful woman as other men use a sword or rifle, a fabulous character whose adventures packed the vital reality of history. {inaudible} from official records formed the basis for all the stories of the Gray Ghost. He was a valiant fighting man but, first of all, an American. When the long terrible slaughter ended and the Reconstruction period started, it was John Mosby who became one of President Grant's closest advisers, to help in binding the nation's wounds. Yes, the life and times of John Singleton Mosby will find their way into the hearts of all Americans. For he was all that they love, the underdog who usually won, brave, loyal, daring, sincere, and, above all, believable, because the Gray Ghost comes right off the romantic pages of our nation's most colorful history.

There was some truth to these claims. More important, the sales pitch for station executives and potential audiences included all the necessary mythic hooks the producers sought to exploit. Mosby represented the American spirit and was a national hero, not just a Confederate guerrilla. The pilot film was also pitching the value of history as entertainment. The Gray Ghost would ride right out of the pages of the history books—romantic pages, not the dull, fact-laden pages of unreadable textbooks. "Give us a chance," the producers seemed to promise, "and Mosby will warm your hearts like *Davy Crockett* or *Old Yeller*."

THE CIVIL WAR CENTENNIAL AND THE COLD WAR

The Gray Ghost preceded the Civil War Centennial by only three years, and the coming anniversary was a factor in the original decision to produce the series. On September 7, 1957, Congress had established the Civil War Centennial Commission to coordinate national observances of the anniversary of the war. President Eisenhower invited "all of the people of our country to take a direct and active part." One of Eisenhower's appointees to the commission was CBS chairman William S. Paley.[10]

Awareness of the war was growing, and it would continue to develop over the next several years. According to the commission, by the time the Centennial observances commenced, "It could be said that the whole country was saturated in the lore and legend of the Civil War period." Like all politically constructed agencies, the commission had an agenda and was not without internal discord. The central metaphors to be advanced were heroism and national unity. According to John E. Bodnar, officials "desperately wanted to avoid rekindling any feelings of regionalism or any other forms of disunity. Their goal was to reinforce loyalty to the nation in an era when it was ostensibly threatened internally and externally by foreign ideologies."[11]

Foreign ideologies were much on the minds of Americans in the post-World War II years, and especially in 1957, during the height of the Cold War. McCarthyism, although in retreat after the U.S. Senate's censuring of Sen. Joseph McCarthy on December 2, 1954, and the senator's death on May 2, 1957, remained an active force in American politics. On September 4, 1957, the desegregation controversy boiled over when national guardsmen called out by Arkansas governor Orval A. Faubus barred nine black students from entering all-white Central High School in Little Rock. The threat of mob violence caused President Eisenhower to send 1,000 federal paratroopers to Little Rock. Civil War Centennial chairman Allan Nevins said that the commission "had the disadvantage of doing its work while a new crisis in the long history of racial irritations in America gripped parts of the country, presenting embarrassments that could be avoided only with anxious precaution and tact."[12]

On October 4, 1957, the Soviet Union launched *Sputnik*, the first manmade satellite. Its appearance in the skies, and its passage over the United States seven times each day, profoundly disturbed American society, because its presence seemed to prove that the nation was falling behind the Soviet Union in science and, perhaps, defense. The segregation controversy and *Sputnik* were explicitly linked in the public mind, as the Soviets sought to turn Little Rock into a Cold War symbol. The Soviets stressed that the satellite would pass over both Bandung, Indonesia, the site of a conference of nonaligned states, and Little Rock. A powerful symbolism was being conjured up, and internal disturbances were ripe for exploitation. The international press was generally critical of the racial turmoil in Little Rock, and charged the United States with hypocrisy at a time when it was trying to export American democratic values, especially to developing nations. The State Department was closely monitoring both foreign and domestic press reactions during this period.[13]

The Gray Ghost first arrived on the nation's television screens on October 10, 1957, only six days after *Sputnik* was launched, and with the Little Rock crisis still on the front pages. In many ways, the timing could not have been worse. A *New York Times* critic later commented that sponsoring a Civil War program "at a moment in history when Federal troops were in Little Rock seemed as perspicacious an idea as one to serialize the life of Joseph Stalin as a situation comedy."[14]

The Gray Ghost, however, may also have arrived with some impressive Cold War credentials. Mosby, to some degree at least, had anticipated modern guerrilla warfare in his behind-the-lines harassment of Union forces, although Bruce Catton, in his foreword to *Gray Ghosts and Rebel Raiders*, wildly overstates the case when he claims that "the Virginia Confederates, generations ahead of their time, had stumbled onto one of the secrets of ultramodern war."[15]

Nevertheless, with the creation of Army Special Forces or Green Beret units in 1954, the role of the ranger was changing from partisan to counterinsurgency warfare. Early American involvement in Vietnam and other hot spots increased the demand for elite troops that could potentially combat Communist rebellions, their mission being "not to make a revolution but to suppress one." The Green Berets and the U.S. Marine Corps based their martial mythology on guerrilla units that had fought in American conflicts from the time of the American Revolution. Richard Slotkin argues that, rather than being an exception to American military tradition, ranger tactics had been well established as the standard for military operations on the American frontier. The fighting style of "the Indian-fighter and the Civil War partisan guerrilla emphasized pragmatic improvisation, borrowing tactics from the enemy, and disdain of parade-ground regularity; and this style became an important strain in the complex of institutional traditions that shaped the American officer's concept of his own character and role." Closer to home, Fidel Castro's guerrilla army was beginning the final assaults that would lead to Havana by the end of 1958.

The Gray Ghost may have capitalized on this interest, too. In the opening sequences, Mosby and his men ride through rugged Virginia countryside (in California). Mosby is at the center of the screen and is gradually joined by Rangers riding in from the periphery, symbolically gathering his fighting flock along with the audience as he rides toward the nation's living rooms. Andrews somberly narrates a lyric as if Mosby were speaking from the historical present:

> We took our men from Texas, Virginia, Kentucky,
> the mountains, the backwoods and the plains.
> We put them under orders—guerrilla fighting orders—and
> what we lacked in numbers, we made up in speed and brains.
> Both Reb and Yankee strangers, they called us Mosby's Rangers.
> Both North and South, they knew our fame.
> Gray Ghost is what they called me.
> John Mosby is my name.[16]

But John Mosby's name and fame turned out to be as troublesome in 1957 and 1958 as they were almost a century earlier. In May 1954 the U.S. Supreme Court had ruled in *Brown v. Board of Education* that racial segregation of public schools was unconstitutional. The next decade was especially turbulent in the South, and some white Southerners embraced social myths, "mental pictures that portray the pattern of what a people think they are (or ought to be) or what somebody else thinks they are. They tend to develop abstract ideas in more or less concrete and dramatic terms," according to George Tindall. The South differs from other regions, Paul Gaston explains, in "the degree to which myths have been spawned and the extent to which they have asserted their hegemony over the Southern mind." A traditional Southern mythic hero was the gallant cavalier.

The cavalier myth began to flower at about the time of Mosby's birth, due in part to the popularity of Sir Walter Scott's Waverley novels, which Mosby read as a boy, and other romantic literature. After the war was lost, many Southerners came to explain the war as a defense of aristocratic virtues represented by the cavalier. The cavalier transformed the Confederacy into a lost republic that would linger in Southern mythology for more than a century. Exploitation of this myth may not have been what Parsons, Moore, or Jones intended, but as the locus of their "Western" moved from the stage sets of California to historical Virginia, its mythology moved as well. In numerous episodes, Mosby's compassionate chivalry was emphasized more than his fighting skills.[17]

The 1950s were fertile times for mythmaking. *The Gray Ghost* was just another symbol of the anxiety that was in the wind as social myths clashed with new technologies. *Sputnik*, the civil rights movement, the Cold War, UFOs, and a small group of Confederate cavalrymen fighting to defend a government that sought to perpetuate slavery—all had to be processed at once in the public's mind.

Just how *The Gray Ghost* works as social myth can be seen in an episode called "The Humanitarian." One of Mosby's soldiers is critically wounded in enemy territory. Mosby must decide whether to leave the soldier behind or risk the safety of his command and the fulfillment of his mission to rescue him. The soldier will die without medical attention. Mosby rides for a physician, leaving the victim in a farmhouse occupied by an old man who awaits an opportunity to betray the Confederates, for a price, to Union soldiers seeking Mosby.

Reaching a physician's house, Mosby learns that the doctor lost an arm when an aid station was shelled inadvertently by Confederates. The physician can only operate with the assistance of his daughter, who despises the Confederates for maiming her father. The physician agrees to treat the wounded soldier, affirming that his duty is to aid the wounded regardless of their uniform. But the daughter refuses and accompanies Mosby only at gunpoint. As the doctor begins surgery, the old farmer seizes a weapon and flees to alert the Union troops, leaving the woman to guard the Confederates. Mosby walks toward her, confident that she, a healer, cannot take away life. She recants and successfully completes the surgery. With Union soldiers approaching, Mosby and his guerrillas make their escape, having imparted the moral and helped the nurse transcend the scourge of war.

Mosby risks capture rather than abandon one of his wounded men in this *Gray Ghost* episode, "The Humanitarian." After attacking a Yankee patrol, Mosby solicits the help of a physician who had recently lost an arm to a Confederate bullet. The doctor and his daughter save the Rebel's life. Raymond Greenleaf had just starred in the film *When Gangland Strikes* when he appeared in this episode. Judith Ames played the daughter. *Photofest*

Mosby's compassion, betrayal, and deliverance provide a mythic parable suitable for a cavalier knight-errant fully consistent with Andrews's interpretation of Mosby. As portrayed by Andrews, Mosby had a conscience about killing. The actor tried carefully to put his admiration for Mosby in a neutral context: "Since getting interested in Mosby, I've come to have a pretty warm feeling for the South and for the tradition of courage on both sides that made the war the fascinating human struggle it was." This comment was of the sort that might have pleased the Civil War Centennial Commission, which wanted to emphasize themes of heroism and reconciliation. The television Mosby was simply a commodity that had to be sold to advertisers, however, and that deal depended on reconciling social myths with raw commerce.[18]

THE GHOST DEPARTS

During its first season, the series was praised lavishly in Southern newspapers. The president of the United Daughters of the Confederacy made a television film commending *The Gray Ghost*. Andrews went on a promotional tour of the South in the spring of 1958. "They greeted me as if I were Robert E. Lee reincarnated," he said. *The Raleigh News and Observer* commented: "Now on television, to the infinite delight of millions, the heroic ranger proves weekly that one Reb is better than a regiment of Yankees." *The Walton Tribune* in Monroe, Georgia, admitted to "a heady, if belated, pleasure in watching Mosby's band outsmart the bluecoats on every turn." The program also gave the impression that the fight was one-sided. Andrews tried to put the series in a historical context: "Yankees sometimes complain that we're rewriting history, that the South always wins. I have to explain that we're doing the story from Mosby's viewpoint, and that he did carry off a lot of successful raids." The program did strain credibility, as audiences grew accustomed to seeing bungling soldiers in the uniform of the U.S. Army giving way week after week to the gray commandos and their clever leader. For some reason, the producers felt it was necessary to unfurl the Confederate battle flag at every opportunity. It was hard to get around the fact that at least one American army, the U.S. Army, was losing battles, and the series became, perhaps unintentionally, good propaganda for the Confederacy. Eventually, this regional triumphalism may have frightened advertisers in some markets and hurt the series. *Variety* said as much, speculating that hot-blooded editorials in Southern newspapers might be scaring CBS away from producing more episodes.[19]

Jones expected the series to continue, and DeWitt had already completed outlines for another year's scripts. Jones recalled: "CBS informed me I should remain ready to go back to Hollywood at any time. Two or three times I received phone calls alerting me. Then, to my surprise and disappointment, I was informed that the series would not be continued." CBS grumbled that the show would have been booked solid if Little Rock had not scared away some Northern sponsors. Parsons felt that "the pros and cons of the Civil War belonged to history, and that entertainment with a historical background would be welcomed. It was. But that was before the Little Rock court decision." Parsons also attributed the cancellation to pressure by the National Association for the Advancement of Colored People (NAACP) on sponsors: "Some of the blacks said *The Gray Ghost* glorified the whites and white supremacy." DeWitt also had encountered pressure: "A delegation came to me and said they didn't want blacks depicted as servants. I told them that if we used them, we would use them as they were during the war. When they didn't accept that, I told them we wouldn't use them at all. That was unfortunate because in the next season's shows we had two or three episodes in which blacks were heroes. I told them there would be no attempt to put them down."[20]

Variety discounted loose talk that any program remotely connected with the Civil War would run into trouble. *Variety* cited sponsorship of *MacKenzie's Raiders* in numerous Southern cities and reported that many network series were being readied for the Civil War Centennial. *MacKenzie's Raiders* fit the earlier pattern, however, by focusing on events in the West well after the war. In any case, it, too, was soon canceled. J. Fred MacDonald, in his history of African Americans in television, concluded that *The Gray Ghost* was a casualty of the segregation issue, although it never had dealt with slavery. He contended that even local sponsors feared that mounting tensions might cause "a misunderstanding of the sponsorship of a series in which the white southern heroes seldom lost. Just as advertisers shunned association with black causes, they also avoided open affiliation with white southern intransigence."[21]

Variety, however, claimed that the program succeeded at the local level because local sponsors were more in touch with their audiences than national advertisers. In most markets, sponsors initially did not think the program would pose a problem. In September 1958, *The Gray Ghost* was still being carried on 190 stations, but the lack of new episodes slowly began eroding its popularity. The decision not to produce more episodes eventually killed the series.

"Again," *Newsweek* said, "the South had won the battles but lost the war." Parsons claimed that CBS received twenty-five hundred letters protesting the cancellation. DeWitt stated that five Southern governors tried to keep the show on the air. He bemoaned the network's lack of sensitivity to historical programming: "CBS hasn't any more courage than a dead chicken. They canceled the show. The U.S. has a history, an exciting history, but nobody has ever done anything with it."[22]

The Gray Ghost television series came along at a time when television was relatively young and innocent, as were many of those who enjoyed the program. William C. Davis is only half-correct when he says it was "aimed largely at a juvenile audience." Even the august Edmund Wilson apparently took a serious interest in *The Gray Ghost* while he was writing *Patriotic Gore*. The commotion caused in the press after its cancellation suggests the program was much more than fodder for children and a few bigots. The intense national interest in the Civil War at the time of the Centennial practically guaranteed a large and diverse audience. It continued to appear in reruns well into the 1970s, and bootleg copies of episodes were still available then. Greg Biggs, who wrote an article about the series for *Blue & Gray Magazine* in 1994, claimed its episodes "are among the most sought after on the video tape trading market." In 2000 a three-volume video collection containing ten episodes became available and could be obtained from Belle & Blade, a Dover, New Jersey, firm selling home videos by mail.[23]

Although the number of people interested in collecting episodes of the series is probably rather small, an indeterminately larger number of middle-aged people have heard about the program and, accordingly, know something about Mosby. Biggs says that although he was only four years old when the program was first broadcast, he remembers seeing it. And according to Ramage, "Today, when Mosby's name is mentioned, almost anyone who watched television in the 1950s will say, 'Oh, the Gray Ghost; I saw him on television.' His fame soared to new heights. . . . Once each week for thirty minutes, in thirty-nine episodes, Mosby thrilled families throughout the nation with his daring and cunning raids against the Union army."[24]

THE GRAY GHOST AS IDEOLOGY

The Gray Ghost was inherently elitist in its presentation of Mosby as a cavalier. By scrupulously avoiding all the larger problems associated with the war—slavery, draft riots, atrocities, desertions, profiteering, class struggles, economic upheavals—the series could deal only with questions of private morality. Mosby's Rangers, while pursuing historicity, had to circumvent history with a nod and a wink. The presentation of the Civil War from the Southern point of view seemed out of place to many viewers after thousands of African Americans had died defending the United States in the Second World War and in the Korean conflict.

Although attempts had been made to separate slavery and racism from the Civil War, it ultimately proved impossible to disassociate entertainment from ideology. As a 1954 study of the Civil War and American memory concluded, "Disagreement over the meaning of the Civil War experience was matched, in the middle of the twentieth century, by sharp controversy in the arena of politics over issues related to those of Civil War days." David M. Potter summarized the work of historians writing on the Civil War between 1940 and 1959 as follows:

> Perhaps the most pervasive quality which it all has in common is that it continues to be explicitly or implicitly controversial. Not only have historians failed to agree as to whether slavery furnished the basic motive for the war or whether it provided a smoke-screen for concealing the basic motives; they have also disagreed as to the nature of the society of the Old South, the nature of slavery, the motivation and character of the antislavery movement, and the interpretation of every link in the chain of sectional clashes which preceded the final crisis.[25]

Mosby might have predicted the difficulties his video surrogate would face. He had said it was better that slavery had been abolished and the Union restored; it was wrong for Southerners to believe that their honor rested on a justification of the right of secession or the defense of slavery. Mosby would have been less than pleased to be remembered as the personification of the Southern cause. Once asked if he admitted fighting on the wrong side, he answered firmly: "I do not—I may have fought on the side that was wrong, but I fought on the right side." Undoubtedly, many of those who enjoyed the series saw the gallant Rangers as resistance fighters in a continuing struggle to preserve not only noble Southern traditions but also white supremacy and the primacy of state over nation, regardless of the intention of the program's producers.

It was unreasonable to blame African-American organizations or sponsors for objecting to *The Gray Ghost*, even if there was little or no explicit racism in the series. The program was implicitly racist in its glorification of those who defended slavery, even if their primary motivation was the defense of their state's right to separate from the Union. In the context of the times, any program resurrecting the Confederacy carried within it the manifest content of sectionalism and the historical baggage of the period. Mosby, as a Confederate icon, was always available to groups that misrepresented him. At least one White Citizens Council used Mosby as a poster boy for its cause during the civil rights upheavals. As a symbol of resistance, he could be exploited for causes he undoubtedly would have resisted himself.[26] At least he would have had the satisfaction of knowing that he had lasted longer on television than *Custer*, an ABC offering that began September 6, 1967, and was canceled after December 27, 1967.[27]

POST–*GHOST* TELEVISION

Parsons doubted that another Civil War series could succeed: "The emerging minorities would make the thing very difficult. You'd have to straddle a lot of issues." And yet the Civil War has often reemerged on the television screen. *Lee at Gettysburg*, a play by Alvin Sapinsley, appeared on the *Omnibus* series in 1957, the same year *The Gray Ghost* was unveiled. *The Americans* (NBC, 1961) recounted the adventures of two brothers from Virginia fighting on opposite sides, although the series was soon canceled. David L. Wolper's *Appointment with Destiny* documentary series (1972), and miniseries and movies such as *The Blue and the Gray* (1982), *North and South* (1985–86), *Gettysburg* (1993), and *Andersonville* (1995), were well received by audiences if not always by historians. *Roots* (1977) and *Roots: The Next Generations* (1979) were the most widely watched miniseries in history, with audiences estimated as high as 140 million. *Roots,* based on Alex Haley's best-seller, told a family's story of slavery and its legacy. Ken Burns's 1990 PBS documentary, *The Civil War,* probably did more to stimulate interest in the period than any production since *Gone With the Wind.*

Lincoln has been a frequent subject for television documentaries and drama since James Agee set a high standard with his acclaimed *Abraham Lincoln—The Early Years,* broadcast in four parts on *Omnibus* in 1952 and 1953. Other notable Lincoln productions included *Sandburg's Lincoln* (1974), *Gore Vidal's Lincoln* (1988), *The Perfect Tribute* (1991), and *Lincoln* (1992). In 1996, Turner Network Television launched *The Lazarus Man,* a kind of Civil War *X-Files* featuring some ghoulish Confederates called the Blood Knights. The complex plot involved a Union soldier assigned to guard Lincoln and a conspiracy with supernatural overtones. The series was soon canceled. Perhaps inspired by the Blood Knights, a 1997 television pilot episode for the short-lived *The Magnificent Seven* offered a similar group of crazed Confederates, who look like drugged zombies on horseback. They terrorize a Seminole village harboring some former slaves somewhere in the West after the war. During the 1998–99 season, *The Secret Diary of Desmond Pfeiffer* was carried by the United Paramount Network. The improbable plot involved a black English nobleman who had served as Lincoln's butler. Some African Americans complained that the program made light of slavery, and the series was canceled after the NAACP picketed UPN. Given the controversy that surrounded *The Gray Ghost,* it is remarkable that such a program could even be attempted. By the end of the century, however, cable channels had so fragmented the television market that audiences could be found for practically anything. TNT also released *The Hunley: The True Story of the Civil War's Most Secret Weapon,* a Confederate submarine, on its cable channel in 1999. None of these programs, with the possible exception of *The Hunley,* really attempted to make a hero out of a Southerner or to romanticize the Southern cause. In *The Lazarus Man* and the pilot episode for *The Magnificent Seven,* the Confederates are incarnations of a palpable evil. Perhaps a lesson had been learned from *The Gray Ghost* after all.[28]

TELEVISION AND HISTORY

Many who watched *The Gray Ghost* simply enjoyed seeing an exciting historical program on television, and Mosby took his unambiguous place along with Davy Crockett, Daniel Boone, and other heroic figures who had appeared on the screen in the 1950s. For an entire generation, Mosby became synonymous with the Civil War, in the same way that Bat Masterson, the Cartwrights, Wyatt Earp, Marshal Dillon, and other television characters of the 1950s and 1960s, historically based or imaginary, came to represent the American West.

Television is a form of history that essentially has no history. There was no significant evolution of function or style, or of audience expectation or familiarity with the form, at least in the twentieth century. Accordingly, the audience has had no expectations or standards for judging the history it absorbs from television. The standard becomes other television fare, so history is judged against sitcoms, news, and drama. Walter Lippmann said myths reduce all "truth and error, fact and fable, report and fantasy [to] the same plane of credibility," and this is exactly what television does. Oral and written history, by contrast, developed over centuries. Television is intolerant of complexity and ambiguity. Storylines, plots, and characters have to be simple. *The Gray Ghost* was often not simple because military tactics required complexity. Anyone who has tried to understand a battle by reading historical markers placed around a battlefield realizes the difficulty involved in trying to reconstruct the complex interplay of mobile forces. The scriptwriters sometimes were unable to provide enough context for small-unit engagements to make any sense to the viewer. Television also must maximize visuals and minimize text. The form must fit into blocs of thirty-minute intervals.

Historical programs on television began to appear with greater frequency in the 1990s, partly as a response to the increasing demand for content to fill time on the many cable and satellite networks, including the History Channel and the A&E Network. Much of the content is documentary programing, which is relatively easy and cheap to produce and can be rebroadcast indefinitely. In fact, programing becomes more "historical" with the passing of time. The problem is that all history becomes equally important to the audience. A documentary about a baseball team or the sinking of the *Titanic*, a biography of Marilyn Monroe, or a series on the Battle of Britain all serve equally well. Everything takes on a "gee-whiz" quality, because the typical American audience knows so little about history to begin with. Complex events are reduced to a clash of personalities, much like television news.[29]

Television history thrives on disasters and war, especially twentieth-century war. We usually look no farther back than the Civil War, which has the first real visual record. In between, we have the vast terrain of the frontier, the homeland of the Western. An important theme in American historiography was Frederick Jackson Turner's closing of the frontier in the 1890s. But television opened the frontier back up. It will live forever as a source of American mythology.

The Gray Ghost was an anomaly because television history is an anomaly. As long as the program could be contained within the conventional Western mythology, it was acceptable. But as Civil War history, simplistic perhaps—and in most ways conventional—it crashed through the gates of the television corral and challenged social myths on the open range of remembrance without meaning to do so. The Mosby Myth was too large for television, but not too large for the popular culture from which it emerged.

MOSBY'S MARAUDERS

Willie and the Yank was released in three one-hour segments on *Walt Disney's Wonderful World of Color* on January 8, 15, and 22, 1967, from 7:30 to 8:30 P.M. on Sunday evenings on NBC opposite the first half hour of the *Ed Sullivan Show* and preceding, by thirty minutes, *Bonanza*. Audiences who tuned in on those winter evenings to the NBC network had grown accustomed over the years to seeing Walt Disney introduce each episode of the program, which had previously been called *Disneyland* and *Walt Disney Presents*, but Disney had died on December 15, 1966. He had long been associated with historical programing, beginning with *Davy Crockett, Indian Fighter*, first broadcast on December 15,

1954. Disney had effectively invented the miniseries. The series was later made into a feature film, *Davy Crockett, King of the Wild Frontier*, released on May 25, 1955, and Crockett became a national sensation, with millions of children wearing coonskin caps and carrying Davy Crockett lunch boxes to school. Television critic Leonard Maltin notes the peculiarity of the Crockett myth, which may shed some light on Mosby's appeal two years later: "Though he is an admirable man, he is violent when he has to be, as in the hand-to-hand fights, as well as the initial Indian battle, where he is seen bayoneting various red men, hollering 'Give it to 'em, boys!' and such. He is also shown to have a not inconsiderable ego." Another historical figure developed by Disney was Mosby's own hero, General Francis Marion, in *The Swamp Fox*, featured in eight episodes during the 1959–60 and 1960–61 seasons.[30]

Disney claimed credit for originating the first hour-long Western series, the *Davy Crockett* episodes for ABC, and he later complained that "the network was flooded with other Westerns. They made so much money for ABC that before long I found myself in a straitjacket. . . . They kept insisting that I do more and more Westerns and my show became loaded with Elfego Baca, the Swamp Fox, Texas John Slaughter, Daniel Boone. I found myself competing with *Maverick*, *Wyatt Earp* and every other Western myth."[31]

Civil War series such as *Andrews' Raiders (The Great Locomotive Chase)* (which originated as a theatrical feature), in 1961, and *Johnny Shiloh*, in 1963, were especially popular. Like all such Disney offerings, the programs were aimed at a young audience accustomed to talking mice, heroic dogs, and clever crickets. Preceding *Willie and the Yank* as Disney selections were such one-episode programs as *Concho, the Coyote Who Wasn't*, *Minado the Wolverine*, *Ida the Offbeat Eagle*, *The Wahoo Bobcat*, *Sancho the Homing Steer*, *The Wetback Hound*, and the feature film *Old Yeller*. Many of these programs were released theatrically in overseas markets, and *Willie and the Yank* was released as *Mosby's Marauders*, a seventy-nine-minute feature film directed by Michael O'Herlihy and written by Harold Swanton. Kurt Russell, later a prominent film actor, starred as Willie Prentiss, a youthful Confederate soldier from Loudoun County who served under Mosby, played by

Jack Ging. Donald Hannon played Stoughton as a pompous, comic figure who needed a comeuppance.

Mosby's Marauders loosely ties together some historical events such as the Fairfax Raid and the capture of Stoughton, but little attention is given to accuracy. Mosby basically kidnaps Stoughton only to stop Stuart from disbanding the Rangers. The film adaptation of the series is awkward because of its episodic structure, which was intended to allow breaks for television commercials. The story anticipates nothing so much as *The Waltons*, the long-running 1970s series, or one of the Frontierland segments of earlier Disney television programing. Ging plays Mosby with suitable box-office, leading-man panache and cowboy-hero theatricality, and with less moral complexity than Tod Andrews's interpretation. The film includes minimorality plays and Civil War cinematic clichés. For example, Willie decides to rescue Nick Adams from a quicksand bog even though he knows the sergeant wants to hang him.

Actor Jack Ging played an imperious Mosby in the Disney feature film *Mosby's Marauders*, originally televised as *Willie and the Yank*. © Disney Enterprises, Inc. *Courtesy Disney Enterprises, Inc., and Jack Ging.*

The obligatory romance between a Union soldier and a Rebel farmgirl is included. Willie gets to shake the hand of Robert E. Lee after he finds the gap in the Union picket lines during the Fairfax Raid, fulfilling the Disney conceit that boys can do great things if given the chance. The Civil War is merely a joust between friends and brothers that builds a stronger America. The film is a much slicker production than *The Gray Ghost* but takes itself less seriously. Disney rebroadcast *Willie and the Yank* on August 23, 30, and September 6, 1970.

FROM COLLECTIBLES TO CABERNET

Contemporary artists who specialize in producing collectible prints for the Civil War art market have found Mosby a stimulating subject. The genre typically places the subject, usually a recognizable military figure, at the center of the composition, with the surrounding landscape realistically detailed. Don Troiani's *Ranger Mosby* is one of the most popular illustrations. Mosby appears in a forest clearing on a fall afternoon with his Rangers and is obtaining information from two captured Union soldiers. Mort Künstler's *The Fairfax Raid* shows Mosby, pistol in hand, astride a rearing horse in front of the Fairfax courthouse, riding beside the captured General Stoughton. Mosby is at the center of the painting, bathed in light cast from the courthouse and reflecting off the snow-covered landscape. Künstler, who favors winter scenes, worked from period photographs of the courthouse and the uniform Mosby was wearing during the raid. His *While the Enemy Rests* depicts Mosby and a squad of Rangers on Paris Mountain, Virginia, on December 1, 1864, looking at enemy campfires in the Shenandoah Valley. Mosby is bearded in both Küntsler paintings.

One of the best paintings, by Gordon Phillips, depicts Mosby and one of his Rangers observing a train from the brow of a snow-covered hill. Another by Phillips shows Mosby, coffee cup in hand, conferring with several Raiders warming themselves by a fire in a snow-covered field. Dale Gallon's stunning *Welcome to Mosby's Confederacy*, released in 1986, depicts Mosby and his Rangers preparing to attack a train traversing a golden landscape. Gallon's *Mosby Reports*, released in 1987, shows Mosby reporting to Stuart as his horsemen ride through a village with admiring townsfolk looking on. One of the most interesting Mosby paintings is by David Wright, who says he's "always been partial to the South's side in the war and I paint portraits of Confederate leaders who have been longtime heroes of mine." His *Stuart and Mosby*, released in 1999, depicts the two soldiers walking their horses across a rainy field in Virginia during the fall of 1862, when Mosby was a scout on Stuart's staff. Stuart is to Mosby's left and is fully attired in the familiar cloak and plumed hat, a cavalry saber strapped to his side. Mosby, a smaller figure, wears a plain gray coat and an unadorned slouch hat. He is diminished by the elegant Stuart, but he seems to be imparting important information. Other riders observe them from a respectful distance, indicating that Mosby enjoys Stuart's confidence. There is little to indicate that this Mosby will become the Gray Ghost. John Paul Strain's *Fire in the Valley*, released in 2001, depicts Mosby leading a detachment of Rangers in the Berryville Raid on August 13, 1864. Mounted on horseback, Mosby, pistol drawn, is in the foreground in front of a burning wagon. Behind him, a rider carries the battalion's new flag.

Fire in the Valley, by John Paul Strain. *Courtesy John Paul Strain*

A very different representation can be found on a sign above Mosby's Tavern, a former blacksmith's shop in Middleburg. Mosby, on horseback, is reaching to embrace a damsel in the moonlight in a scene right out of the pages of a gothic novel. Mosby and his men had, in fact, once ridden into Middleburg and found, as he wrote, many young women "as pure and as

Mosby's Tavern in Middleburg, Virginia, was originally a blacksmith's shop. The tavern's sign commemorates an occasion when Mosby and his men once rode into town like knights in shining armor "to avenge the wrongs of distressed damsels." Stuart and Mosby once met in the nearby Red Fox Inn. Photograph by Paul Ashdown.

bright as any pearl that ever shone in Oman's green water. Their beauty had won the hearts of many of my men. To avenge the wrongs of distressed damsels is one of the vows of knighthood; so we spurred on to overtake the Federal cavalry." Mosby's image also appears on a wide variety of Civil War kitsch, including T-shirts, coffee mugs, whiskey decanters, postcards, baubles, signs, maps, monuments, tourist pamphlets, and statues. Cornell and Diehl, an online retailer, markets a Mosby pipe tobacco. The John Singleton Mosby Heritage Area has been developed in the region surrounding what was once "Mosby's Confederacy," and the old Little River Turnpike, U.S. Highway 50, was designated the John S. Mosby Highway 50 in 1980. Gray Ghost Winery in Amissville, Virginia, managed by Al and Cheryl Kellert, produces some excellent premium wines. The winery is open for tours and offers clothing and glassware with the vineyard's Gray Ghost logo. Portraits of Mosby hang on the showroom walls and in the tasting room.[32]

The Gray Ghost did have a brief life as a comic book series issued by the Dell Publishing Company in 1958 and 1959. Stories were inspired by episodes from the television program and featured well-drawn characters engaged in action-oriented stories. Several photographs from the program were used as cover art. In "Point of Honor," Mosby keeps a promise to fight a Union colonel from Ireland whom he forces to help rescue a female spy.

Gray Ghost Winery in Amissville, Virginia, features a gift shop and a tasting room devoted to Mosby, who generally avoided all forms of alcohol. Late in life, he did occasionally drink imported wines. Photograph by Paul Ashdown.

Mosby wins a saber fight with the colonel, who then joins the Confederate army because he realizes it offers more "romance" than the Union army. "Problem of Command" involves a love affair between a Ranger and his prewar sweetheart who is a Northern sympathizer. In "The Missing Colonel," Mosby captures a Union officer so he can be exchanged for a son of General Lee who had been taken prisoner by the Union army. In "Horses for Stuart," a Cherokee tries to become a Ranger by using some irregular tactics to save Mosby. The stories portray Mosby as a comic-book superhero like "The Lone Ranger" or "Batman." Always an honorable adversary, he deplores killing and respects his opponents. He is capable of extraordinary feats and is always accompanied by his chubby sidekick, Sergeant Miles Magruder. Little attention is given to historical accuracy. Mosby, for example, as we know, disdained the use of a saber.[33]

WAR AS BOARD GAME

The Gray Ghost Adventure Game, inspired by the series, was produced by Transogram Inc., a New York manufacturer of board games, in 1958. Transogram was making board games, such as the *Adventures of Rin-Tin-Tin*, as spinoffs to popular television programs of the 1950s. The box for *The Gray Ghost Adventure Game* promised potential buyers that the game was full of real battle thrills and hazards—pursuit, capture, imprisonment, victory. Each player is a "rebel raider" who "must accomplish a 'secret mission,' harass the enemy lines and capture his quota of enemy soldiers. Pretested for educational play value, this lively pursuit game, designed for youngsters 7 to 12, teaches them authentic Civil War events, names and places."

The comic book Mosby was a kind of action superhero, a Civil War "Mosbyman" who could perform superhuman feats. *The Gray Ghost* comics were printed by Dell Publishing Company.

It is not difficult to see why *The Gray Ghost* was suitable for a board game. It offers a clear objective (a quota of captured soldiers) and obstacles that prevent the achievement of that objective (pursuit, capture, imprisonment). Children playing the game are not wasting time (after all, the game is "pretested for educational play value"), but learning history while vicariously experiencing the thrills of combat. Victory Games, Inc., a New York firm, also manufactured a board game, *Mosby's Raiders: Guerrilla Warfare in the Civil War*. Mosby himself on several occasions had written of war as entertainment. ("I never enjoyed myself so much in my life"; "The true secret was that it was a fascinating life"; "That summer night was a carnival of fun.") This "carnival of fun" aspect is what youngsters found attractive about the game.[34] And Mosby, the lithe cavalryman, was a much better subject than more prominent military figures. It is difficult to imagine a successful board game based on Grant ("50,000 casualties in the Wilderness. Go back three spaces.") or Hood ("7,000 casualties in five hours at Franklin. You will soon be relieved of command.") or Albert Sidney Johnston ("You have bled to death at Shiloh. Game over.").

THE BRENTMOOR CONTROVERSY

Perhaps the ultimate artistic expression of the Mosby legacy is Brentmoor, Mosby's two-story, Italianate villa-style Warrenton house, constructed in 1859, and now listed on the National Register of Historic Landmarks. In 1998, a group of citizens in Warrenton established the John Singleton Mosby Foundation in order to preserve Brentmoor, also known as the Mosby House. Mosby had purchased the property in 1875 and sold it in 1878. The town bought the house with the intention of turning it into a museum and Chamber of Commerce headquarters. The purchase has caused considerable controversy. Although most of those present at a town council meeting to discuss the purchase in 1999 were for the project, arguing that it would be a stimulus to tourism, there was some dissent. The president of the Fauquier County Afro-American Historical Association said, "The concept of a museum in the name of a famous Confederate hero is not charming to all. That era is still painful for many of our residents. If adults are discouraged and even angered at a museum dedicated to a Confederate hero, what will the children think?" Another resident pointed out that Mosby "was not universally loved. Some of the old southern officers felt he was a bushwhacker and they did not approve of his methods." Others noted that he had lived in the house for only two years. Mayor George Fitch was strongly behind the project, which he predicted would generate new tax revenue and boost the local economy by $3 million per year. The town later considered selling the property and abandoning the controversial project. The Mosby Foundation remained optimistic and released the first issue of its newsletter, *The Mosby Messenger*, on January 21, 2000. Plans called for a grand opening of the museum in late 2002.[35]

Even Mosby's ghost is still able to polarize and provoke—a city official, like a Confederate officer nearly a century and a half ago, looks to Mosby to bring in the loot. But another part of society is aghast that someone would resurrect and lionize a man who defended slavery, by virtue of association, even if he later criticized the institution. The argument is reminiscent of those who damned Mosby during the war as a mere bandit and killer. It is a principled position, and it will lose. Because, even though a stalemate may be the condition of the moment, the Gray Ghost is already well established on the periphery and making inroads, having been on television and in comic books, the subject of pulp fiction, a theme drawn on by the literati, and on T-shirts and coffee mugs. One can travel the Mosby Highway, check landmarks on a Mosby map, turn in to the Mosby Tavern, drink some Mosby wine from a Mosby cup while killing some time playing a Mosby board game and smoking Mosby pipe tobacco, rent a Mosby movie, watch episodes of *The Gray Ghost* television series, and, for good measure, pick up a few Mosby novels for bedtime reading beneath a Mosby painting hung on the wall, as a Mosby reenactor gallops by the front door. The opposition may be holding the Gray Ghost at bay with well-orchestrated and larger forces, but it simply cannot prevent successful raids into the American imagination.

The Mosby Monument on Courthouse Square near Warrenton's Old Jail and the Fauquier County Courthouse pays tribute to the town's famous Reconstruction-era resident. Photograph by Paul Ashdown.

EPILOGUE: MOSBY REDUX

Don C. Seitz recalled seeing Mosby in his last years, when his face "was one of the coldest and calmest I ever saw." Mosby's friend George Cary Eggleston made this assessment shortly after the old raider's death: "No man was ever gentler or more considerate of others; no man was ever readier to meet a challenge of any kind with a fight. No man was readier to forgive a fault confessed—no man more merciless toward wrong-doing unrepented."[36]

When he was a small boy, John S. Patton, who later became a librarian at the University of Virginia, caught a glimpse of the aging Gray Ghost in Charlottesville and never forgot it: "I had the happiness of seeing the real, sure-enough John Singleton Mosby. I viewed him with the tense feeling that only boys know, but with a sense of loss. The plumed hat was gone."[37]

Were Seitz and Patton remembering a myth or a man? Or were they one and the same?

NOTES

1. Marc Ferro, *Cinema and History* (Detroit: Wayne State University Press, 1988), 146–53; Robert F. Horowitz, "History Comes to Life and You Are There," in *American History/American Television: Interpreting the Video Past*, ed. John E. O'Connor (New York: Frederick Ungar, 1983), 89; Spears, *Civil War on the Screen*, 11–116; John M. Cassidy, *Civil War Cinema* (Missoula, MT: Pictorial Histories Publishing Co., 1986); Roy Kinnard, *The Blue & Gray on the Silver Screen* (Secaucus, NJ: Birch Lane Press, 1996); Brian Steel Wills, "Films and Television," in *The American Civil War: A Handbook of Literature and Research*, ed. Steven E. Woodworth (Westport, CT: Greenwood Press, 1996); William C. Davis, *The Lost Cause: Myths and Realities of the Confederacy* (Lawrence: University Press of Kansas, 1996), 193.

2. Cassidy, *Civil War Cinema*, 150; Slotkin, *Gunfighter Nation*, 348; Richard West, *Television Westerns* (Jefferson, NC: McFarland & Co., 1987); Rita Parks, *The Western Hero in Film and Television* (Ann Arbor, MI: UMI Research Press, 1982), 31; David Buxton, *From the Avengers to Miami Vice: Form and Ideology in Television Series* (Manchester, England: Manchester University Press, 1981), 31.

3. Parks, *Western Hero*, 47; Cassidy, *Civil War Cinema*, 150; Davis, *The Lost Cause*, 31; Buxton, *From Avengers to Miami Vice*, 27–28; Cullen, *Civil War*, 9.

4. Horace Newcomb, "Toward a Television Aesthetic," in *Television: The Critical View*, ed. Horace Newcomb (New York: Oxford University Press, 1976), 284–85.

5. J. Fred MacDonald, *Who Shot the Sheriff?* (New York: Praeger, 1987), 1; Paula S. Fass, "Television as Cultural Document: Promises and Problems," in *Television as a Cultural Force*, ed. Richard Adler and Douglass Cater (New York: Praeger, 1976), 56.

6. Tom Moore to authors, telephone interview, July 5, 1978; *TV Guide* (August 30, 1958): 29–30; Greg Biggs, "Gray Ghost Story," 31–33; Virgil Carrington Jones to authors, personal letter, May 19, 1976.

7. Jones, letter; Jeff Rovin, *The Great Television Series* (South Brunswick, NJ: A.S. Barnes, 1977), 54; Tim Brooks and Earle Marsh, *The Complete Directory to Prime Time Network and Cable TV Shows, 1946–Present* (New York: Ballantine, 1995), 415. Details of DeWitt's life were provided by Michael T. George, in a personal letter, August 4, 1978.

8. *Variety*, September 18, 1957, 34–35; *TV Guide* (August 30, 1958): 29–30.

9. Moore, interview; Richard F. Shepard, " 'The Gray Ghost' Rides Again," *New York Times*, September 28, 1958.

10. Civil War Centennial Proclamation by Dwight D. Eisenhower, President of the United States of America, December 8, 1960, in Civil War Centennial Commission, *The Civil War Centennial: A Report to the Congress* (Washington, DC, 1968).

11. U.S. Civil War Centennial Commission, *The Civil War Centennial*, 1–6; John E. Bodnar, *Remaking America: Public Memory, Commemoration, and Patriotism in the Twentieth Century* (Princeton, NJ: Princeton University Press, 1992), 208–9.

12. Nevins, quoted in *Civil War Centennial*, 1.

13. K. Smirnov, "This Must Be Said!" *Izvestia*, September 13, 1957, *Current Digest of Soviet Press* 9, no. 37: 25–26; Andrew H. Berding, "Balance Sheet in the War of Ideas," *Department of State Bulletin* 39, no. 1016 (December 15, 1958): 955; Richard Lentz, "Media, Symbols, and Propaganda: The 1957 Little Rock Desegregation Crisis as Cold War Event," a paper presented at the Western Journalism Historians Conference, University of California, Berkeley, February 27, 1998; see also: Mary L. Dudziak, "Desegregation and the Cold War Imperative," *Stanford Law Review* 41 (1988): 61–120; idem, "The Little Rock Desegregation Crisis and Foreign Affairs: Race, Resistance, and the Image of American Democracy," *Southern California Law Review* 70 (1997): 1641–716; idem, *Cold War Civil Rights* (Princeton, NJ: Princeton University Press, 2000); John David Skrentny, "The Effect of the Cold War on African-American Civil Rights: America and the World Audience," *Theory and Society* 27 (1998): 237–85.

14. Shepard, " 'Gray Ghost' Rides Again." *The Gray Ghost* appeared at 9:30 P.M. on WPIX-TV in New York City on Thursday, October 10, 1957.

15. Jones, in Preface, *Memoirs*; Catton, Foreword, Jones's *Gray Ghosts and Rebel Raiders*, viii.

16. Slotkin, *Gunfighter Nation*, 453–61; *Variety*, October 16, 1957, 52.

17. George Tindall, "Mythology: A New Frontier in Southern History," in *The Idea of the South: Pursuit of a Central Theme*, ed. Frank E. Vandiver (Chicago: University of Chicago Press, 1964), 1–2; Paul M. Gaston, *The New South Creed: A Study in Southern Mythmaking* (New York: Alfred A. Knopf, 1970), 8; Daniel Joseph Singal, *The War Within: From Victorian to Modernist Thought in the South, 1919–1945* (Chapel Hill: University of North Carolina Press, 1982), 11–33.

18. Rovin, *Great Television Series*, 54.

19. Ibid.; "Why No 'Gray Ghost,' " *Newsweek* (August 4, 1958): 65; *Variety*, July 30, 1958, 29; " 'Gray Ghost' Haunts CBS Films," *Variety*, October 22, 1958, 31.

20. Jones, letter, May 19, 1976; *Newsweek* (August 4, 1958): 65; Jack DeWitt to authors, telephone interview, July 5, 1978; Lindsley Parsons to authors, telephone interview, July 5, 1978.

21. *Variety*, September 10, 1958, 115; Shepard, " 'Gray Ghost' Rides Again"; J. Fred MacDonald, *Blacks and White TV: Afro-Americans in Television since 1948* (Chicago: Nelson-Hall, 1983), 69.

22. *Variety*, October 16, 1957.

23. Ten episodes of the series are available from Belle & Blade, 124 Penn Avenue, Dover, NJ 07801. See http://www.belleandblade.com; Davis, *The Lost Cause*, 197; *Newsweek* (August 4, 1958).

24. Biggs, "Gray Ghost Story," 31–33; Ramage, *Gray Ghost*, 342.

25. David M. Potter, quoted in Thomas J. Pressly, *Americans Interpret Their Civil War* (Princeton, NJ: Princeton University Press, 1954), 10.

26. JSM to Spottswood Campbell, February 25, 1909, Special Collections, University of California, Santa Barbara, quoted in Siepel, *Rebel*, 282–83; see also Mosby's Rangers.com (http://www.mosbys rangers. com/biolpopculture.htm).

27. Alex McNeil, *Total Television: A Comprehensive Guide to Programming from 1948 to the Present*, 3d ed. (New York: Penguin Books, 1991), 173.

28. MacDonald, *Blacks and White TV*, 215; Alvin Sapinsley, *Lee at Gettysburg*, in *Great Television Plays* , selected by William I. Kaufman (New York: Dell Publishing CO., 1969), 33–80; Daniel Lyons, "NAACP's War on Television," *Christian Science Monitor*, July 29, 1999.

29. Neal Gabler, "History's Prime Time," *TV Guide* (August 23, 1997): 18–21.

30. Leonard Maltin, *The Disney Films* (New York: Crown Publishers, 1984), 122–24, 320–24; McNeil, *Total Television*, 812–14.

31. Disney, in *TV Guide*, n.d., quoted by Maltin, *Disney Films*, 319–20.

32. Phillips, *Daring Raiders*, 55 (on Künstler's *Ranger Mosby*), 56, 124 (on Gordon Phillips); Küntsler's *The Fairfax Raid* is used as a jacket cover illustration for Ramage's *Gray Ghost*; promotional flyers, American Print Gallery, Gettysburg, Pennsylvania, and Gray Stone Press, Nashville; *Mosby's War Reminiscences*, 49; John Paul Strain's *Fire in the Valley* may be viewed in color on his Web site, www.johnpaulstrain.com or in a double-page advertisement, *Civil War Times Illustrated* 40, no. 3 (June

2001): 22–23; Cornell and Diehl, Inc. (http://cornellanddiehl.com/premium_blends.htm).

33. *The Gray Ghost*, No. 911 (New York: Dell Publishing Co., 1958); *The Gray Ghost*, No. 1000 (New York: Dell Publishing Co., 1959).

34. *Mosby's War Reminiscences*, 45, 232; JSM to Pauline Mosby, June 16, 1862, *Letters*, 24–25.

35. *The Mosby Messenger* (Warrenton, Va.), January 21, 2000; George Fitch, "Mosby House Purchase a Safe Bet," *Fauquier Times-Democrat*, January 1, 1999; Brian Minter, "Council Holds off on 'Mosby House,' " *Fauquier Times-Democrat*, January 13, 1999; Graeme Zielinski, "Warrenton's Planned Mosby Museum a Thing of the Past?" *Washington Post*, June 13, 1999.

36. Seitz, *Uncommon Americans*, 145–46.

37. John S. Patton, "Mosby the Ranger as a College Student," *Baltimore Sun*, January 15, 1911; Ramage, *Gray Ghost*, 338.

BIBLIOGRAPHY

Alexander, John H. *Mosby's Men*. New York: Neale Publishing Co., 1907.

Anderson, Michael R. "Col. John Mosby and the Southern Code of Honor." American Studies class project, University of Virginia, 1997. http://roads.virginia.edu/~class/am483_97/projects/anderson/intro.html

Ashdown, Paul. "Confederates on Television: The Cavalier Myth and the Death of 'The Gray Ghost,' " *Studies in Popular Culture* 2, no. 1 (Spring 1979): 11–22.

Beaty, John O. *John Esten Cooke, Virginian*. 1922. Reprint, Port Washington, NY: Kennikat Press, 1965.

Beller, Susan Provost. *Mosby and His Rangers*. Cincinnati, OH: Betterway Books, 1992.

Bellow, Saul. *Mosby's Memoirs and Other Stories*. New York: Viking Press, 1968.

Berding, Andrew H. "Balance Sheet in the War of Ideas." *Department of State Bulletin* 39, no. 1016 (December 15, 1958).

Bergland, Renee L. *The National Uncanny: Indian Ghosts and American Subjects*. Hanover, NH: University Press of New England, 2000.

Bergreen, Laurence. *James Agee: A Life*. New York: E. P. Dutton, 1984.

Biggs, Greg. "The Gray Ghost Story." *Blue & Gray Magazine* (April 1994): 31–33.

Blackford, William Willis. *War Years with Jeb Stuart*. New York: Charles Scribner's Sons, 1945.

Blight, David W. *Race and Reunion: The Civil War in American Memory*. Cambridge, MA: Harvard University Press, 2001.

Blumenson, Martin. *Patton: The Man behind the Legend, 1885–1945*. New York: Berkeley Books, 1985. Reprint, New York: Morrow, 1985.

Bodnar, John E. *Remaking America: Public Memory, Commemoration, and Patriotism in the Twentieth Century*. Princeton, NJ: Princeton University Press, 1992.

Boritt, Gabor S., ed. *The Gettysburg Nobody Knows*. New York: Oxford University Press, 1997.

Brandt, Nat. *The Man Who Tried to Burn New York*. Syracuse, NY: Syracuse University Press, 1986.

Brilliant, Richard. *Portraiture*. Cambridge, MA: Harvard University Press, 1991.

Brindle, Paul W. *Ancestry of William Sperry Bunk*. N.p., privately printed, 1974.

Brooks, Tim, and Earle Marsh. *The Complete Directory to Prime Time Network and Cable TV Shows, 1946–Present*. New York: Ballantine, 1995.

Bryan, J., III. *The Sword over the Mantel: The Civil War and I*. New York: McGraw-Hill, 1960.

Buxton, David. *From the Avengers to Miami Vice: Form and Ideology in Television Series*. Manchester, England: Manchester University Press, 1981.

Cassidy, John M. *Civil War Cinema*. Missoula, MT: Pictorial Histories Publishing Co., 1986.

Catton, Bruce. *Terrible Swift Sword*. Garden City, NY: Doubleday, 1963.

_____. Foreword to *Gray Ghosts and Rebel Raiders* by Virgil Carrington Jones. Reprint, New York: Galahad Books, 1995.

Chiniquy, Charles. *Fifty Years in the Church of Rome*. 1886. Reprint, Grand Rapids, MI: Baker Book House, 1958.

Churchill, Winston Spencer. *The River War. An Historical Account of the Reconquest of the Soudan*. 2 vols. Edited by Col. F. Rhodes. London: Longmans, Green, and Co., 1899.

Coleman, Christopher K. *Ghosts and Haunts of the Civil War: Authentic Accounts of the Strange and Unexplained*. Nashville: Rutledge Hill Press, 1999.

Comte de Paris, Louis-Philippe-Albert d'Orleans. *History of the Civil War in America*. Philadelphia: J. H. Coates, 1876.

Cooke, John Esten. *Wearing of the Gray*. 1867. Edited by Philip van Doren Stern. Reprint, Bloomington: Indiana University Press, 1959.

_____. *Surry of Eagle's-Nest*. 1866. Reprint, Ridgewood, NJ: Gregg Press, 1968.

Cords, Nicholas, and Patrick Gerster, eds. *Myth and the American Experience*. 2 vols. New York: Glencoe Press, 1973.

Cotter, Bill. *The Wonderful World of Disney Television: A Complete History*. New York: Hyperion, 1997.

Crawford, J. Marshall. *Mosby and His Men*. New York: G. W. Carleton and Co., 1867.

Cullen, Jim. *The Civil War in Popular Culture*. Washington, DC: Smithsonian Institution Press, 1995.

Czitrom, Daniel J. *Media and the American Mind*. Chapel Hill: University of North Carolina Press, 1982.

Daniels, Jonathan. *John Singleton Mosby, Gray Ghost of the Confederacy*. Philadelphia: J. B. Lippincott Co., 1959.

Dannett, Sylvia G. L., and Rosamond H. Burkhart. *Confederate Surgeon, Aristides Monteiro*. New York: Dodd, Mead & Co., 1969.

Dasher, Thomas E. "John Esten Cooke." *Antebellum Writers in New York and the South*. Edited by Joel Myerson. *Dictionary of Literary Biography* 3:64–71. Detroit: Gale Research, 1979.

Davis, William C. *The Lost Cause: Myths and Realities of the Confederacy*. Lawrence: University Press of Kansas, 1996.

_____, Brian C. Pohanka, and Don Troiani, eds. *Civil War Journal: The Leaders*. Nashville: Rutledge Hill, 1997.

Dudziak, Mary L. *Cold War Civil Rights*. Princeton, NJ: Princeton University Press, 2000.

_____. "Desegregation and the Cold War Imperative." *Stanford Law Review* 41 (1988): 61–120.

_____. "The Little Rock Desegregation Crisis and Foreign Affairs: Race, Resistance, and the Image of American Democracy." *Southern California Law Review* 70 (1997): 1641–716.

Durrill, Wayne K. *War of Another Kind: A Southern Community in the Great Rebellion*. New York: Oxford University Press, 1990.

Dutton, Robert R. *Saul Bellow*. Boston: Twayne Publishers, 1982.

Eicher, David J. *The Civil War in Books*. Urbana: University of Illinois Press, 1997.

Emerson, Edward W. *Life and Letters of Charles Russell Lowell*. Reprint, Port Washington, NY, 1971.

Evans, Edna Hoffman. *Sunstar and Pepper*. Chapel Hill: University of North Carolina Press, 1947.

Evans, Thomas J., and James M. Moyer. *Mosby's Confederacy: A Guide to the Roads and Sites of Colonel John Singleton Mosby*. Shippensburg, PA: White Mane Publishers, 1991.

Fahs, Alice. *The Imagined Civil War: Popular Literature of the North and South, 1861–1865*. Chapel Hill: University of North Carolina Press, 2001.

Farago, Ladislas. *Patton: Ordeal and Triumph*. New York: Ivan Obolensky, 1963.

Fass, Paula S. "Television as a Cultural Document: Promises and Problems." In *Television as Cultural Force*. Edited by Richard Adler and Douglass Cater. New York: Praeger, 1976.

Fellman, Michael. *Inside War: The Guerrilla Conflict in Missouri during the American Civil War*. New York: Oxford University Press, 1989.

Ferro, Marc. *Cinema and History*. Detroit: Wayne State University Press, 1988.

Fisher, Noel C. *War at Every Door: Partisan Politics and Guerrilla Violence in East Tennessee, 1860–1869*. Chapel Hill: University of North Carolina Press, 1997.

Fitzgerald, F. Scott. *Tender Is the Night*. Edited by Malcolm Cowley. 1934, 1951. Reprint, Harmondsworth, England: Penguin, 1955.

Foster, Gaines M. *Ghosts of the Confederacy*. New York: Oxford University Press, 1987.

Freeman, Douglas Southall. *Lee's Lieutenants: A Study in Command*. 3 vols. New York: Charles Scribner's Sons, 1942–1944.

Frye, Dennis E. " 'I Resolved to Play a Bold Game': John S. Mosby as a Factor in the 1864 Valley Campaign." In *Struggle for the Shenandoah: Essays on the 1864 Valley Campaign*. Edited by Gary W. Gallagher, 107–26. Kent, OH: Kent State University Press, 1991.

Fussell, Paul. *The Great War and Modern Memory*. New York: Oxford University Press, 1975.

Gabler, Neal. "History's Prime Time." *TV Guide* (August 23, 1997): 18–21.

Garner, Stanton. *The Civil War World of Herman Melville*. Lawrence: University Press of Kansas, 1993.

Gaston, Paul M. *The New South Creed: A Study in Southern Mythmaking*. New York: Alfred A. Knopf, 1970.

Grant, Carl E. "Partisan Warfare, Model 1861–1865." *Military Review* (November 1958): 42–49.

Grant, Ulysses S. *Personal Memoirs of U. S. Grant*. New York: Charles L. Webster & Co., 1886.

Guy, Anne Welsh. *John Mosby, Rebel Raider of the Civil War*. New York: Abelard-Schuman, 1965.

Harris, Brayton. *Blue and Gray in Black and White: Newspapers in the Civil War*. Dulles, VA: Batsford Brassey, 1999.

Hartigan, Richard Shelly. *Lieber's Code and the Law of War*. Chicago: Precedent, 1983.

Head, James W. *History of Loudoun County Virginia*. N.p., Park View Press, 1908.

Hogan, Ray. *The Ghost Raider*. New York: Pyramid Publications, 1960.

———. *Hell to Hallelujah*. New York: Macfadden, 1962.

———. *Mosby's Last Raid*. New York: Macfadden, 1966.

———. *Night Raider*. New York: Avon, 1964. Reprint, Bath, England: Chivers Press, 1992.

———. *Raider's Revenge*. New York: Pyramid Publications, 1960.

———. *Rebel Ghost*. New York: Macfadden, 1964. Reprint, Toronto: PaperJacks, 1987.

———. *Rebel in Yankee Blue*. New York: Avon, 1962.

_____. *Rebel Raid*. New York: Berkeley, 1961. Reprint, Bath, England: Chivers Press, 1988.

Holzer, Harold, and Mark E. Neely Jr. *Mine Eyes Have Seen the Glory: The Civil War in Art*. New York: Orion, 1993.

_____. "Aristocratic Company: Colonel John S. Mosby and the French Artistes." *Virginia Cavalcade* 41 (Spring 1992): 148.

Horowitz, Robert F. "History Comes to Life and You Are There." *American History/American Television: Interpreting the Video Past*. Edited by John E. O'Connor. New York: Frederick Ungar, 1983.

Horwitz, Tony. *Confederates in the Attic*. New York: Random House, 1998. Reprint, New York: Vintage Books, 1999.

Hunter, Alexander. *The Women of the Debatable Land*. Washington, DC: Corden Publishing Co., 1912.

Icenhower, Joseph B. *The Scarlet Raider*. Philadelphia and New York: Chilton Book Co., 1961.

Jakes, John. *On Secret Service*. New York: E. P. Dutton, 2000.

Joes, Anthony James. *Guerrilla Conflict before the Cold War*. Westport, CT: Praeger, 1996.

_____. *Guerrilla Warfare: A Historical, Biographical and Bibliographical Sourcebook*. Westport, CT: Greenwood, 1996.

Johnson, Paul. *A History of the American People*. 1998. Reprint, New York: HarperPerennial, 1999.

Jones, Virgil Carrington. *Gray Ghosts and Rebel Raiders*. 1956. Reprint, New York: Galahad Books, 1995.

_____. *Ranger Mosby*. Chapel Hill: University of North Carolina Press, 1944.

_____, "Ranger Mosby in Albemarle." *Papers of the Albemarle County Historical Society* (Charlottesville, VA) 5 (June 1945): 36–46.

Kammen, Michael. *A Season of Youth*. New York: Alfred A. Knopf, 1978.

Karnow, Stanley. *Vietnam: A History*. New York: Penguin Books, 1983.

Keen, Hugh C., and Horace Mewborn. *43rd Battalion Virginia Cavalry: Mosby's Command*. Lynchburg, VA: H. E. Howard, 1993.

Kinnard, Roy. *The Blue & Gray on the Silver Screen*. Secaucus, NJ: Birch Lane Press, 1996.

Kramer, Aaron. *Melville's Poetry: Toward the Enlarged Heart*. Rutherford, NJ: Fairleigh Dickinson University Press, 1972.

Lagard, Garald. *Scarlet Cockerel*. New York: William Morrow, 1948.

Lang, J. Stephen, and Michael Caplanis. *Drawn to the Civil War*. Winston-Salem, NC: John F. Blair, 1999.

Lentz, Richard. "Media, Symbols, and Propaganda: The 1957 Little Rock Desegregation Crisis as Cold War Event." A paper presented at the Western Journalism Historians Conference, University of California, Berkeley, February 27, 1998.

Le Vot, Andre. *F. Scott Fitzgerald*. New York: Doubleday, 1983.

Limon, John. *Writing after War*. New York: Oxford University Press, 1994.

Lippmann, Walter. *Public Opinion*. 1922. Reprint, New York: Free Press, 1965.

Lively, Robert A. *Fiction Fights the Civil War*. Chapel Hill: University of North Carolina Press, 1957.

Lock, John D. *To Fight with Intrepidity: The Complete History of the U.S. Army Rangers, 1622 to Present*. New York: Pocket Books, 1998.

Lule, Jack. *Daily News, External Stories: The Mythological Role of Journalism*. New York: Guilford Press, 2001.

Lyons, Daniel. "NAACP's War on Television." *Christian Science Monitor*, July 29, 1999.

MacDonald, J. Fred. *Blacks and White TV: Afro-Americans in Television since 1948*. Chicago: Nelson-Hall, 1983.

———. *Who Shot the Sheriff?* New York: Praeger, 1987.

Maltin, Leonard. *The Disney Films*. New York: Crown Publishers, 1984.

Marling, Karal Ann. *George Washington Slept Here: Colonial Revivals and American Culture, 1876–1986*. Cambridge, MA: Harvard University Press, 1988.

Mayo, Bernard. *Myths and Men*. Athens: University of Georgia Press, 1959.

McCarthy, Eugene. Foreword to *Rebel: The Life and Times of John Singleton Mosby*, by Kevin H. Siepel. New York: Da Capo Press, 1997.

McCarty, Burke. *The Suppressed Truth about the Assassination of President Lincoln*. Philadelphia, 1924.

McLean, James. *Californian Sabers: The 2nd Massachusetts Cavalry in the Civil War*. Indianapolis: Indiana University Press, 2000.

McNeil, Alex. *Total Television: A Comprehensive Guide to Programming from 1948 to the Present*, 3d ed. New York: Penguin Books, 1991.

Melville, Herman. *Battle-Pieces and Aspects of the War*. New York: Harper & Bros., 1866.

Menendez, Albert J. *Civil War Novels: An Annotated Bibliography*. New York: Garland, 1986.

Mewborn, Horace. "The Operations of Mosby's Rangers." *Blue & Gray Magazine* 17, no. 4 (Spring 2000): 6–20, 22, 38–50.

Mitchell, Adele H., ed. *The Letters of John S. Mosby*. 2d ed. N.p., Stuart-Mosby Historical Society, 1986.

Monteiro, A. *War Reminiscences by the Surgeon of Mosby's Command.* 1890. Reprint, Gaithersburg, MD: Butternut Press, n.d.

Morris, Roy, Jr. *Sheridan: The Life and Wars of General Phil Sheridan.* New York: Crown, 1992.

Mosby, John S. *The Memoirs of Colonel John S. Mosby.* Edited by Charles Wells Russell. 1917. Reprint, Nashville: J. S. Sanders & Co., 1959.

_____. *Mosby's War Reminiscences and Stuart's Cavalry Campaigns.* 1887. Reprint, New York: Pageant, 1958.

_____. "Personal Recollections of General J. E. B. Stuart." *Munsey's Magazine* (April 1913): 35–41.

_____. "Stuart's Cavalry in the Gettysburg Campaign." *Belford's Monthly* (October 1891): 149–69; (November 1891): 261–75.

_____. *Stuart's Cavalry in the Gettysburg Campaign.* New York: Moffat, Yard & Co., 1908.

Mosby's Rangers.com. http://www.mosbysrangers.com/bio/popculture.htm.

Muller, Herbert J. *The Uses of the Past: Profiles of Former Societies.* 1952. Reprint, New York: Schocken Books, 1985.

Munson, John W. "Recollections of a Mosby Guerrilla." *Munsey's Magazine* (September 1904): 845–56.

_____. *Reminiscences of a Mosby Guerrilla.* 1906. Reprint, Washington, DC: Zenger Publishing Co., 1983.

Newall, Walter S. *A Memoir.* Philadelphia, 1864.

Newcomb, Horace, ed. *Television: The Critical View.* New York: Oxford University Press, 1976.

Nimmo, Dan, and James E. Combs. *Mediated Political Realities.* New York: Longman, 1983.

Noyes, Beppie. *Mosby, the Kennedy Center Cat.* Washington, DC: Acropolis Books, 1978.

Nye, Russel. *The Unembarrassed Muse.* New York: Dial Press, 1970.

Park, David. "Picturing the War: Visual Genres in Civil War News." *The Communication Review* 3, no. 4 (1999): 287–321.

Parks, Rita. *The Western Hero in Film and Television.* Ann Arbor, MI: UMI Research Press, 1982.

Peavey, James Dudley, ed. *Confederate Scout: Virginia's Frank Stringfellow.* N.p., privately published, 1956.

Perry, James M. *A Bohemian Brigade: The Civil War Correspondents.* New York: John Wiley & Sons, 2000.

Peterson, Merrill D. *Lincoln in American Memory.* New York: Oxford University Press, 1994.

Phillips, David L. *Daring Raiders.* New York: Friedman/Fairfax, 1998.

Phillips, V. N. *Bristol, Tennessee/Virginia: A History, 1852–1900.* Johnson City, TN: Overmountain Press, 1992.

Pifer, Ellen. *Saul Bellow against the Grain.* Philadelphia: University of Pennsylvania Press, 1990.

Poulter, Keith. "A Word in Edgeways." *North & South* 3, no. 1 (November 1999): 18–19.

Pressly, Thomas J. *Americans Interpret Their Civil War.* Princeton, NJ: Princeton University Press, 1954.

Prindle, Paul W. *Ancestry of William Sperry Beinecke.* N.p., privately published, 1974.

Pullen, John J. *Joshua Chamberlain.* Mechanicsburg, PA: Stackpole Books, 1999.

Rachal, William M. E., ed. "Petitions concerning the Pardon of John S. Mosby in 1853." *Papers of the Albemarle County Historical Society* (Charlottesville, VA) 19 (1948–49): 13–41.

Ramage, James A. *Gray Ghost: The Life of Col. John Singleton Mosby.* Lexington: University Press of Kentucky, 1999.

———. "Mosby in the Valley." *North & South* 3, no. 1 (November 1999): 10–22.

Richards, A. E. "Mosby's Partizan Rangers." In *Famous Adventures and Prison Escapes of the Civil War.* Edited by G. W. Cable et al., 102–15. 1885. Reprint, London: T. Fisher Unwin, 1894.

Robertson, James I., Jr. *General A. P. Hill: The Story of a Confederate Warrior.* New York: Random House, 1987.

———. *Stonewall Jackson: The Man, the Soldier, the Legend.* New York: Macmillan, 1997.

Robertson, James Oliver. *American Myth, American Reality.* New York: Hill and Wang, 1980.

Rosa, Joseph G. *The Gunfighter: Man or Myth.* Norman: University of Oklahoma Press, 1969.

Rovin, Jeff. *The Great Television Series.* South Brunswick, NJ: A. S. Barnes, 1977.

Safire, William. *The New Language of Politics: A Dictionary of Catchwords, Slogans, and Political Usage.* 1968. Reprint, New York: Collier Books, 1972.

Sanders, William. *The Wild Blue and the Gray.* New York: Warner Books, 1991.

Sapinsley, Alvin. *Lee at Gettysburg.* In *Great Television Plays.* Selected by William I. Kaufman. New York: Dell Publishing Co., 1969.

Sconce, Jeffrey. *Haunted Media: Electronic Presence from Telegraphy to Television.* Durham, NC: Duke University Press, 2000.

Scott, John. *Partisan Life with Col. John S. Mosby.* 1867. Reprint, Gaithersburg, MD: Butternut Press, 1985.

Siepel, Kevin H. *Rebel: The Life and Times of John Singleton Mosby.* 1983. Reprint, New York: Da Capo Press, 1997.

Seitz, Don C. *Uncommon Americans: Pencil Portraits of Men and Women Who Have Broken the Rules.* Indianapolis: Bobbs-Merrill, 1925.

Singal, Daniel Joseph. *The War Within: From Victorian to Modernist Thought in the South, 1919–1945.* Chapel Hill: University of North Carolina Press, 1982.

Skimin, Robert. *Gray Victory.* New York: St. Martin's Press, 1988.

Skrentny, John David. "The Effect of the Cold War on African-American Civil Rights: America and the World Audience." *Theory and Society* 27 (1998): 237–85.

Slotkin, Richard. *Gunfighter Nation: The Myth of the Frontier in Twentieth-Century America.* New York: Atheneum, 1992.

Smirnov, K. "This Must Be Said!" *Izvestia*, September 13, 1957. In *Current Digest of Soviet Press* 9, no. 37, 25–26.

Sneden, Robert Knox. *Eye of the Storm.* Edited by Charles E. Bryan Jr. and Nelson D. Lankford. New York: Free Press, 2000.

Spears, Jack. *The Civil War on the Screen, and Other Essays.* South Brunswick, NJ: A. S. Barnes, 1977.

Starr, Louis M. *Bohemian Brigade: Civil War Newsmen in Action.* New York: Alfred A. Knopf, 1954.

Summers, Neil. *The Official TV Western Book.* Vienna, WV: The Old West Shop Publishing, 1992.

Tate, J. O. Foreword to *The Memoirs of Colonel John S. Mosby*, by John S. Mosby, vii–xxi. 1917. Reprint, Nashville: J. S. Sanders & Co., 1995.

Taylor, James E. *With Sheridan Up the Shenandoah Valley in 1864: Leaves from a Special Artist's Sketchbook and Diary.* Edited by George Skoll, Martin F. Graham, and Dennis E. Frye. Dayton, OH: Morningside House, 1989.

Taylor, Michael W. "In a Small Virginia Stable Yard, a Quick-Shooting Union Lieutenant Bested Five of Mosby's Rangers." *America's Civil War* 13, no. 6 (January 2001): 12, 14, 16, 77.

Thomas, Emory. "Eggs, Aldie, Shepherdstown and J. E. B. Stuart." In *The Gettysburg Nobody Knows.* Edited by Gabor S. Boritt. New York: Oxford University Press, 1997, 101–21.

———. "Jeb Stuart." *Encyclopedia of Southern Culture.* Edited by Charles Reagan Wilson and William Ferris. Chapel Hill: University of North Carolina Press, 1989, 703.

Tibbets, Paul W. *Return of the Enola Gay.* Columbus, OH: Midcoast Marketing, 1998.

Tidwell, William A. *April '65: Confederate Covert Action in the American Civil War.* Kent, OH: Kent State University Press, 1995.

_____. With James O. Hall and David Winfred Gaddy. *Come Retribution: The Confederate Secret Service and the Assassination of Lincoln.* Jackson: University Press of Mississippi, 1988.

Tindall, George. "Mythology: A New Frontier in Southern History." In *The Idea of the South: Pursuit of a Central Theme,* 1–15. Edited by Frank E. Vandiver. Chicago: University of Chicago Press, 1964.

Turtledove, Harry. *Guns of the South: A Novel of the Civil War.* New York: Ballantine Books, 1993.

Tuska, Jon, and Vicki Piekarski, eds. *Encyclopedia of Frontier and Western Fiction.* New York: McGraw-Hill, 1983.

U.S. Civil War Centennial Commission. *The Civil War Centennial: A Report to the Congress.* Washington, DC, 1968.

Venable, Clarke. *Mosby's Night Hawk.* Chicago: Reilly & Lee, 1931.

The War of the Rebellion: A Compilation of the Official Records of the Union and Confederate Armies. 70 vols., 4 series. Washington, DC, 1880–1901.

Ward, Geoffrey C., with Ric Burns and Ken Burns. *The Civil War: An Illustrated History.* New York: Alfred A. Knopf, 1990.

Ward, James A. *Railroads and the Character of America, 1820–1887.* Knoxville: University of Tennessee Press, 1986.

Weaver, Richard M. *The Southern Essays of Richard M. Weaver.* Edited by George M. Curtis III and James J. Thompson Jr. Indianapolis: Liberty Press, 1987.

Wellman, Manly Wade. *Harpers Ferry, Prize of War.* Charlotte, NC: McNally, 1960.

Wert, Jeffry D. *Mosby's Rangers.* New York: Simon & Schuster, 1990.

West, Richard. *Television Westerns.* Jefferson, NC: McFarland & Co., 1987.

Wheeler, Tom. *Leadership Lessons from the Civil War: Winning Strategies for Today's Managers.* New York: Doubleday, 2000.

Wheelwright, Jere Hungerford. *Gentlemen, Hush!* New York: Charles Scribner's Sons, 1948.

Wiley, Bell Irvin, and Hurst D. Milhollen. *Embattled Confederates.* New York: Harper & Row, 1964.

Wilkinson, Rupert. *American Tough.* Westport, CT: Greenwood Press, 1984.

Williamson, James J. *Mosby's Rangers.* New York: Ralph B. Kenyon, 1896.

Wills, Brian Steel. "Films and Television." In *The American Civil War: A Handbook of Literature and Research,* 613–19. Edited by Steven E. Woodworth. Westport, CT: Greenwood Press, 1996.

Wilson, Edmund. *Patriotic Gore.* New York: Oxford University Press, 1962.

Winik, Jay. *April 1865: The Month That Saved America*. New York: HarperCollins, 2001.

Wistar, Isaac J. *Autobiography of Isaac Jones Wistar, 1827–1905*. New York: Wistar Institute of Anatomy and Biology, 1937.

Worsham, James J., and R. B. Anderson. "Mosby: The Model Partisan." *Special Warfare* (Winter 1989): 34.

INDEX

231

106-7,
49,